global

intermediate teacher's book

Lindsay Clandfield & Rebecca Robb Benne

MACMILLAN

Macmillan Education
Between Towns Road, Oxford OX4 3PP
A division of Macmillan Publishers Limited
Companies and representatives throughout the world

ISBN: 978-0-230-03305-4

First published 2011

Designed by eMC Design Limited
Cover design by Macmillan Publishers Limited

Teacher's Resource Disc
Illustration by Celia Hart and Stephen Dew

Motion clips kindly provided by
BBC Motions Gallery
ITN Source

Printed and bound in Thailand

2015 2014 2013 2012
10 9 8 7 6 5 4 3 2

Contents

Coursebook contents map

EV – Extend your vocabulary (P) – Pronunciation

Components for the learner

Coursebook
see pages viii-xiii

eWorkbook
see pages xiv-xv

Components for the teacher

Teacher's Book & Teacher's Resource Disc

see page xvi

Class Audio CDs

see page xvii

Global Website

see page xvii

Global Digital

see pages xviii-xix

Coursebook: lessons 1 and 2 of a unit

Unit structure

Each unit is divided into six two-page lessons. The first four lessons are the core part of the unit. The last two lessons include additional material (eg Study skills, Review). In this unit, the first two lessons are about 'lost', the next two lessons are about 'found'.

Headings

Clear headings throughout the book show what you are teaching at each stage of the lesson.

Grammar explanations

Short grammar explanations are provided on the page, with a cross reference to further explanation and practice at the back of the book.

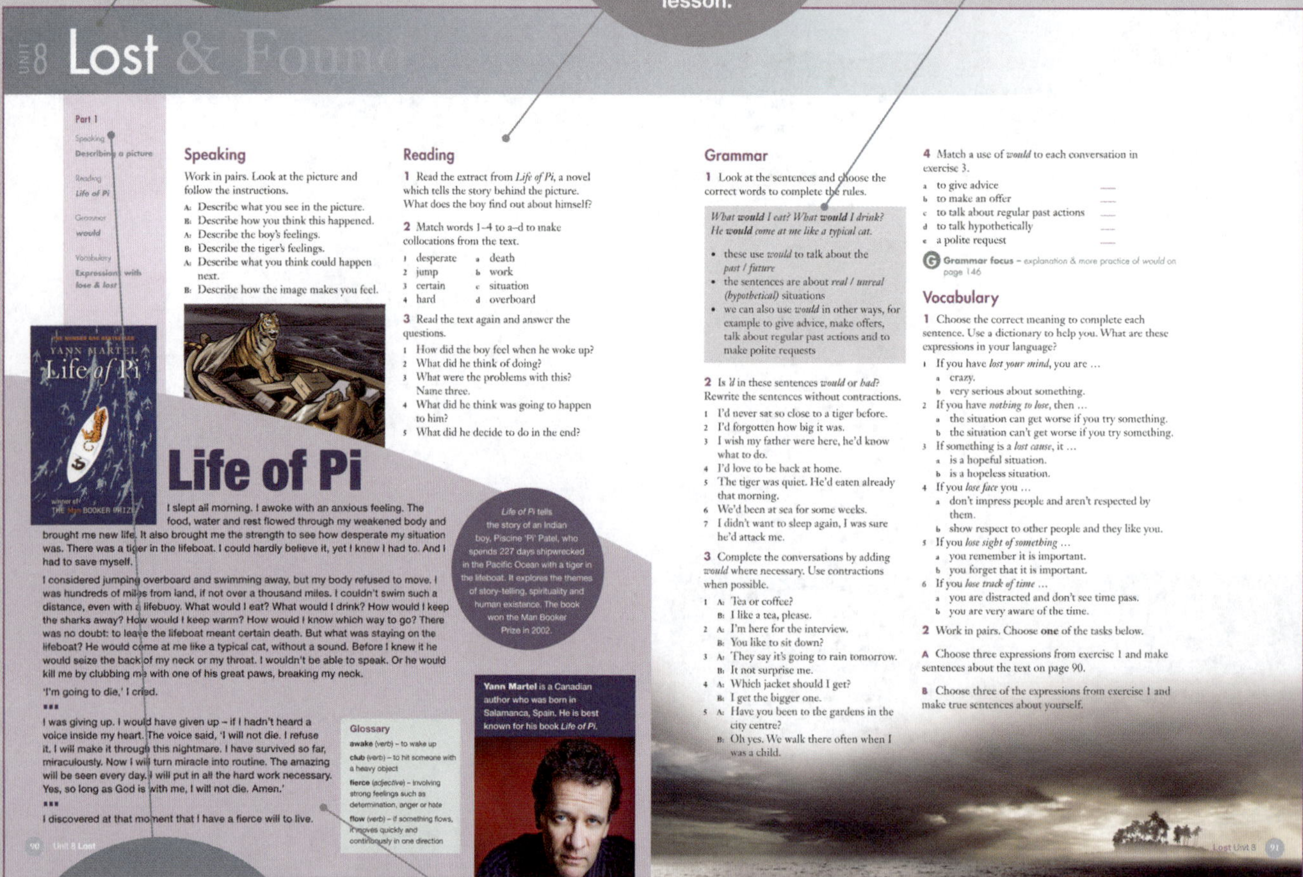

UNIT 8 Lost & Found

Part 1

Speaking
Describing a picture

Reading
Life of Pi

Grammar
would

Vocabulary
Expressions with lose & lost

Speaking

Work in pairs. Look at the picture and follow the instructions.

A: Describe what you see in the picture.
B: Describe how you think this happened.
A: Describe the boy's feelings.
B: Describe the tiger's feelings.
A: Describe what you think could happen next.
B: Describe how the image makes you feel.

Reading

1 Read the extract from *Life of Pi*, a novel which tells the story behind the picture. What does the boy find out about himself?

2 Match words 1–4 to a–d to make collocations from the text.

1 desperate a death
2 jump b work
3 certain c situation
4 hard d overboard

3 Read the text again and answer the questions.

1 How did the boy feel when he woke up?
2 What did he think of doing?
3 What were the problems with this? Name three.
4 What did he think was going to happen to him?
5 What did he decide to do in the end?

YANN MARTEL Life of Pi
winner of THE Man BOOKER PRIZE

Life of Pi

I slept all morning. I awoke with an anxious feeling. The food, water and rest flowed through my weakened body and brought me new life. It also brought me the strength to see how desperate my situation was. There was a tiger in the lifeboat. I could hardly believe it, yet I knew I had to. And I had to save myself.

I considered jumping overboard and swimming away, but my body refused to move. I was hundreds of miles from land, if not over a thousand miles. I couldn't swim such a distance, even with a lifebuoy. What would I eat? What would I drink? How would I keep the sharks away? How would I keep warm? How would I know which way to go? There was no doubt: to leave the lifeboat meant certain death. But what was staying on the lifeboat? He would come at me like a typical cat, without a sound. Before I knew it he would seize the back of my neck or my throat. I wouldn't be able to speak. Or he would kill me by clubbing me with one of his great paws, breaking my neck.

'I'm going to die,' I cried.

■■■

I was giving up. I would have given up – if I hadn't heard a voice inside my heart. The voice said, 'I will not die. I refuse it. I will make it through this nightmare. I have survived so far, miraculously. Now I will turn miracle into routine. The amazing will be seen every day. I will put in all the hard work necessary. Yes, so long as God is with me, I will not die. Amen.'

■■■

I discovered at that moment that I have a fierce will to live.

Life of Pi tells the story of an Indian boy, Piscine 'Pi' Patel, who spends 227 days shipwrecked in the Pacific Ocean with a tiger in the lifeboat. It explores the themes of story-telling, spirituality and human existence. The book won the Man Booker Prize in 2002.

Yann Martel is a Canadian author who was born in Salamanca, Spain. He is best known for his book *Life of Pi*.

Glossary
awake (*verb*) – to wake up
club (*verb*) – to hit someone with a heavy object
fierce (*adjective*) – involving strong feelings such as determination, anger or hate
flow (*verb*) – if something flows, it moves quickly and continuously in one direction

90 Unit 8 Lost

Grammar

1 Look at the sentences and choose the correct words to complete the rules.

What **would** *I eat? What* **would** *I drink?*
He **would** *come at me like a typical cat.*

- these use *would* to talk about the *past / future*
- the sentences are about *real / unreal (hypothetical)* situations
- we can also use *would* in other ways, for example to give advice, make offers, talk about regular past actions and to make polite requests

2 Is *'d* in these sentences *would* or *had*? Rewrite the sentences without contractions.

1 I'd never sat so close to a tiger before.
2 I'd forgotten how big it was.
3 I wish my father were here, he'd know what to do.
4 I'd love to be back at home.
5 The tiger was quiet. He'd eaten already that morning.
6 We'd been at sea for some weeks.
7 I didn't want to sleep again, I was sure he'd attack me.

3 Complete the conversations by adding *would* where necessary. Use contractions when possible.

1 A: Tea or coffee?
B: I like a tea, please.
2 A: I'm here for the interview.
B: You like to sit down?
3 A: They say it's going to rain tomorrow.
B: It not surprise me.
4 A: Which jacket should I get?
B: I get the bigger one.
5 A: Have you been to the gardens in the city centre?
B: Oh yes. We walk there often when I was a child.

4 Match a use of *would* to each conversation in exercise 3.

a to give advice ___
b to make an offer ___
c to talk about regular past actions ___
d to talk hypothetically ___
e a polite request ___

G **Grammar focus** – explanation & more practice of would on page 146

Vocabulary

1 Choose the correct meaning to complete each sentence. Use a dictionary to help you. What are these expressions in your language?

1 If you have *lost your mind*, you are …
a crazy.
b very serious about something.
2 If you have *nothing to lose*, then …
a the situation can get worse if you try something.
b the situation can't get worse if you try something.
3 If something is a *lost cause*, it …
a is a hopeful situation.
b is a hopeless situation.
4 If you *lose face* you …
a don't impress people and aren't respected by them.
b show respect to other people and they like you.
5 If you *lose sight of something* …
a you remember it is important.
b you forget that it is important.
6 If you *lose track of time* …
a you are distracted and don't see time pass.
b you are very aware of the time.

2 Work in pairs. Choose **one** of the tasks below.

A Choose three expressions from exercise 1 and make sentences about the text on page 90.

B Choose three of the expressions from exercise 1 and make true sentences about yourself.

Lost Unit 8 91

Contents sidebar

Content is summarised on every spread so you can see at a glance what the lesson is about.

Literary texts

Short extracts from modern literature are included, with information about the author and the book.

Topics and texts

Topics and texts are chosen to appeal to the learners' intellectual curiosity. Texts are authentic, with information about the real world. Attractive and stylish design makes the text more attractive and motivating to read.

Listening

Every lesson has a reading or listening text. Listening texts are supported by different tasks for gist and specific listening. The listening texts in *Global* include a variety of genres, including lectures and presentations as well as interviews and dialogues.

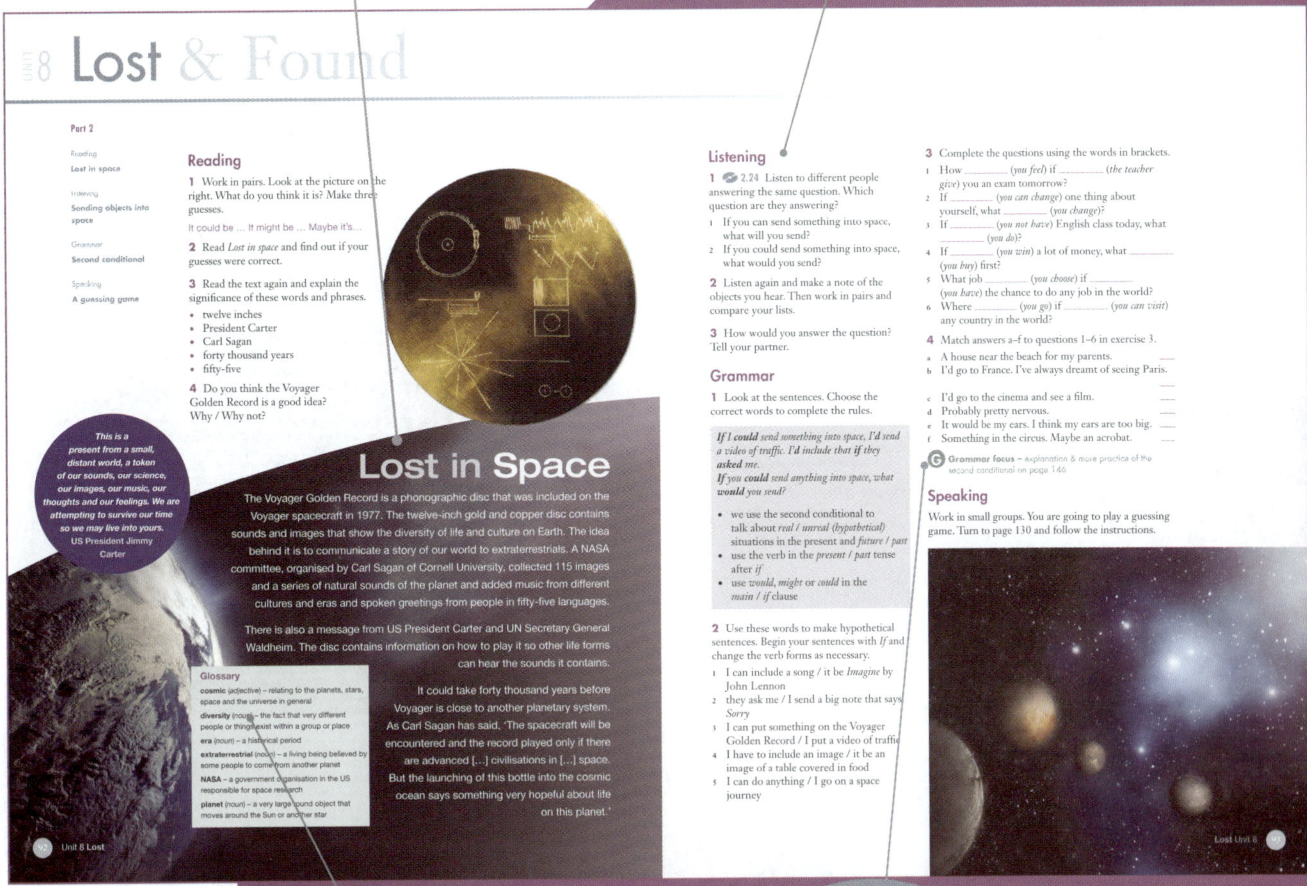

UNIT 8 Lost & Found

Part 2

Reading
Lost in space

Listening
Sending objects into space

Grammar
Second conditional

Speaking
A guessing game

Reading

1 Work in pairs. Look at the picture on the right. What do you think it is? Make three guesses.

It could be … It might be … Maybe it's…

2 Read *Lost in space* and find out if your guesses were correct.

3 Read the text again and explain the significance of these words and phrases.

- twelve inches
- President Carter
- Carl Sagan
- forty thousand years
- fifty-five

4 Do you think the Voyager Golden Record is a good idea? Why / Why not?

This is a present from a small, distant world, a token of our sounds, our science, our images, our music, our thoughts and our feelings. We are attempting to survive our time so we may live into yours.
US President Jimmy Carter

Lost in Space

The Voyager Golden Record is a phonographic disc that was included on the Voyager spacecraft in 1977. The twelve-inch gold and copper disc contains sounds and images that show the diversity of life and culture on Earth. The idea behind it is to communicate a story of our world to extraterrestrials. A NASA committee, organised by Carl Sagan of Cornell University, collected 115 images and a series of natural sounds of the planet and added music from different cultures and eras and spoken greetings from people in fifty-five languages.

There is also a message from US President Carter and UN Secretary General Waldheim. The disc contains information on how to play it so other life forms can hear the sounds it contains.

It could take forty thousand years before Voyager is close to another planetary system. As Carl Sagan has said, 'The spacecraft will be encountered and the record played only if there are advanced […] civilisations in […] space. But the launching of this bottle into the cosmic ocean says something very hopeful about life on this planet.'

Glossary

cosmic (*adjective*) – relating to the planets, stars, space and the universe in general
diversity (*noun*) – the fact that very different people or things exist within a group or place
era (*noun*) – a historical period
extraterrestrial (*noun*) – a living being believed by some people to come from another planet
NASA – a government organisation in the US responsible for space research
planet (*noun*) – a very large round object that moves around the Sun or another star

Unit 8 Lost

Listening

1 2.24 Listen to different people answering the same question. Which question are they answering?

1 If you can send something into space, what will you send?
2 If you could send something into space, what would you send?

2 Listen again and make a note of the objects you hear. Then work in pairs and compare your lists.

3 How would you answer the question? Tell your partner.

Grammar

1 Look at the sentences. Choose the correct words to complete the rules.

*If I **could** send something into space, I'**d** send a video of traffic. I'**d** include that **if** they **asked** me.*
*If you **could** send anything into space, what **would** you send?*

- we use the second conditional to talk about *real / unreal (hypothetical)* situations in the present and *future / past*
- use the verb in the *present / past* tense after *if*
- use *would*, *might* or *could* in the *main / if* clause

2 Use these words to make hypothetical sentences. Begin your sentences with *If* and change the verb forms as necessary.

1 I can include a song / it be *Imagine* by John Lennon
2 they ask me / I send a big note that says *Sorry*
3 I can put something on the Voyager Golden Record / I put a video of traffic
4 I have to include an image / it be an image of a table covered in food
5 I can do anything / I go on a space journey

3 Complete the questions using the words in brackets.

1 How ______ (*you feel*) if ______ (*the teacher give*) you an exam tomorrow?
2 If ______ (*you can change*) one thing about yourself, what ______ (*you change*)?
3 If ______ (*you not have*) English class today, what ______ (*you do*)?
4 If ______ (*you win*) a lot of money, what ______ (*you buy*) first?
5 What job ______ (*you choose*) if ______ (*you have*) the chance to do any job in the world?
6 Where ______ (*you go*) if ______ (*you can visit*) any country in the world?

4 Match answers a–f to questions 1–6 in exercise 3.

a A house near the beach for my parents. ___
b I'd go to France. I've always dreamt of seeing Paris. ___
c I'd go to the cinema and see a film. ___
d Probably pretty nervous. ___
e It would be my ears. I think my ears are too big. ___
f Something in the circus. Maybe an acrobat. ___

Grammar focus – explanation & more practice of the second conditional on page 146

Speaking

Work in small groups. You are going to play a guessing game. Turn to page 130 and follow the instructions.

Lost Unit 8

Glossary

Many texts include a short glossary of difficult words.

Grammar focus

Grammar focus sections at the back of the book provide reference and extra practice.

Coursebook: lessons 3 and 4 of a unit

Pronunciation

A focus on sounds, stress and intonation is included at regular intervals in *Global*. Pronunciation is integrated into the language points of the lesson. The aim is for students to achieve international intelligibility.

Texts

Texts are either information rich or excerpts from literary texts, modern and classic, with background information about the book and the author provided to give students extra cultural information. All the literary texts are also on the class audio, so students can read and listen to them.

Real world people

Reading and listening texts in *Global* are about real people and the real world.

UNIT 8 Lost & Found

Part 3

Vocabulary
Expressions with *make* & *do*

Reading
Top five inventions and discoveries made by accident

Grammar
Third conditional

Pronunciation
Expressing blame, intonation

Writing
How would your life have been different?

Vocabulary

1 Are these nouns used with *make* or *do*?

decisions   a difference   a discovery   an experiment   a favour   a job   a test   a mistake   nothing   progress   sense

2 Complete the sentences with words in the box in exercise 1.

1 I always put off making ______ until the last moment, especially important ones.
2 If I do ______ for somebody, then I think that person should do something for me.
3 I just love sitting around and doing ______ at the weekend.
4 I love my work. I think I'm doing ______ that really makes ______ to people's lives.
5 I don't understand this crazy world. Sometimes I think nothing makes ______.

3 Choose three sentences from exercise 2. Then work in pairs and tell your partner if the sentences are true for you. Explain why.

Reading

1 Read *Top five inventions and discoveries made by accident*. Do you agree with the order? Which is the most important for you?

2 Which discovery or discoveries …

1 was/were made outside a laboratory?
2 was/were a result of not cleaning up?
3 can save lives?
4 developed out of a failed idea?
5 was/were a result of a different experiment?
6 was/were a result of two lucky events?

Extend your vocabulary – with or without a plan

If you do something without a plan, you do it *by mistake* (negative), *by chance* (positive) or *by accident* (positive or negative).

Benedictus broke the flask by accident

If you do something with an aim or plan, you do it *on purpose*, *deliberately* or *intentionally*.

Fleming didn't leave the dish out on purpose.

Think of something you've done recently by accident. Has anything happened to you by chance?

94 Unit 8 Found

Grammar

If Spencer ***hadn't invented*** *the microwave, modern eating habits* ***might have been*** *very different.*
This ***wouldn't have been*** *significant* ***if*** *Fleming* ***hadn't noticed*** *one important thing.*

- we use the third conditional to imagine unreal situations in the past
- use the past perfect in the *if* clause
- use *would/may/might/could have* and a past participle in the main clause

1 Complete the sentences using information from the text on page 95.

1 If Alexander Fleming hadn't been so messy, he wouldn't have …
2 Arthur Fry wouldn't have invented sticky notes if he …
3 If Edouard Benedictus hadn't knocked over a glass flask, he …
4 Percy LeBaron Spencer wouldn't have … if a chocolate bar …
5 If Jacques E Brandenburger …

2 Think about how history would have been different if the things in the box hadn't been invented. Then work in pairs and compare your ideas.

the car   the computer   the printing press   the telephone   the TV

If the computer hadn't been invented the internet wouldn't have been developed.
If the printing press hadn't been invented ordinary people wouldn't have been able to read books.

G **Grammar focus** – explanation & more practice of the third conditional on page 146

Pronunciation

1 2.25 Look at the situation in the box and read and listen to the sentences. Notice the pronunciation of *would have* and *wouldn't have*. Then listen again and repeat.

You've forgotten to get the shopping for dinner.

1 If my boss hadn't made me work late, I would have got to the shops in time.
2 If you'd written me a note, I wouldn't have forgotten.

2 Work in pairs. Choose three situations and write sentences making excuses.

- You're late for a job interview.
- You didn't go to your friend's party.
- You haven't done the housework.
- You've missed a deadline at work.
- You haven't got enough money to pay the bills.
- You've forgotten your best friend's birthday.

3 Read your sentences to the class, paying attention to your pronunciation.

Writing

1 Make a list of important events in your life.

2 Write a paragraph describing how your life would have been different if the events you wrote hadn't happened.

In 2002 I got a job in Madrid. If I hadn't got this job, I'd have stayed in my home town. I wouldn't have got to know some of my best friends. And I wouldn't have met my wife …

Top five inventions and discoveries made by accident

1 Penicillin

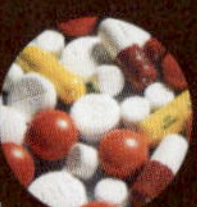

The laboratory of Scottish scientist Alexander Fleming was extremely untidy. One day in 1928 he came back from holiday and saw that mould had grown on a dish containing bacteria. However this wouldn't have been significant if Fleming hadn't noticed one important thing: that no bacteria were growing in the areas covered by mould. In later experiments Fleming proved that the mould could kill the bacteria that cause human infections. Using this discovery, Howard Florey and Ernst Boris Chain later developed penicillin for use as a medicine. In 1945 the three scientists shared the Nobel Prize for Medicine.

2 Sticky notes

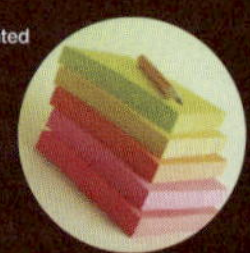

In 1968 Spencer Silver, an American research chemist, wanted to invent a strong glue. Instead he created a weak glue that stuck to objects but could be taken off again. A few years later a colleague of Silver's, Arthur Fry, was singing in church. His bookmarks kept falling out of his song book and suddenly he remembered Silver's glue. He successfully tried the glue on his bookmarks and later developed his idea into sticky notes.

3 The microwave oven

While Percy Spencer was working on radar research in 1946, he made an interesting discovery. He was testing a magnetron (a tube which produces microwaves) when he noticed a chocolate bar in his pocket had melted. Spencer did some experiments and found out that microwaves can cook food much more quickly than conventional ovens, because the food is cooked from inside, not by warming the air around it. If Spencer hadn't invented the microwave, modern eating habits might have been very different. Today more than 90% of households in the US have a microwave oven.

4 Safety glass

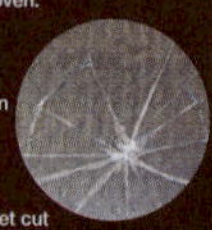

In 1903 the French scientist Edouard Benedictus broke a glass flask by accident. To his surprise he saw that the glass had broken into many small pieces – but the pieces had stayed together. He found out that liquid plastic in the flask had evaporated and left a thin film of plastic inside. By chance, in the same week Benedictus read a newspaper article about how many drivers get cut by broken glass in car accidents. He realised that he had made a useful discovery.

5 Cellophane

Swiss chemist Jacques E Brandenburger worked for a textile company. When he saw wine spilt on a restaurant tablecloth, he was inspired to make a tablecloth that wouldn't stain. He used a waterproof spray, but the experiment didn't work; the tablecloth became too stiff. Brandenburger noticed, however, that the thin plastic film came off the cloth easily. Today his discovery, cellophane, is used for wrapping up food.

Glossary

bookmark (*noun*) – something that you put inside a book so that you can find the page you want
evaporate (*verb*) – if liquid evaporates it changes into gas
film (*noun*) – a very thin layer of something that forms on a surface
glue (*noun*) – a sticky substance that you use to fix things to each other
mould (*noun*) – a green, blue or white substance which grows on food that is not fresh, or things that are not kept clean and dry.
waterproof (*adjective*) – something that is waterproof does not get damaged by water

Found Unit 8 95

Developing critical thinking

Reading tasks and discussion questions for texts encourage reflection and critical thinking.

Extend your vocabulary

Regular *Extend your vocabulary* boxes draw on language in the unit and help students gain a deeper word knowledge. Word families, easily confused words and different ways of expressing concepts are covered in these sections throughout the book.

Short writing tasks

Some lessons end with a short writing task to give students the opportunity to develop fluency in writing as well as speaking.

Balance of skills

Each lesson has a balance of skills work and language work.

Grammar practice

Grammar practice is highly contextualised and meaningful, often in texts that provide additional information about the topic of the lesson. Many grammar practice exercises are designed in a similar way to the reading texts.

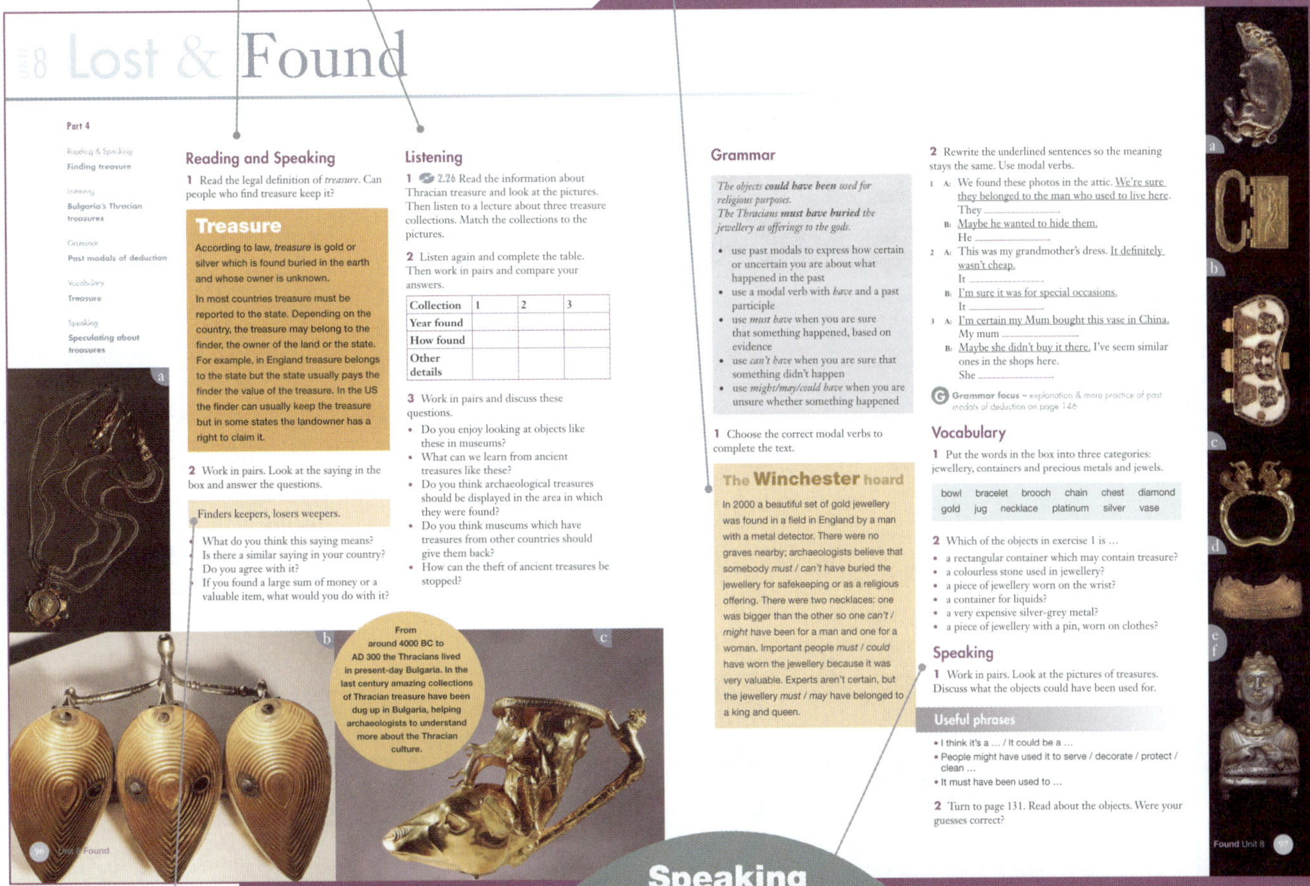

UNIT 8 Lost & Found

Part 4

Reading & Speaking
Finding treasure

Listening
Bulgaria's Thracian treasures

Grammar
Past modals of deduction

Vocabulary
Treasure

Speaking
Speculating about treasures

Reading and Speaking

1 Read the legal definition of *treasure*. Can people who find treasure keep it?

Treasure

According to law, *treasure* is gold or silver which is found buried in the earth and whose owner is unknown.

In most countries treasure must be reported to the state. Depending on the country, the treasure may belong to the finder, the owner of the land or the state. For example, in England treasure belongs to the state but the state usually pays the finder the value of the treasure. In the US the finder can usually keep the treasure but in some states the landowner has a right to claim it.

2 Work in pairs. Look at the saying in the box and answer the questions.

Finders keepers, losers weepers.

- What do you think this saying means?
- Is there a similar saying in your country?
- Do you agree with it?
- If you found a large sum of money or a valuable item, what would you do with it?

Listening

1 2.26 Read the information about Thracian treasure and look at the pictures. Then listen to a lecture about three treasure collections. Match the collections to the pictures.

2 Listen again and complete the table. Then work in pairs and compare your answers.

Collection	1	2	3
Year found			
How found			
Other details			

3 Work in pairs and discuss these questions.

- Do you enjoy looking at objects like these in museums?
- What can we learn from ancient treasures like these?
- Do you think archaeological treasures should be displayed in the area in which they were found?
- Do you think museums which have treasures from other countries should give them back?
- How can the theft of ancient treasures be stopped?

From around 4000 BC to AD 300 the Thracians lived in present-day Bulgaria. In the last century amazing collections of Thracian treasure have been dug up in Bulgaria, helping archaeologists to understand more about the Thracian culture.

Grammar

The objects ***could have been*** *used for religious purposes.*
The Thracians ***must have buried*** *the jewellery as offerings to the gods.*

- use past modals to express how certain or uncertain you are about what happened in the past
- use a modal verb with *have* and a past participle
- use *must have* when you are sure that something happened, based on evidence
- use *can't have* when you are sure that something didn't happen
- use *might/may/could have* when you are unsure whether something happened

1 Choose the correct modal verbs to complete the text.

The Winchester hoard

In 2000 a beautiful set of gold jewellery was found in a field in England by a man with a metal detector. There were no graves nearby; archaeologists believe that somebody *must / can't* have buried the jewellery for safekeeping or as a religious offering. There were two necklaces: one was bigger than the other so one *can't / might* have been for a man and one for a woman. Important people *must / could* have worn the jewellery because it was very valuable. Experts aren't certain, but the jewellery *must / may* have belonged to a king and queen.

2 Rewrite the underlined sentences so the meaning stays the same. Use modal verbs.

1 A: We found these photos in the attic. We're sure they belonged to the man who used to live here.
They ....
B: Maybe he wanted to hide them.
He ....
2 A: This was my grandmother's dress. It definitely wasn't cheap.
It ....
B: I'm sure it was for special occasions.
It ....
3 A: I'm certain my Mum bought this vase in China.
My mum ....
B: Maybe she didn't buy it there. I've seem similar ones in the shops here.
She ....

Grammar focus – explanation & more practice of past modals of deduction on page 146

Vocabulary

1 Put the words in the box into three categories: jewellery, containers and precious metals and jewels.

bowl bracelet brooch chain chest diamond
gold jug necklace platinum silver vase

2 Which of the objects in exercise 1 is …

- a rectangular container which may contain treasure?
- a colourless stone used in jewellery?
- a piece of jewellery worn on the wrist?
- a container for liquids?
- a very expensive silver-grey metal?
- a piece of jewellery with a pin, worn on clothes?

Speaking

1 Work in pairs. Look at the pictures of treasures. Discuss what the objects could have been used for.

Useful phrases

- I think it's a … / It could be a …
- People might have used it to serve / decorate / protect / clean …
- It must have been used to …

2 Turn to page 131. Read about the objects. Were your guesses correct?

96 Unit 8 Found

Found Unit 8 97

Speaking

A wide variety of speaking tasks are presented in the book. Support is given in the form of vocabulary (useful language) and constructions (useful phrases).

Many speaking tasks include an element of choice (students can choose from different tasks or questions). This gives the teacher and students flexibility and can be used in mixed ability classes.

Informal language

Informal language and idioms are introduced and discussed throughout *Global*.

Coursebook: extra material at the end of a unit

Function globally

Every unit includes a *Function globally* section. This contains frequent functional and situational language that is immediately useful outside the classroom.

Global English

Every other unit contains an extra reading lesson called *Global English* featuring a text by David Crystal, which provides interesting information about the English language.

Global voices

Every other unit contains a listening section featuring authentic and unscripted recordings of a wide range of native and non-native speakers of English, which expose learners to real English as it is being used around the world today.

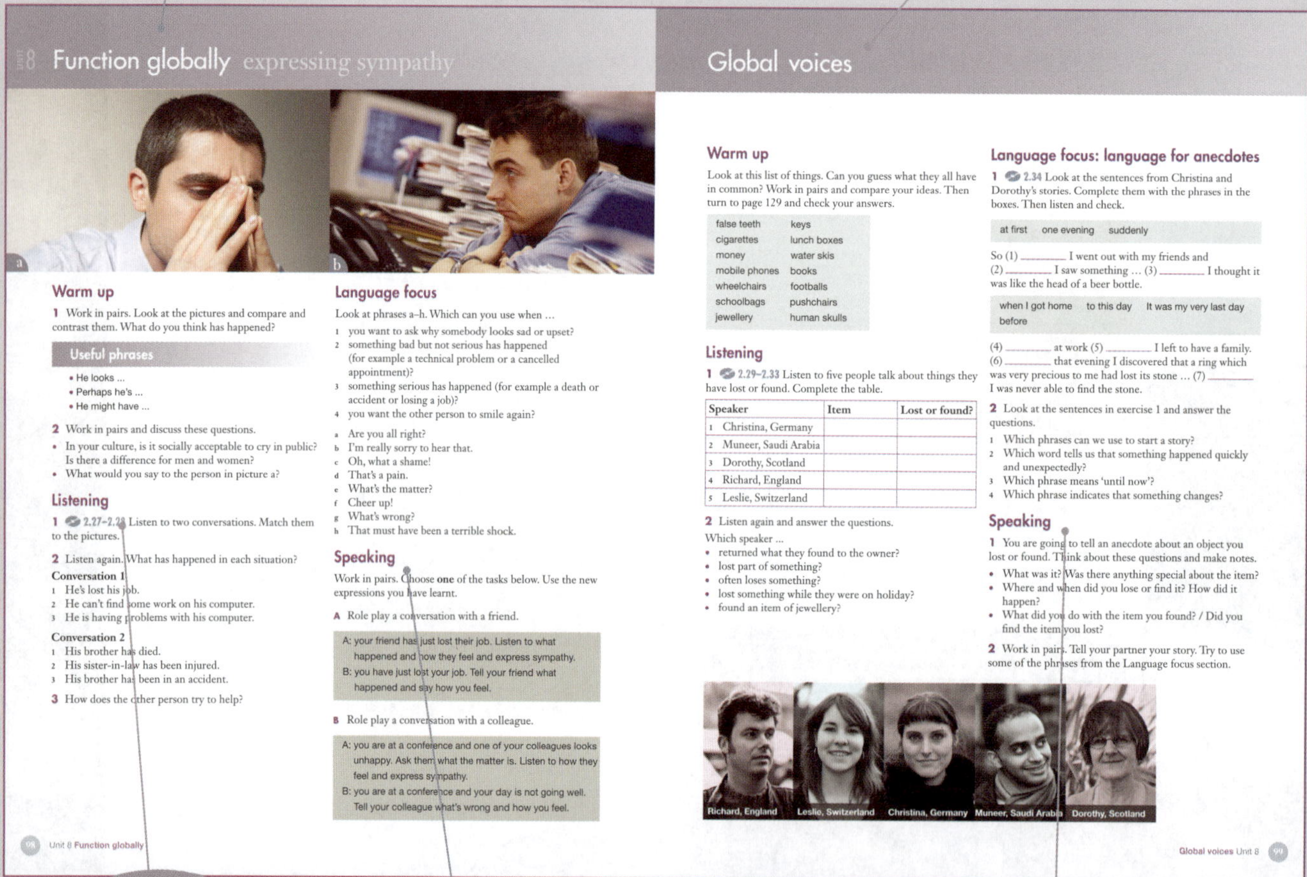

UNIT 8 Function globally expressing sympathy

Warm up

1 Work in pairs. Look at the pictures and compare and contrast them. What do you think has happened?

Useful phrases

- He looks ...
- Perhaps he's ...
- He might have ...

2 Work in pairs and discuss these questions.

- In your culture, is it socially acceptable to cry in public? Is there a difference for men and women?
- What would you say to the person in picture a?

Listening

1 2.27–2.28 Listen to two conversations. Match them to the pictures.

2 Listen again. What has happened in each situation?

Conversation 1

1 He's lost his job.
2 He can't find some work on his computer.
3 He is having problems with his computer.

Conversation 2

1 His brother has died.
2 His sister-in-law has been injured.
3 His brother has been in an accident.

3 How does the other person try to help?

Language focus

Look at phrases a–h. Which can you use when ...

1 you want to ask why somebody looks sad or upset?
2 something bad but not serious has happened (for example a technical problem or a cancelled appointment)?
3 something serious has happened (for example a death or accident or losing a job)?
4 you want the other person to smile again?

a Are you all right?
b I'm really sorry to hear that.
c Oh, what a shame!
d That's a pain.
e What's the matter?
f Cheer up!
g What's wrong?
h That must have been a terrible shock.

Speaking

Work in pairs. Choose **one** of the tasks below. Use the new expressions you have learnt.

A Role play a conversation with a friend.

A: your friend has just lost their job. Listen to what happened and how they feel and express sympathy.
B: you have just lost your job. Tell your friend what happened and say how you feel.

B Role play a conversation with a colleague.

A: you are at a conference and one of your colleagues looks unhappy. Ask them what the matter is. Listen to how they feel and express sympathy.
B: you are at a conference and your day is not going well. Tell your colleague what's wrong and how you feel.

Unit 8 Function globally

Global voices

Warm up

Look at this list of things. Can you guess what they all have in common? Work in pairs and compare your ideas. Then turn to page 129 and check your answers.

false teeth	keys
cigarettes	lunch boxes
money	water skis
mobile phones	books
wheelchairs	footballs
schoolbags	pushchairs
jewellery	human skulls

Listening

1 2.29–2.33 Listen to five people talk about things they have lost or found. Complete the table.

Speaker	Item	Lost or found?
1 Christina, Germany		
2 Muneer, Saudi Arabia		
3 Dorothy, Scotland		
4 Richard, England		
5 Leslie, Switzerland		

2 Listen again and answer the questions.

Which speaker ...

- returned what they found to the owner?
- lost part of something?
- often loses something?
- lost something while they were on holiday?
- found an item of jewellery?

Language focus: language for anecdotes

1 2.34 Look at the sentences from Christina and Dorothy's stories. Complete them with the phrases in the boxes. Then listen and check.

at first one evening suddenly

So (1) ________ I went out with my friends and (2) ________ I saw something ... (3) ________ I thought it was like the head of a beer bottle.

when I got home to this day It was my very last day before

(4) ________ at work (5) ________ I left to have a family. (6) ________ that evening I discovered that a ring which was very precious to me had lost its stone ... (7) ________ I was never able to find the stone.

2 Look at the sentences in exercise 1 and answer the questions.

1 Which phrases can we use to start a story?
2 Which word tells us that something happened quickly and unexpectedly?
3 Which phrase means 'until now'?
4 Which phrase indicates that something changes?

Speaking

1 You are going to tell an anecdote about an object you lost or found. Think about these questions and make notes.

- What was it? Was there anything special about the item?
- Where and when did you lose or find it? How did it happen?
- What did you do with the item you found? / Did you find the item you lost?

2 Work in pairs. Tell your partner your story. Try to use some of the phrases from the Language focus section.

Richard, England Leslie, Switzerland Christina, Germany Muneer, Saudi Arabia Dorothy, Scotland

Global voices Unit 8

Listening

Students hear conversations in various situations which help contextualise the language and provide a model.

Putting it into practice

This is followed by a choice of speaking activity so that students can put the new language to use immediately.

Extended speaking

Each *Global voices* page ends with an extended speaking task, allowing students to personalise the language.

Coursebook: extra material at the end of a unit

Writing

Each unit focuses on a specific writing skill and a language point, presented within a particular genre. Learners' critical ability is developed by reading, analysing and correcting one aspect of a model writing text.

Global review

Revision is crucial for language learning. Each unit contains review activities that cover the main grammar and vocabulary points.

Study skills

Developing effective study skills and strategies is an essential part of language learning. The *Study skills* section in each unit focuses on a particular skill or strategy.

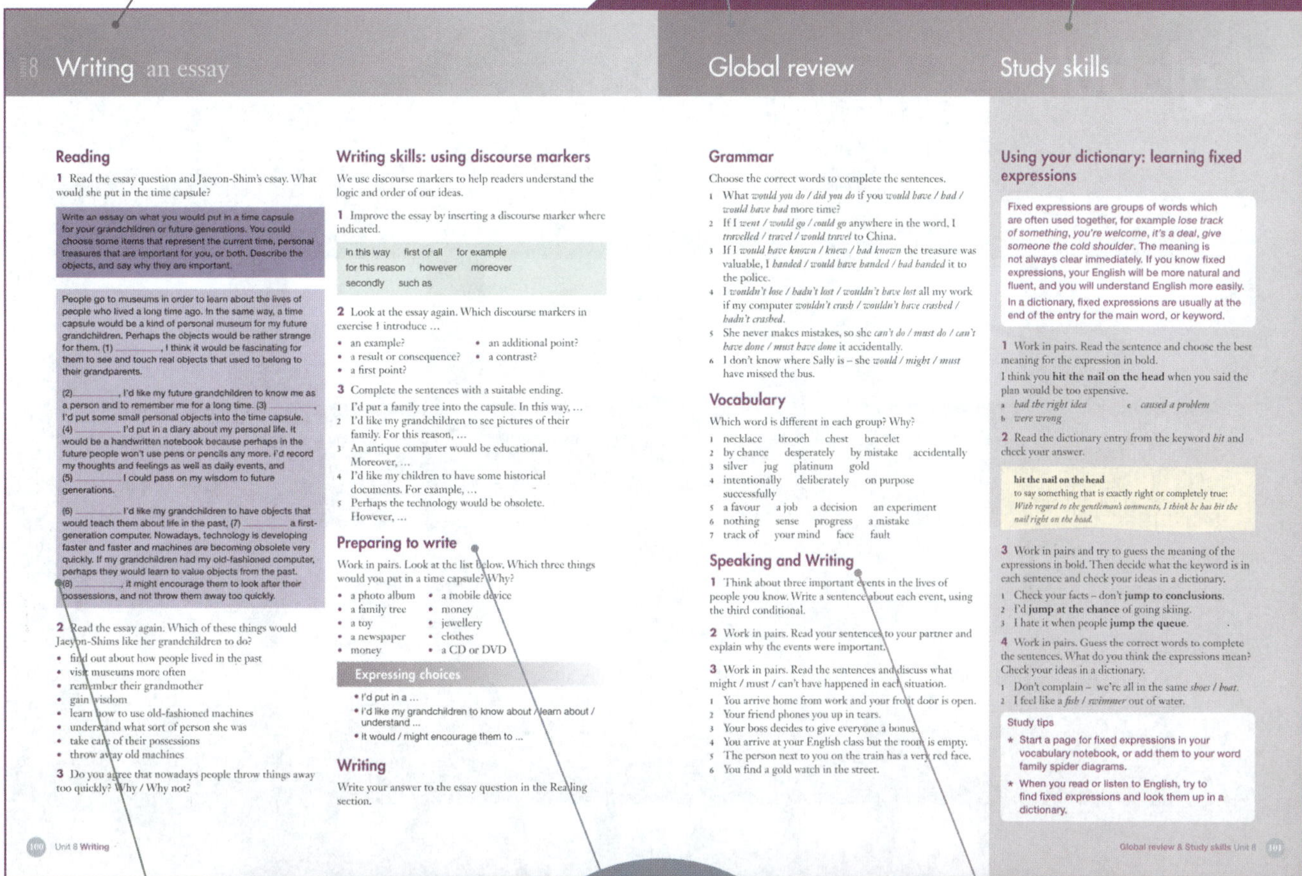

8 Writing an essay

Reading

1 Read the essay question and Jaeyon-Shim's essay. What would she put in the time capsule?

Write an essay on what you would put in a time capsule for your grandchildren or future generations. You could choose some items that represent the current time, personal treasures that are important for you, or both. Describe the objects, and say why they are important.

People go to museums in order to learn about the lives of people who lived a long time ago. In the same way, a time capsule would be a kind of personal museum for my future grandchildren. Perhaps the objects would be rather strange for them. (1) ________, I think it would be fascinating for them to see and touch real objects that used to belong to their grandparents.

(2) ________, I'd like my future grandchildren to know me as a person and to remember me for a long time. (3) ________, I'd put some small personal objects into the time capsule. (4) ________ I'd put in a diary about my personal life. It would be a handwritten notebook because perhaps in the future people won't use pens or pencils any more. I'd record my thoughts and feelings as well as daily events, and (5) ________ I could pass on my wisdom to future generations.

(6) ________ I'd like my grandchildren to have objects that would teach them about life in the past, (7) ________ a first-generation computer. Nowadays, technology is developing faster and faster and machines are becoming obsolete very quickly. If my grandchildren had my old-fashioned computer, perhaps they would learn to value objects from the past. (8) ________, it might encourage them to look after their possessions, and not throw them away too quickly.

2 Read the essay again. Which of these things would Jaeyon-Shims like her grandchildren to do?

- find out about how people lived in the past
- visit museums more often
- remember their grandmother
- gain wisdom
- learn how to use old-fashioned machines
- understand what sort of person she was
- take care of their possessions
- throw away old machines

3 Do you agree that nowadays people throw things away too quickly? Why / Why not?

Writing skills: using discourse markers

We use discourse markers to help readers understand the logic and order of our ideas.

1 Improve the essay by inserting a discourse marker where indicated.

in this way   first of all   for example   for this reason   however   moreover   secondly   such as

2 Look at the essay again. Which discourse markers in exercise 1 introduce ...

- an example?
- a result or consequence?
- a first point?
- an additional point?
- a contrast?

3 Complete the sentences with a suitable ending.

1 I'd put a family tree into the capsule. In this way, ...
2 I'd like my grandchildren to see pictures of their family. For this reason, ...
3 An antique computer would be educational. Moreover, ...
4 I'd like my children to have some historical documents. For example, ...
5 Perhaps the technology would be obsolete. However, ...

Preparing to write

Work in pairs. Look at the list below. Which three things would you put in a time capsule? Why?

- a photo album
- a family tree
- a toy
- a newspaper
- money
- a mobile device
- money
- jewellery
- clothes
- a CD or DVD

Expressing choices

- I'd put in a ...
- I'd like my grandchildren to know about / learn about / understand ...
- It would / might encourage them to ...

Writing

Write your answer to the essay question in the Reading section.

Global review

Grammar

Choose the correct words to complete the sentences.

1 What *would you do / did you do* if you *would have / had / would have had* more time?
2 If I *went / would go / could go* anywhere in the word, I *travelled / travel / would travel* to China.
3 If I *would have known / knew / had known* the treasure was valuable, I *handed / would have handed / had handed* it to the police.
4 I *wouldn't lose / hadn't lost / wouldn't have lost* all my work if my computer *wouldn't crash / wouldn't have crashed / hadn't crashed*.
5 She never makes mistakes, so she *can't do / must do / can't have done / must have done* it accidentally.
6 I don't know where Sally is – she *would / might / must* have missed the bus.

Vocabulary

Which word is different in each group? Why?

1 necklace   brooch   chest   bracelet
2 by chance   desperately   by mistake   accidentally
3 silver   jug   platinum   gold
4 intentionally   deliberately   on purpose   successfully
5 a favour   a job   a decision   an experiment
6 nothing   sense   progress   a mistake
7 track of   your mind   face   fault

Speaking and Writing

1 Think about three important events in the lives of people you know. Write a sentence about each event, using the third conditional.

2 Work in pairs. Read your sentences to your partner and explain why the events were important.

3 Work in pairs. Read the sentences and discuss what might / must / can't have happened in each situation.

1 You arrive home from work and your front door is open.
2 Your friend phones you up in tears.
3 Your boss decides to give everyone a bonus.
4 You arrive at your English class but the room is empty.
5 The person next to you on the train has a very red face.
6 You find a gold watch in the street.

Study skills

Using your dictionary: learning fixed expressions

Fixed expressions are groups of words which are often used together, for example *lose track of something, you're welcome, it's a deal, give someone the cold shoulder*. The meaning is not always clear immediately. If you know fixed expressions, your English will be more natural and fluent, and you will understand English more easily.

In a dictionary, fixed expressions are usually at the end of the entry for the main word, or keyword.

1 Work in pairs. Read the sentence and choose the best meaning for the expression in bold.

I think you **hit the nail on the head** when you said the plan would be too expensive.

a *had the right idea*
b *were wrong*
c *caused a problem*

2 Read the dictionary entry from the keyword *hit* and check your answer.

hit the nail on the head
to say something that is exactly right or completely true: *With regard to the gentleman's comments, I think he has hit the nail right on the head.*

3 Work in pairs and try to guess the meaning of the expressions in bold. Then decide what the keyword is in each sentence and check your ideas in a dictionary.

1 Check your facts – don't **jump to conclusions**.
2 I'd **jump at the chance** of going skiing.
3 I hate it when people **jump the queue**.

4 Work in pairs. Guess the correct words to complete the sentences. What do you think the expressions mean? Check your ideas in a dictionary.

1 Don't complain – we're all in the same *shoes / boat*.
2 I feel like a *fish / swimmer* out of water.

Study tips

★ Start a page for fixed expressions in your vocabulary notebook, or add them to your word family spider diagrams.
★ When you read or listen to English, try to find fixed expressions and look them up in a dictionary.

Writing models

Texts are based on authentic pieces of writing from international students at Intermediate level, reflecting the interests of a worldwide audience and providing a realistic model within their capabilities.

Preparation

Structured preparation tasks, useful language and paired activities guide students towards production of a final piece of writing.

Extra speaking and writing practice

Speaking and writing tasks based on the unit topic provide an extra opportunity to revise and consolidate the language from the unit in a freer and more open-ended format.

eWorkbook

Comprehensive component for self-study

The *Global* eWorkbook represents an evolution in self-study materials for learners. Within a rich multimedia environment it provides a wealth of resources for the learner, enabling them to continue their studies at their own pace, and in their own time.

Language work

The eWorkbook contains a wide range of activities which allow for extra practice and review of the language presented in the Coursebook. These activities cover all aspects of language learning. Grammar, vocabulary, listening and pronunciation practice activities are available both as fully interactive activities and in a printable pen-and-paper format. There are also worksheets to practise reading and writing skills.

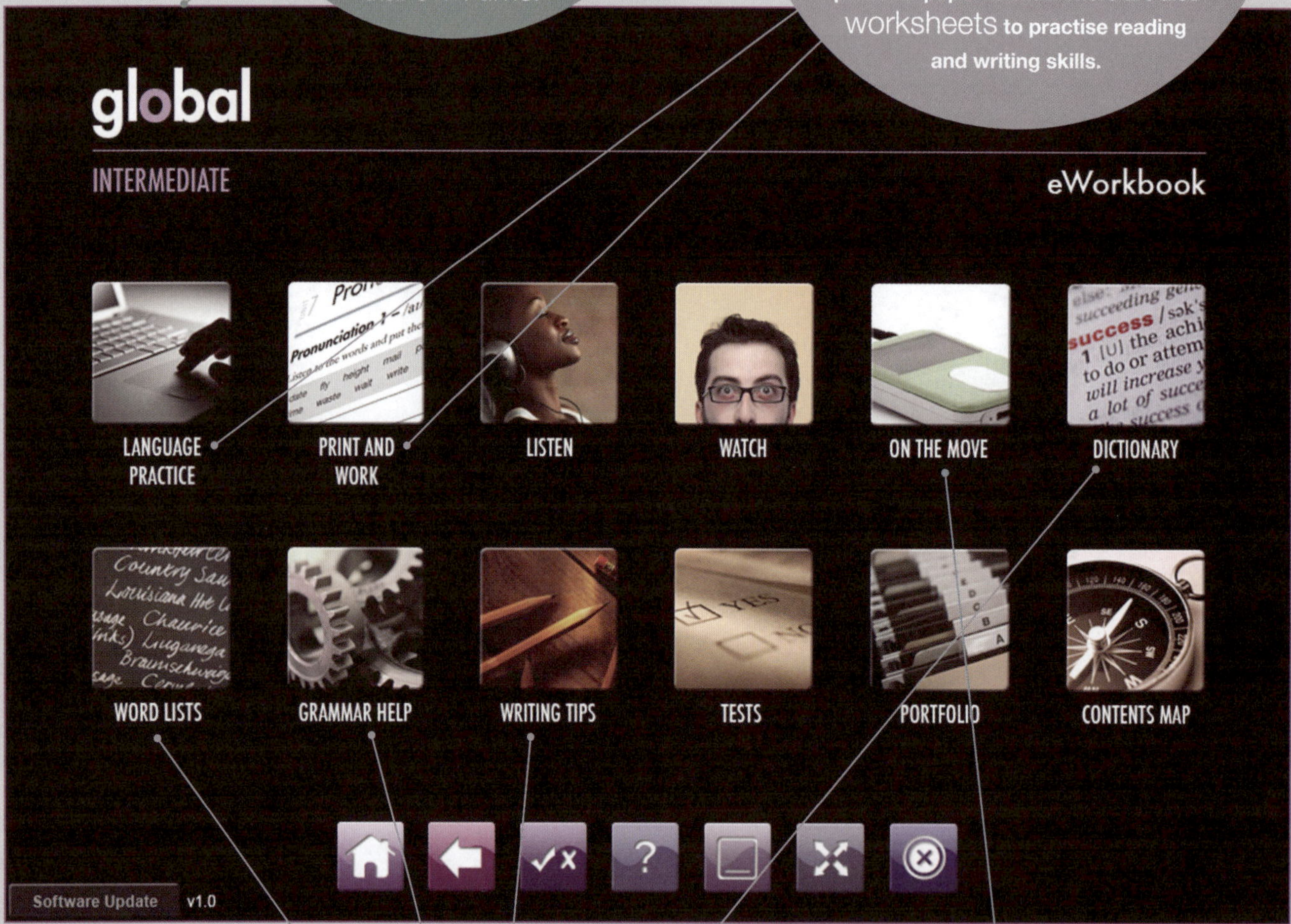

Tools for reference and support

The eWorkbook offers all the support the learner may need. For instance, links to the Macmillan English Dictionary Online, Word Lists per unit and Grammar Help organised by topic. The Writing Tips section includes information on general aspects of writing, such as spelling, punctuation, paragraphing, etc.

Learning on the move

The *Global* eWorkbook provides a wide variety of authentic extra listening and video materials supplied in commonly used file formats, so learners can load them onto their portable music and video players and study and review 'on the go'.

Interactive activities

Meaningful practice.

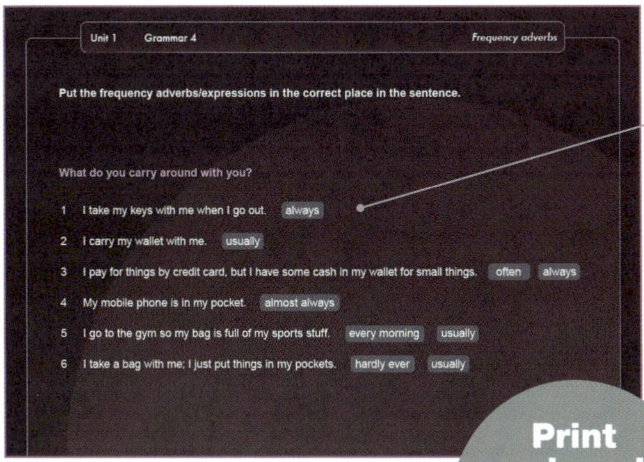

Video

Extracts from BBC and other programmes as well as original videos that can be downloaded and used on the move.

Print and work

For those who prefer to work offline.

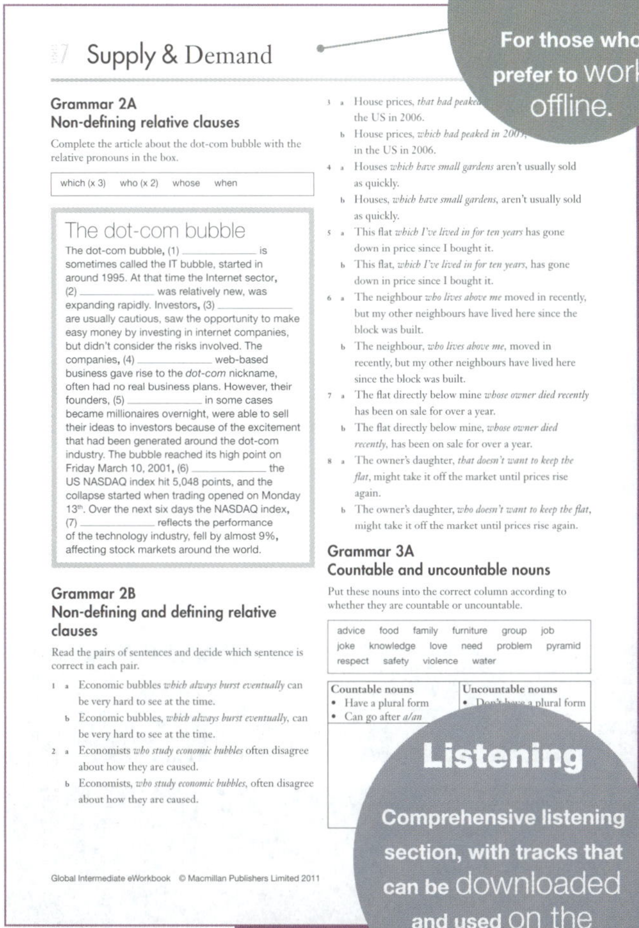

Supply & Demand

Grammar 2A
Non-defining relative clauses

Complete the article about the dot-com bubble with the relative pronouns in the box.

which (x 3) who (x 2) whose when

The dot-com bubble

The dot-com bubble, (1) ________ is sometimes called the IT bubble, started in around 1995. At that time the Internet sector, (2) ________ was relatively new, was expanding rapidly. Investors, (3) ________ are usually cautious, saw the opportunity to make easy money by investing in internet companies, but didn't consider the risks involved. The companies, (4) ________ web-based business gave rise to the *dot-com* nickname, often had no real business plans. However, their founders, (5) ________ in some cases became millionaires overnight, were able to sell their ideas to investors because of the excitement that had been generated around the dot-com industry. The bubble reached its high point on Friday March 10, 2001, (6) ________ the US NASDAQ index hit 5,048 points, and the collapse started when trading opened on Monday 13th. Over the next six days the NASDAQ index, (7) ________ reflects the performance of the technology industry, fell by almost 9%, affecting stock markets around the world.

Grammar 2B
Non-defining and defining relative clauses

Read the pairs of sentences and decide which sentence is correct in each pair.

1 a Economic bubbles *which always burst eventually* can be very hard to see at the time.
b Economic bubbles, *which always burst eventually*, can be very hard to see at the time.
2 a Economists *who study economic bubbles* often disagree about how they are caused.
b Economists, *who study economic bubbles*, often disagree about how they are caused.
3 a House prices, *that had peaked* ... the US in 2006.
b House prices, *which had peaked in 2007*, ... in the US in 2006.
4 a Houses *which have small gardens* aren't usually sold as quickly.
b Houses, *which have small gardens*, aren't usually sold as quickly.
5 a This flat *which I've lived in for ten years* has gone down in price since I bought it.
b This flat, *which I've lived in for ten years*, has gone down in price since I bought it.
6 a The neighbour *who lives above me* moved in recently, but my other neighbours have lived here since the block was built.
b The neighbour, *who lives above me*, moved in recently, but my other neighbours have lived here since the block was built.
7 a The flat directly below mine *whose owner died recently* has been on sale for over a year.
b The flat directly below mine, *whose owner died recently*, has been on sale for over a year.
8 a The owner's daughter, *that doesn't want to keep the flat*, might take it off the market until prices rise again.
b The owner's daughter, *who doesn't want to keep the flat*, might take it off the market until prices rise again.

Grammar 3A
Countable and uncountable nouns

Put these nouns into the correct column according to whether they are countable or uncountable.

advice food family furniture group job joke knowledge love need problem pyramid respect safety violence water

Countable nouns	Uncountable nouns
• Have a plural form • Can go after a/an	• Don't have a plural form

Global Intermediate eWorkbook © Macmillan Publishers Limited 2011

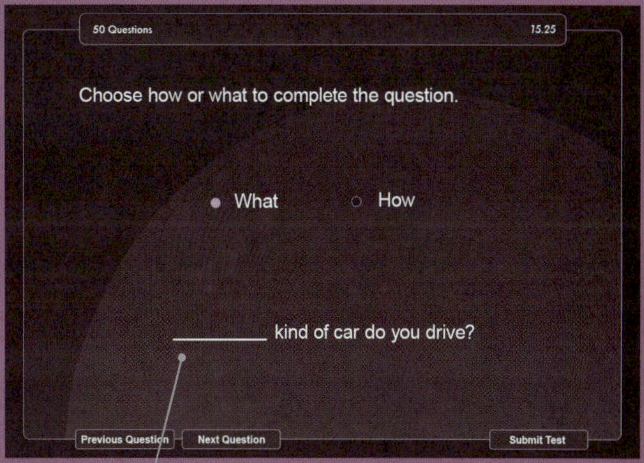

Listening

Comprehensive listening section, with tracks that can be downloaded and used on the move.

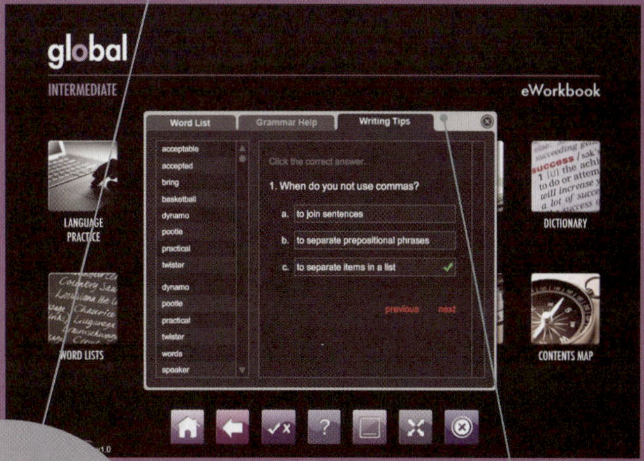

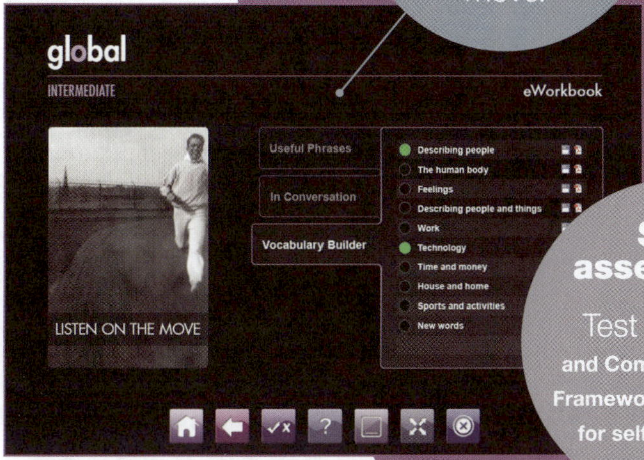

Self-assessment

Test generator and Common European Framework checklists for self-assessment.

Tools

Comprehensive tools for self-study.

Teacher's Book

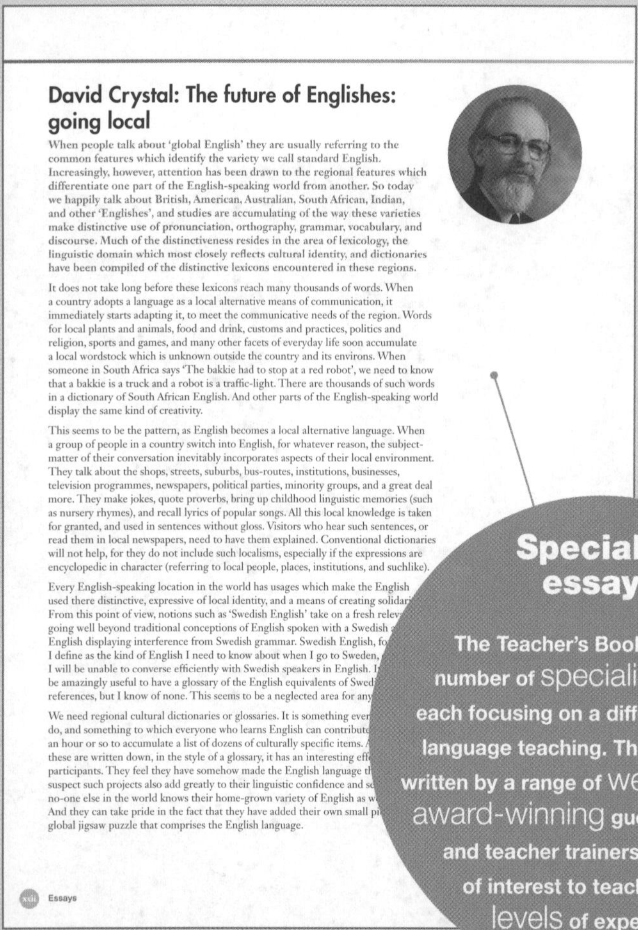

David Crystal: The future of Englishes: going local

When people talk about 'global English' they are usually referring to the common features which identify the variety we call standard English. Increasingly, however, attention has been drawn to the regional features which differentiate one part of the English-speaking world from another. So today we happily talk about British, American, Australian, South African, Indian, and other 'Englishes', and studies are accumulating of the way these varieties make distinctive use of pronunciation, orthography, grammar, vocabulary, and discourse. Much of the distinctiveness resides in the area of lexicology, the linguistic domain which most closely reflects cultural identity, and dictionaries have been compiled of the distinctive lexicons encountered in these regions.

It does not take long before these lexicons reach many thousands of words. When a country adopts a language as a local alternative means of communication, it immediately starts adapting it, to meet the communicative needs of the region. Words for local plants and animals, food and drink, customs and practices, politics and religion, sports and games, and many other facets of everyday life soon accumulate a local wordstock which is unknown outside the country and its environs. When someone in South Africa says 'The bakkie had to stop at a red robot', we need to know that a bakkie is a truck and a robot is a traffic-light. There are thousands of such words in a dictionary of South African English. And other parts of the English-speaking world display the same kind of creativity.

This seems to be the pattern, as English becomes a local alternative language. When a group of people in a country switch into English, for whatever reason, the subject-matter of their conversation inevitably incorporates aspects of their local environment. They talk about the shops, streets, suburbs, bus-routes, institutions, businesses, television programmes, newspapers, political parties, minority groups, and a great deal more. They make jokes, quote proverbs, bring up childhood linguistic memories (such as nursery rhymes), and recall lyrics of popular songs. All this local knowledge is taken for granted, and used in sentences without gloss. Visitors who hear such sentences, or read them in local newspapers, need to have them explained. Conventional dictionaries will not help, for they do not include such localisms, especially if the expressions are encyclopedic in character (referring to local people, places, institutions, and suchlike).

Every English-speaking location in the world has usages which make the English used there distinctive, expressive of local identity, and a means of creating solidari[…] From this point of view, notions such as 'Swedish English' take on a fresh relev[…] going well beyond traditional conceptions of English spoken with a Swedish a[…] English displaying interference from Swedish grammar. Swedish English, fo[…] I define as the kind of English I need to know about when I go to Sweden, […] I will be unable to converse efficiently with Swedish speakers in English. I[…] be amazingly useful to have a glossary of the English equivalents of Swed[…] references, but I know of none. This seems to be a neglected area for any[…]

We need regional cultural dictionaries or glossaries. It is something ever[…] do, and something to which everyone who learns English can contribute[…] an hour or so to accumulate a list of dozens of culturally specific items. […] these are written down, in the style of a glossary, it has an interesting eff[…] participants. They feel they have somehow made the English language th[…] suspect such projects also add greatly to their linguistic confidence and se[…] no-one else in the world knows their home-grown variety of English as w[…] And they can take pride in the fact that they have added their own small pi[…] global jigsaw puzzle that comprises the English language.

xiii Essays

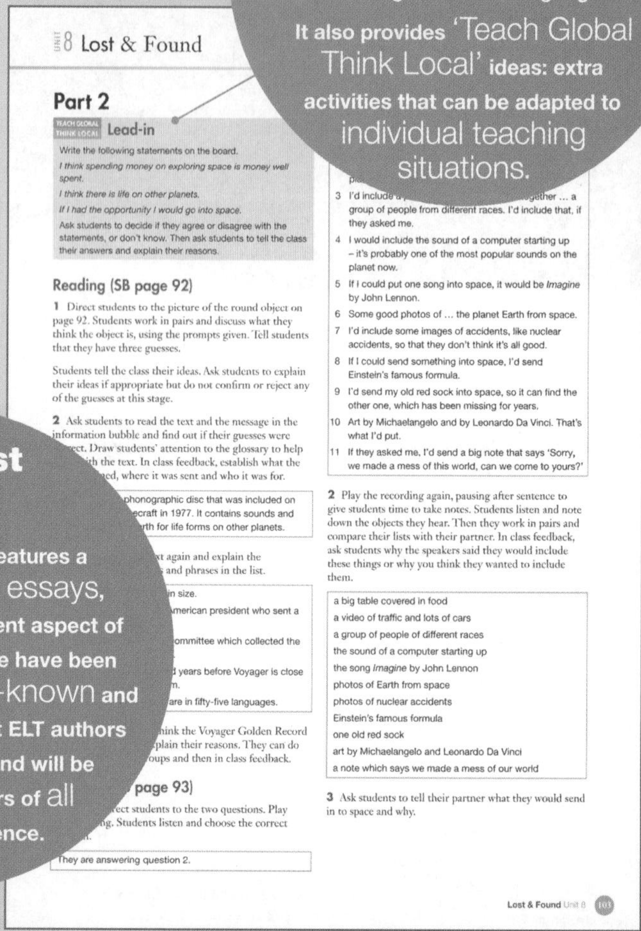

UNIT 8 Lost & Found

Part 2

TEACH GLOBAL THINK LOCAL **Lead-in**

Write the following statements on the board.

I think spending money on exploring space is money well spent.

I think there is life on other planets.

If I had the opportunity I would go into space.

Ask students to decide if they agree or disagree with the statements, or don't know. Then ask students to tell the class their answers and explain their reasons.

Reading (SB page 92)

1 Direct students to the picture of the round object on page 92. Students work in pairs and discuss what they think the object is, using the prompts given. Tell students that they have three guesses.

Students tell the class their ideas. Ask students to explain their ideas if appropriate but do not confirm or reject any of the guesses at this stage.

2 Ask students to read the text and the message in the information bubble and find out if their guesses were […]ect. Draw students' attention to the glossary to help […]ith the text. In class feedback, establish what the […]ed, where it was sent and who it was for.

[…] phonographic disc that was included on […]ecraft in 1977. It contains sounds and […]rth for life forms on other planets.

[…]xt again and explain the […] and phrases in the list.

[…]n size.
[…]merican president who sent a
[…]ommittee which collected the
[…] years before Voyager is close […]n.
[…]are in fifty-five languages.

[…]hink the Voyager Golden Record […]plain their reasons. They can do […]oups and then in class feedback.

[…] page 93)

[…]ect students to the two questions. Play […]ng. Students listen and choose the correct […]

They are answering question 2.

3 I'd include a […]gether … a group of people from different races. I'd include that, if they asked me.
4 I would include the sound of a computer starting up – it's probably one of the most popular sounds on the planet now.
5 If I could put one song into space, it would be *Imagine* by John Lennon.
6 Some good photos of … the planet Earth from space.
7 I'd include some images of accidents, like nuclear accidents, so that they don't think it's all good.
8 If I could send something into space, I'd send Einstein's famous formula.
9 I'd send my old red sock into space, so it can find the other one, which has been missing for years.
10 Art by Michaelangelo and by Leonardo Da Vinci. That's what I'd put.
11 If they asked me, I'd send a big note that says 'Sorry, we made a mess of this world, can we come to yours?'

2 Play the recording again, pausing after sentence to give students time to take notes. Students listen and note down the objects they hear. Then they work in pairs and compare their lists with their partner. In class feedback, ask students why the speakers said they would include these things or why you think they wanted to include them.

a big table covered in food
a video of traffic and lots of cars
a group of people of different races
the sound of a computer starting up
the song *Imagine* by John Lennon
photos of Earth from space
photos of nuclear accidents
Einstein's famous formula
one old red sock
art by Michaelangelo and Leonardo Da Vinci
a note which says we made a mess of our world

3 Ask students to tell their partner what they would send in to space and why.

Lost & Found Unit 8 103

Teach Global Think Local

The Teacher's Book includes comprehensive teaching notes with answer keys and audioscripts, and detailed background and language notes. It also provides 'Teach Global Think Local' ideas: extra activities that can be adapted to individual teaching situations.

Specialist essays

The Teacher's Book features a number of specialist essays, each focusing on a different aspect of language teaching. These have been written by a range of well-known and award-winning guest ELT authors and teacher trainers, and will be of interest to teachers of all levels of experience.

Teacher's Resource Disc

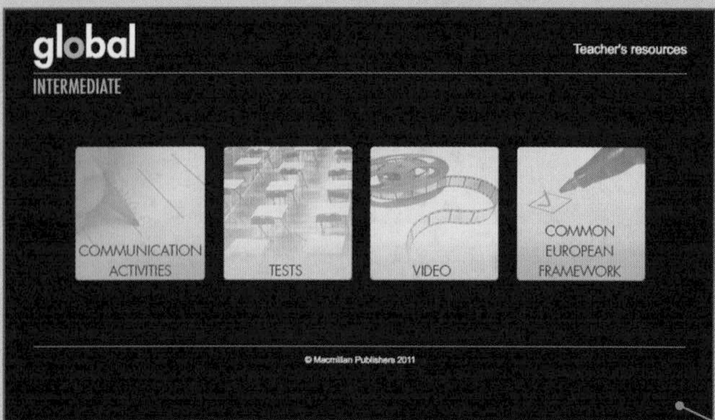

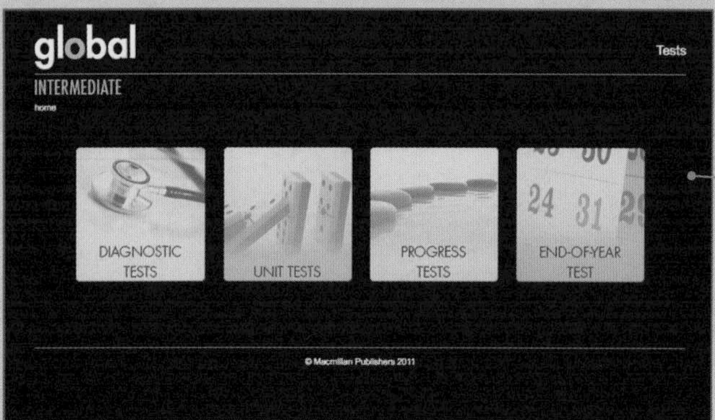

Communication activities, tests, videos

The Teacher's Resource Disc includes printable communication activity worksheets that practise areas of language from the Coursebook units and printable communication activity worksheets to do at different stages of the course. In addition, it provides a wide range of tests (diagnostic tests, progress tests, end-of-year tests, etc) and additional video clips and video worksheets for the teacher.

Class Audio CDs

The *Global* Intermediate class audio is contained on two CDs. They include the listening material from the Coursebook and recordings of the literary extracts featured in the book.

Website

The *Global* website consists of author blogs, teaching tips, extra resources and much more.

www.macmillanenglish.com/global

Global Digital

Enhancing the teaching experience in the classroom

Global Digital is a digital component designed for classroom use. It can be used with an interactive whiteboard or with a computer and projector.

The Digital Book

The Digital Book allows the teacher to access and display an interactive version of any page from the Coursebook in front of the class. All of the relevant audio, video and reference materials are instantly accessible right on the page.

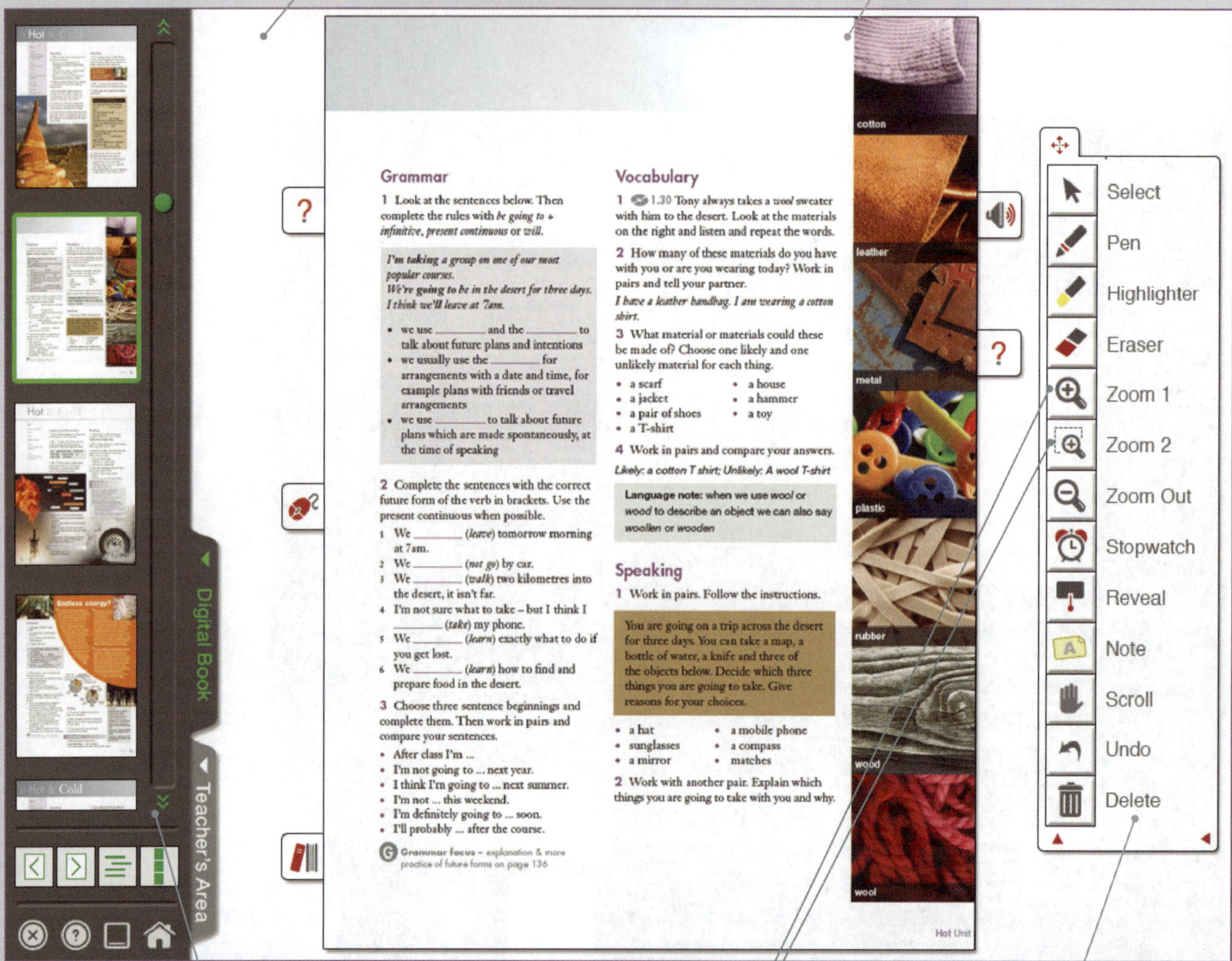

Navigation pane

The navigation pane allows you to select a page from anywhere in the book.

Zooming in and out

The Zoom tools allow you to zoom in either on pre-defined areas or any part of the page that you choose.

Toolbox

The toolbox provides a number of tools which enable you to interact with the Digital book page.

The Teacher's Area

The Teacher's Area can be used to create your own material either before or during the class. You can insert and edit text and images, add links to pages from the digital book and insert audio and website links.

Navigation pane

The navigation pane displays thumbnails of the pages you have created in the Teacher's area.

Games section

The games section provides interactive game templates to which you can add your own content.

Toolbox

A toolbox which includes some different tools from the ones for the digital book enables you to make annotations and create and edit materials.

Specialist essays

Introduction

Ideas about language teaching, like languages themselves, are subject to change. For much of the twentieth century different 'methods' were presented as the best way to learn or acquire a new language. Some argue that we are now 'beyond methods', or in a 'post-method' condition in the twenty-first century. However, suggestions and approaches, useful tips, techniques and advice for good teaching practice are still as important as they ever were.

We know that language teachers often like to be informed of the newest developments in our field. With current technology we know more about the English language than ever before. Additionally, we as teachers are harnessing technology and the internet in new and exciting ways that help us help our students in ways we could not have imagined twenty years ago. And yet, there are some things that remain the same in the classroom.

What follows are a series of short essays, each written by experts in the field. The aim of these essays is to provide you, the language teacher, with up-to-date information about your subject matter. Like the material in *Global* itself, they are thought-provoking pieces. We also believe that learning more about what we do is extremely useful for our ongoing professional development. We hope you find them useful.

Lindsay Clandfield

Contents

Lindsay Clandfield: Why *Global*?

Every book is a product of its times. Nowhere is this truer than in educational materials. Notions of how people learn, of what they learn and of what is important are shaped by the world around us and the period we live through. What then, are the times that have shaped *Global*?

We live in an era of fast communication. More and more people are gaining access to internet and quicker communications technology. This means that we are writing and reading more than before, be it emails, text messages, blogs or web pages. Language learners need to work on quick and unplanned writing (writing for fluency) just as they do for speaking.

We live in an era of information. New technologies enable us to communicate more and with more people, but they have also made more and more information available than ever before – and it is available faster. Much of this information is still in English. Students need to be able to access information and assimilate it quickly.

We live in an era of uncertainty. Precisely because so much information is out there, we are often unsure what is accurate and what is opinion or even misleading. To succeed in an information-rich world one has to learn how to discern, analyse and evaluate what one sees or hears. Fostering critical thinking skills has long been an important goal of educaton.

We live in an era of global English. One of the most important realisations in the field of English Language Teaching of the past decade or so is that English is an international language, spoken all over the world, by people with different accents and different 'Englishes'. A learner is just as likely, if not more likely, to use his or her English with another non-native speaker as with a native speaker.

Given all this, the goals of *Global* are threefold:

1 For your students to **learn English**. This, as for any language course, is the primary goal of *Global*, which reflects modern developments in language teaching and learning. There is a strong lexical focus as well as a complete grammar syllabus, language presentation and practice is highly contextualised with many opportunities for personalisation, and there is plenty of meaningful communicative practice which in *Global* extends to mean writing as well as speaking fluency. *Global* includes a wide variety of reading and listening genres and practises a range of reading and listening skills. With the addition of sections to develop functional language, writing and study skills and review language, we are confident this course provides your students with the tools to become competent users of the language.

2 For your students to **learn through English**. The texts and topics of *Global* are selected so that in every lesson you and your students will be learning something new. We have chosen material that is thought provoking, interesting, intelligent and above all, real. We have also included tasks that encourage students to examine the information they receive critically, and to find out more about a topic if they are interested. Unlike many other courses, texts and topics steer away from the light human interest or celebrity-related story. We use real-world information from a wide variety of domains and the power of literature to unlock students' self-expression.

3 For your students to **learn about English**. This course also includes a focus, through extra reading and listening activities, on the English language as a subject itself. What is it? How is it changing? What kinds of English are appearing around the world? What are the implications of this? We believe these are important questions, worthy of being touched on in the language class. It is why we asked the foremost world expert author on these matters, David Crystal, to contribute to this new and innovative thread of *Global*.

David Crystal: The future of Englishes: going local

When people talk about 'global English' they are usually referring to the common features which identify the variety we call standard English. Increasingly, however, attention has been drawn to the regional features which differentiate one part of the English-speaking world from another. So today we happily talk about British, American, Australian, South African, Indian and other 'Englishes', and studies are accumulating of the way these varieties make distinctive use of pronunciation, orthography, grammar, vocabulary and discourse. Much of the distinctiveness resides in the area of lexicology, the linguistic domain which most closely reflects cultural identity, and dictionaries have been compiled of the distinctive lexicons encountered in these regions.

It does not take long before these lexicons reach many thousands of words. When a country adopts a language as a local alternative means of communication, it immediately starts adapting it, to meet the communicative needs of the region. Words for local plants and animals, food and drink, customs and practices, politics and religion, sports and games and many other facets of everyday life soon accumulate a local wordstock which is unknown outside the country and its environs. When someone in South Africa says 'The bakkie had to stop at a red robot', we need to know that a bakkie is a truck and a robot is a traffic light. There are thousands of such words in a dictionary of South African English. And other parts of the English-speaking world display the same kind of creativity.

This seems to be the pattern, as English becomes a local alternative language. When a group of people in a country switch into English, for whatever reason, the subject matter of their conversation inevitably incorporates aspects of their local environment. They talk about the shops, streets, suburbs, bus routes, institutions, businesses, television programmes, newspapers, political parties, minority groups and a great deal more. They make jokes, quote proverbs, bring up childhood linguistic memories (such as nursery rhymes) and recall lyrics of popular songs. All this local knowledge is taken for granted, and used in sentences without gloss. Visitors who hear such sentences, or read them in local newspapers, need to have them explained. Conventional dictionaries will not help, for they do not include such localisms, especially if the expressions are encyclopedic in character (referring to local people, places, institutions and suchlike).

Every English-speaking location in the world has usages which make the English used there distinctive, expressive of local identity, and a means of creating solidarity. From this point of view, notions such as 'Swedish English' take on a fresh relevance, going well beyond traditional conceptions of English spoken with a Swedish accent, or English displaying interference from Swedish grammar. Swedish English, for example, I define as the kind of English I need to know about when I go to Sweden, otherwise I will be unable to converse efficiently with Swedish speakers in English. It would be amazingly useful to have a glossary of the English equivalents of Swedish cultural references, but I know of none. This seems to be a neglected area for any language.

We need regional cultural dictionaries or glossaries. It is something every region can do, and something to which everyone who learns English can contribute. It takes only an hour or so to accumulate a list of dozens of culturally specific items. And when these are written down, in the style of a glossary, it has an interesting effect upon the participants. They feel they have somehow made the English language their own. I suspect such projects also add greatly to their linguistic confidence and self-esteem, for no-one else in the world knows their home-grown variety of English as well as they do. And they can take pride in the fact that they have added their own small piece to the global jigsaw puzzle that comprises the English language.

David Crystal is honorary professor of linguistics at the University of Bangor, and works from his home in Holyhead, North Wales, as a writer, editor, lecturer and broadcaster. He read English at University College London, specialised in English language studies, then joined academic life as a lecturer in linguistics, first at Bangor, then at Reading, where he became professor of linguistics. He received an OBE for services to the English language in 1995. His books include *The Cambridge Encyclopedia of the English Language* and *The Stories of English*. *Just a Phrase I'm Going Through: My Life in Language* was published in 2009.

Amanda Jeffries: Developing study skills and encouraging learner autonomy

Learner autonomy can be defined as the ability of a learner to take charge of their own learning, not only by learning specific strategies or study skills but also by developing an entirely new attitude to learning. A truly independent learner of English is aware of their learning needs and goals, can reflect on how they learn, has a positive and proactive attitude to language-learning and can make the most of learning opportunities both in and out of class.

Study skills are strategies and approaches that can lead to more effective learning. The *Global* series follows a comprehensive study skills syllabus covering metacognitive strategies (thinking about, planning and evaluating learning) and affective and social strategies (monitoring your attitude to learning and working with others) as well as dictionary and reference skills. It also develops specific strategies for learning and practising listening, speaking, reading, writing, vocabulary and grammar more effectively. All learners are different and research suggests that effective learning depends on choosing the right strategy, or combination of strategies, for the task, the learning context or the particular individual.

Why deal with learner autonomy in class?

Most teachers recognise the importance of learning effectively, but many have reservations about doing learner training or learning awareness activities in class: 'It wouldn't work with my group'; 'There's already too much to do in class'; or 'I wouldn't know where to start'. It is important to remember, however, that a focused and independent learner is not only more efficient but also more motivated. Moreover, learner autonomy activities provide a valuable extra practice opportunity.

How can I help my learners to develop these skills?

You may find some of the following suggestions useful in your teaching situation.

- Include short regular learner training slots in your timetable, so that your learners get used to the idea of study skills as a key part of their learning.
- Offer students a 'menu' of possible strategies for, say, planning an essay, or memorising vocabulary to help them choose the strategy that works best for them. Comparing ideas in pairs or groups can also suggest new and useful ideas. Suggest they try out a new strategy for a week and report back on how effective they found it.
- When doing class activities, share your aims with your students and suggest useful strategies; for example, explain that you are asking them to read primarily to understand the gist of a passage and offer good gist reading tips.
- Ask students regularly to note down or discuss how well they have learned and what they have enjoyed or found puzzling, and make resolutions for how to improve.
- Find out how your students learn. You could ask them to write you a short letter about their progress and write back with suggestions!
- Make students aware of the range of practice opportunities and materials available – in a library or study centre, online, or in the media. Students can also keep a record of work outside class that they can discuss with you.
- More advanced groups might find writing learner diaries a good way to reflect on their learning styles and preferences.
- Above all, show you are convinced that developing good learning habits is a valuable learning focus – that way, your own attitude is more likely to rub off on your students.

Amanda Jeffries teaches university students and works on teacher development programmes in Oxford. She has contributed to the Macmillan *Straightforward* and *New Inside Out* series. She has written the writing, study skills and review pages for the *Global* series, and is the co-author of *Global Advanced*.

Pete Sharma: Blended learning

The term 'blended learning' is a 'buzz' term, yet one that means different things to different people. The 'classic' definition of blended learning is a course consisting of traditional 'face-to-face' language lessons, combined with 'distance learning', ie the opportunity to study 'beyond the classroom'. Such a course can provide many benefits for language learners.

In our book *Blended Learning*, we suggest a broader definition, taking blended learning to mean a combination of classroom teaching and the *appropriate* use of technology. Technology such as an interactive whiteboard can be used inside the classroom to enrich the learning experience. In addition, the students could have 24/7 access to their interactive learning materials, allowing them to study at anytime, anywhere.

Principles

Whichever definition is used, new technology has had a major impact on language teaching and learning. We describe four key principles for successfully integrating technology into language teaching:

- Differentiate the role you play as a teacher, and the role the technology is playing. For example, the teacher can clarify 'fuzzy' areas of grammar. The interactive exercises on a CD-ROM could then offer extra practice in 'crisp' areas of language, with students receiving feedback from the computer.
- Teaching should be principled. In other words, there should be a sound pedagogical reason for using the technology.
- The technology should complement and enhance what the teacher does. It is not a replacement for the teacher.
- 'It's not what it is, but what you do with it'. The interactive whiteboard in itself is just a 'tool'. It is how teachers actually use it, to help provide engaging language lessons, which can lead to better learning outcomes.

Integrating technology into language courses

There are many ways to integrate technology into a language course. A teacher can:

- support their face-to-face teaching with a Virtual Learning Environment, a web based platform which learners can access at any time. The VLE can be used, for example, to post language feedback for students to study after a class discussion.
- run 'learner training' sessions to show students how to benefit from the digital material in the eWorkbook at the back of their course book. For instance, you can download the audio files to their mp3 players to allow learning 'on the go'; use the 'QuickFind' feature on their electronic dictionary and download the free interactive version of the phonemic chart from the web.
- use technology before a class. Before a fluency lesson, email students a pre-discussion reading task to get them thinking about the topic.
- use technology during a class. If you use an interactive whiteboard, you can save the electronic flip-charts you create. This allows you to build up a bank of personalised digital materials including photographs and sound files to support each of the course book units.
- use technology after a class. Students focusing on writing can collaborate together to produce an essay using a wiki, a website which contains editable web pages.

If teachers continue to provide pedagogically sound and interesting lessons, and allow the technology to support learning both inside and outside the classroom, then a blended learning approach can certainly enrich the language learning experience of students.

References

Barrett, B and Sharma, P *Blended Learning* – using technology inside and beyond the language classroom (Macmillan, 2007); Jones, C (1986) 'It's not so much the program, more what you do with it: the importance of methodology in CALL' System 14 / 2, 171-178

Pete Sharma is an associate Lecturer at Oxford Brookes University, UK. He has written books on technology in language teaching, and is co-author of *Blended Learning: using technology in and beyond the language classroom* (Macmillan, 2007). Pete is a Director of Pete Sharma Associates, which runs training in educational technology: www.psa.eu.com. He has edited the *CALL Review*, the newsletter of the Learning Technologies SIG of IATEFL, and blogs on technology at www.te4be.com.

Duncan Foord: How we can develop as teachers

Development means change and change is inevitable. You are not the same teacher (or person) you were a year ago. Working with a new coursebook, new students and colleagues, taking part in in-service training, preparing classes – all of these challenging elements of your day-to-day routine have changed you. You are always developing, you just have to decide how.

Our choices are framed by the culture we live in, the school we work in, government policy, students' expectations and so on. Some schools may encourage and support teacher development, others less so, but you will always have choices to make about how you teach and how you deal with challenges inside and outside the classroom. Focus on what you can do rather than what you can't.

Guiding principles

Just like a lesson, your working life needs some aims to guide your choice of development activities, your development plan, if you like. Here are six which I like.

- Take an interest in my students.
- Enjoy teaching.
- Take on challenges.
- Manage stress.
- Balance work and home life.
- Share my enthusiasm with others.

Give your teaching a 'developmental twist'

Here are some ideas for practical activities which are easy to integrate into your teaching routine and not time-consuming.

- **Get feedback** from your students. Five minutes before the end of the lesson ask the students to write on a piece of paper three things they liked about the class and one thing they didn't like, or a 'suggestion' if they prefer. Thank your students and collect the papers in. In the next class (or via email) respond to the comments.
- **Make a short video** of your class. For this you need a small hand-held camera or mobile phone with video. Get a colleague or student to video your class for about five to ten minutes. Watch the video afterwards more than once. The first few times you will be cringing at your appearance and mannerisms! After that you will notice more interesting things about your choice of language, gestures and facial expressions and get a good idea how your students see you.
- **Try activities out first**. Before you use a speaking activity, try it out with a colleague. Afterwards assess how much time you needed, whether the instructions were clear, if you needed preparation time, what language you used, whether your students would find it easy or difficult and what help they might need. Adjust your lesson plan accordingly.
- **Break your routine**. This can be a very good way to help you understand your teaching better and add an element of surprise and fun to your classes. For example, let one of your students become the teacher for ten minutes and you become a student, move the seating arrangement, supplement the coursebook text with one you find which will particularly interest your students …
- **Create a staff 'sharing board'**. This is a place where you can share materials and teaching ideas with your colleagues. Once it catches on, the board will help build staff rapport as well as provide a source of interesting lessons and save you preparation time.

Duncan Foord is the Director of the teacher training institution OxfordTEFL. He is responsible for teacher training and development in the company and teaches on Trinity Certificate and Diploma courses in the Barcelona centre. He is co-author (with Lindsay Clandfield) of *The Language Teacher's Survival Handbook* (It's Magazines, 2008) and *The Developing Teacher* (Delta Publishing, 2009), winner of the Duke of Edinburgh ESU English Language Award 2009 for Best Entry for Teachers.

Jim Scrivener: Halfway up the mountain? What does it mean to be Intermediate?

The term 'Intermediate' suggests a place somewhere in the middle. But in the middle of what? Does it mean that learners have reached a half-way point? That they have broken the back of the language learning task and will find it increasingly easy from here on?

I recall a comment I heard once that '*All* students are Intermediate'. And, yes, of course, any language learner is always going to be somewhere in the middle of a long route between starting out at the beginning and reaching native speaker-like competence.

The naming of levels suggests that the process of learning a language is a steady path up a mountain, with each new level clearly delineated and signposted as you arrive. Not many will ever reach the peak but there are camps, and even 'plateaus' on the way up where students can pause, looking back over the slopes they have climbed and taking stock of their achievements. Think of the pride in some students as they announce 'I am not Elementary any more. Now I am Pre-intermediate'.

Should we talk about a student's level or a student's levels?

It is important for teachers to be clear that shorthand level names may cover up the real level profile a learner has. They are not the whole story, but simply represent a useful simplification, an *average*. They do not reveal an in-depth portrait. For in fact any learner has many levels rather than one level. A more accurate description of a learner will refer to their knowledge and skills over a range of areas. We could, for example, think about a learner's systems or skills profiles: how much they know of grammar, lexis, pronunciation, functional language and discourse, or how good they are at listening, reading, writing and speaking. Analysing these might reveal significant differences between learners who are nominally at the same 'Intermediate' level. For example, Student A has a very high level in listening and speaking, is Intermediate in reading but has a significantly lower level in writing. With Student B we find a contrasting picture: very weak in listening and speaking, but quite good at reading and writing. Yet these two students are both in the same Intermediate class!

Spiky profiles

Imagine that we plot the four skills levels of each student onto a line graph. We would see some dramatic peaks and valleys as the levels rose and fell. These learners have what are known as 'spiky profiles' – competencies in some areas that are substantially different from others. Thus, rather than being able to assume that Intermediate students must, by definition, resemble each other in level, we may actually find that they can be remarkably different. Their levels average out to Intermediate but when we look closer, we can see that their individual skills may vary dramatically.

Within a school where students have followed similar courses, the peaks and lows of such profiles are more likely to resemble each other than when a teacher works with people who come from different learning backgrounds.

When you go in to teach your new class, it is worth remembering this: whatever the level name is on the cover of your coursebook, the learners inside your class actually have a wide range of levels. You cannot assume that all have reached exactly the same point in each skill or system – you will find that your learners span a wide range of middle points, varying not just from one person to another, but also from one language area to another.

Is this just one more problem for the poor teacher? Or can the learners' diversity of knowledge and skills bring an extra richness to your lessons, and provide the opportunity and incentive for every student to contribute something useful to the class?

Jim Scrivener is Head of Teacher Development for Bell International based at Bedgebury School in Kent, UK, where he developed and runs the Online Delta course. He is the author of *Learning Teaching* (Macmillan), *Oxford Basics: Teaching Grammar* (OUP) as well as the Teacher's Books and Portfolios for the *Straightforward* coursebook series (Macmillan).

Scott Thornbury: Making the most of learner-generated content

Learner-generated content is the language – either spoken or written – that learners produce, naturally and often spontaneously, during the course of a lesson, and which constitutes authentic communication. This distinguishes it from the language that is produced in order to answer comprehension questions and display questions (like 'What is the past of *take*?'), or to do grammar exercises, or to perform roleplays, or to write summaries, and so on.

Why use it?

Using learner output as lesson input is one way of involving learners more directly in the learning–teaching process. And research suggests that when learners have some control of the topic agenda and of the management of classroom talk, the lesson is more likely to match their particular learning needs, as well as being both more meaningful and more memorable.

When?

Learner-generated content can emerge at any stage of the lesson, and is often a by-product of some other activity, such as reading or listening. It can be deliberately prompted by personalisation tasks – that is, tasks that require students to use a pre-taught language item to talk about themselves – or by opinion-seeking tasks, such as when preparing learners to read a text, or by questions eliciting their response to the text they have just read. It can occur in the chat that opens a lesson. It can also be prompted when learners report on group discussions, or on something they have read or heard prior to the lesson. Asking the learners to come prepared to every lesson with an item of interesting news is one way of formalising this procedure. But learners are more likely to generate original content if the classroom dynamic is conducive to informal, personalised talk, and if initiating such talk is welcomed by the teacher.

How do you make the most of it?

First of all, treat the personalisation stage not as a test of pre-taught items but as a potential launch pad for classroom talk. Let's say an individual learner has offered an opinion, or given some personal information, or referred to something going on in the world outside the classroom, and that you feel that this is a comment of general interest, and exploitable for the language 'affordances' (ie learning opportunities) that it offers. Use questions to encourage the learner to elaborate. Try to do this in as natural and conversational a way as possible. If the learner is stuck for words, supply them. Avoid correcting errors if this might inhibit the speaker. Instead, reformulate what the speaker is saying in a way that makes it more target-like. Draw other learners into the conversation. When the topic seems to have run its course, ask the learners, working in pairs or groups, to write a summary of what was talked about, as if writing to an absent classmate. Collect the texts and use these as the basis for a subsequent lesson, eg error correction. This could take the form of extracting a mixture of (unattributed) correct and incorrect sentences and asking the learners first to sort them, and then to correct the incorrect ones.

Set up writing activities that replicate online social networking interactions. Learners can 'chat' to one another in small groups using pen and paper. This conversation can then form the basis of a group 'blog'; these blogs are then passed around the class – or posted on the classroom wall – and commented on, before being returned to their original writers. This material is then available to the teacher for subsequent analysis and development.

Finally, exploit the texts and the topics in your course book as stimuli for learner comment and opinion. Learners may not always respond to the content of a text – but they *never* will if they are not invited to!

Scott Thornbury teaches on an MA TESOL program for the New School, New York, and lives in Spain. He is the author of a number of books on language and methodology, including *Uncovering Grammar, Beyond the Sentence* and *An A-Z of ELT* (all published by Macmillan). His latest book, *Teaching Unplugged* (Delta Publishing), was co-written with Luke Meddings. He is currently the series editor for the Cambridge Handbooks for Teachers.

Rose Senior: Class-centred learning

Class-centred teaching is a framework for understanding the behaviour of effective classroom teachers that can help all language teachers to teach more successfully. As its name suggests, class-centred teaching emphasises the class group and makes the learning and social wellbeing of the class the focal point of the teacher's attention. The holistic notion of class-centred teaching is based on the premise that cohesive classes (characterised by overall feelings of openness, trust, and mutual respect) provide optimum environments for language learning.

The class-centred framework is applicable to all classroom situations, to all teaching contexts, and to all teaching approaches. Although no teacher has a 100% success rate, class-centred teachers have a higher proportion of classes that 'gel' than those who do not. The good news is that all teachers can become class-centred. The starting point involves keeping in mind that each class must sense that it is going on a collective journey towards the achievement of worthwhile learning goals.

How do class-centred teachers behave?

Class-centred teachers:

- develop rapport with their classes, ensuring that their students regard them not only as teachers with a sound knowledge of English but also as integral members of their class groups (who can laugh at themselves or behave spontaneously when something unexpected happens, for example).
- treat all students fairly and with respect, appreciating that learning a new language is a risky business because of the possibility of making mistakes and appearing foolish.
- always maintain their authority while remaining friendly towards their students and establish codes of behaviour that support student learning and enforce them in ways that do not alienate or humiliate individuals.
- understand that once social processes that enhance learning have been set in motion, teachers should find it unnecessary to behave in authoritarian ways that enforce the 'me-versus-them' divide.

How can I teach in class-centred ways?

- Encourage whole-class involvement by engaging your students in a memorable or meaningful way at the start of each new lesson. (At intermediate levels this is particularly important, since the initial excitement of learning English may have worn off.) Think of alternative, engaging ways of having your classes complete mundane tasks such as grammar exercises, remembering that variety is the essence of good teaching and that there are many ways in which learning activities can be 'tweaked'.
- As you move around your class observing students you will find yourself naturally helping small numbers of students on the spot. As the need for additional words or phrases becomes apparent, write these on the board so that other students can benefit from your input. Make a note, too, of what needs to be expanded upon or revised. Then, at a later point, re-teach these items to the class as a whole.
- Remember that although lively behaviour is evidence of student engagement, noisy, fun-filled classrooms may not be reliable indicators either of student learning – or of student satisfaction. There will be times when it is more appropriate for students to be working purposefully and reflectively, either on their own or quietly with a partner. A collective feeling of whole-class learning will prevail when this happens.

The class-centred framework will help you keep in mind that your classes function as groups – and that effective teaching and learning involves keeping every class that you teach as unified as possible for the duration of the course.

Rose Senior is a language teacher, teacher educator and classroom researcher. Author of *The Experience of Language Teaching* (CUP, 2006), Rose presents at conferences, runs professional development workshops and writes on a range of aspects of classroom language teaching in both academic and teacher-oriented journals. She has a regular column in *English Teaching Professional*.

Jonathan Marks: Pronunciation: the right kind and the right time

Teachers sometimes feel unsure about what kind of pronunciation learners should be aiming for – British? American? or something else? – and about what is the right time in a lesson to focus on pronunciation. I hope this short essay will give you some pointers in these two directions.

What kind of pronunciation should my learners aim for?

If English is a global language, it obviously needs to be internationally intelligible. But it would probably be impossible to describe a type of pronunciation that would always guarantee intelligibility between any two speakers from any two parts of the world. It seems that consonant sounds – with the exception of the notorious 'th' sounds! – may be particularly important. A consistent set of distinctions between vowel sounds is important too, but the total number of different vowel sounds probably doesn't need to be as large as in standard native English. Word stress is probably important for intelligibility, and perhaps at least a basic intonation distinction between fall and rise.

There are other factors to consider, too. In some parts of the world there are well-established and widely-used regional pronunciations of English. In some countries, there may be prestige attached to British or American pronunciation, and learners may wish to aim for one of these or even be expected to do so in exams they plan to take.

At the same time, it's important for all learners to have experience of listening to, and 'tuning in' to, a wide variety of different pronunciations from around the world – which is why *Global* has introduced its *Global voices* section.

When is the right time to focus on pronunciation?

1 Planned pronunciation activities

Sometimes you might want to plan and include an activity to practise a particular aspect of pronunciation. For example, if you notice that your learners systematically fail to make the distinction between the vowel sounds in pairs of words like 'cold' and 'called', you might devote a 10-minute spot to practising that distinction.

2 Introducing new language

Whenever you introduce new language, you should think about how it's pronounced, and whether learners are likely to need help with saying it. For example, if they're learning a compound noun such as 'reception desk' they need to know that the stress is on the first element, or if they're learning the idiom 'You must be joking!' they need to know that it has a standardised stress and intonation pattern.

3 Any other time!

A need for a focus on pronunciation can also arise at any other time. Let's say, for example, that a class discussion about different jobs turns to the topic of having to wear a suit at work. Some learners pronounce the word 'suit' correctly, and others say 'sweet' or 'suet'. Because 'suit' has become, for the moment, a key word in the discussion, it would probably be useful to intervene and establish the correct pronunciation. Or, let's say that learners have trouble understanding part of a recording which sounds to them like 'A bing go in there for ages'. You could help them by pointing out that: 'I've' is reduced to /a/, the vowel sound in 'been' is shortened, the last sound of 'been' changes to /ŋ/ to make a smooth link with 'going', and the '-ing' of 'going' is changed to /ɪn/. You could also give them a chance to imitate the pronunciation on the recording – not necessarily in order to learn to speak this way, but because it will help them to develop an awareness of how words can become disguised in fluent speech, and to recognise such 'disguised' words.

Every lesson is a pronunciation lesson, because nobody can speak without pronouncing! Thinking about 'the right kind' and 'the right time' is a first step towards giving learners effective help with their pronunciation.

Jonathan Marks is a freelance teacher trainer, author and translator based in Poland. His publications include *English Pronunciation in Use - Elementary* (CUP, 2007). He is a founder member of the IATEFL Pronunciation Special Interest Group, and currently the group's joint co-ordinator.

Ben Goldstein: Images and critical thinking

Using images in the language classroom is something we take for granted. However, images have been traditionally used as 'pictures' to stimulate or illustrate language, subservient to the written or spoken word, and therefore not always exploited to their full potential. Rather than asking learners simply to describe images, we can encourage them to reflect more deeply on them, to look beyond the frame and start to see images as cultural artefacts open to diverse readings. We can also allow learners to take a more active role by inviting them to bring their own images to class.

What kinds of images?

Digital technology has meant that we can now access and manipulate images as never before. Many of our learners have become experts in visualising experience, some communicate more easily through visual stimuli than verbal – this may be through photos on social networking sites, emoticons in text messages or avatars in virtual worlds. Alongside such images, it is easy for the ones we present in class to look outdated or irrelevant. Our challenge is to provide images that can truly resonate and motivate learners to take part in classroom tasks. To this aim the images in *Global* have been selected with the aim of moving away from typical language teaching representations of reality and to challenge our expectations. This is a fine starting point, but teachers should also be sensitive to local needs and interests when choosing images. Sensible criteria for selecting images might be summed up as: impact (will the images be able to stimulate or engage the learner on an imaginative level?), practicability (how easy is it for learners to access them?), familiarity (how well will the class recognize them or know how to respond?), opportunity for personalisation (how can the learners make these images their own?) and openness to multiple interpretation (how many different readings can be drawn from a certain image?).

Where can you find them?

- Try image-sharing websites which allow you to search via key words or tags and exhibit or edit your own images.
- Create your own class page and ask learners to upload files, inviting them to comment on their own work and that of others.
- Use key words to search for miscellaneous images on the internet.

What can you do with them?

We can analyse images from three different perspectives: the affective, the compositional and the critical. The first is our emotional response to the image – how does it make you feel? The second is how the image can be analysed in terms of its relationship to text, for example the way it has been framed or captured and presented to the viewer. Finally, the critical perspective asks us to bear in mind the broader context in which an image appears, what messages does it convey and how is it intended to be read? Such an approach emphasises the importance of bringing a social critique to our reading of images.

For example, imagine that you wanted to focus on a particular country in class. One idea would be to search for images that reflect something about this country's identity, customs, values, etc. Choose icons such as stamps, money, flags. Analyse these in class and collect different interpretations. Then set learners the task of finding their own visual representations of the place. Finally, source images of the learners' own country to find out how it is portrayed in different media. For example, what images are commonly found in tourist brochures of the learners' country and how representative are these in reality? As such, images can be an excellent way to encourage critical reading and intercultural awareness and consequently challenge stereotyping.

Ben Goldstein is a teacher, teacher trainer and materials writer. He teaches online at the Universitat Oberta de Catalunya in Barcelona and on the MA Tesol Program for the New School, New York. He is the main author of the *New Framework* adult coursebook series (Richmond Publishing) and author of a methodological handbook for teachers *Working with Images* (CUP). His main interests in ELT are the use of images, World Englishes and intercultural issues.

Teaching notes

UNIT 1 # Language & Culture

Coursebook

Unit 1	Language	Texts	Communicative skills
Part 1 SB page 6	Listening and Vocabulary Greetings Pronunciation Intonation and different meanings Grammar State and action verbs Present tenses	Reading *The Hobbit*	Speaking Fantasy stories and films
Part 2 SB page 8	Vocabulary and Pronunciation English for specific purposes Word stress Grammar Present simple and present continuous	Listening English for a specific purpose	Speaking Languages
Part 3 SB page 10	Extend your vocabulary *look* Grammar Questions review Vocabulary and Pronunciation Collocations for describing places, word stress	Listening Capitals of Culture	Speaking Nominating a town
Part 4 SB page 12	Grammar Subject / Object pronouns	Reading and Speaking Towards a definition of culture	Writing and Speaking Culture quiz
Function globally SB page 14	Making recommendations Talking about advantages and disadvantages Asking for recommendations		
Global English SB page 15	A world full of Englishes Varieties of English around the world		
Writing SB page 16	A report Making additional points Planning		
Global review SB page 17	Grammar and vocabulary review Extra speaking and writing practice		
Study skills SB page 17	Understanding your language style		

Additional resources

eWorkbook	Interactive and printable grammar, vocabulary, listening and pronunciation practice Extra reading and writing practice Additional downloadable listening and audio material
Teacher's Resource Disc	Communication activity worksheets to print and photocopy
Go global: ideas for further research	**Language** Ask students to find two different free internet translation programmes and compare them. **Culture** Ask students to find out what the next Cities of Culture are going to be in different continents and prepare a short presentation about one of them.

Part 1

TEACH GLOBAL THINK LOCAL Lead-in

If this is one of your first lessons with the class, ask everyone to stand up and greet the people next to or around them. Tell them first to do this in their *own* language (if you are working with a multilingual class you can still do this – you'll just have more languages flowing around the classroom). Once they have done that, ask them to repeat the activity again, this time in English.

Depending on how much your students know each other and are ready to have some fun, you could ask them to repeat the greeting exercise with the following instructions:

Greet each other in a language that is 1) not your first language and 2) not English.

Greet each other with a whisper.

Greet each other as loudly as possible.

Greet each other using only mime, not words.

Listening and Vocabulary (SB page 6)

1 Books closed. Ask students to make a list of different ways to say *Hello* in English. Give the following examples to get them started: *Hi, Hello …* Students do this first individually. Then ask them to compare answers with a partner. They probably will not be able to make a very long list at this stage. Feed back on the answers, but do not provide extra phrases that the students don't come up with at this stage.

2 **1.01** Tell students they are going to listen to different conversations in which people are greeting each other. Direct their attention to the three questions. Play the first track and go through the questions with the whole class.

Possible answers

Conversation 1
Informal. The speakers know each other and are probably friends. They are in a place where drinks are available, perhaps a cafeteria or bar.

Conversation 2
More formal. One of the speakers doesn't know the other and is being introduced. It could be a business situation, perhaps at an office or the beginning of a meeting.

Conversation 3
Informal. The speakers know each other. Perhaps they have met on the way to work.

Conversation 4
Formal. A man is addressing a group of people, perhaps at the beginning of a conference, meeting or similar event.

3 Play the conversations again and ask students to make notes of all the ways they hear people greeting each other. Ask how many of these they already had. Write the answers on the board in two columns: *Informal* and *Neutral / Formal*. Drill the pronunciation.

Informal:

Hey / Hi / Hiya / How's it going? / Morning / Hi there / How are things?

Neutral / Formal:

Hello / Good evening / Nice to meet you / Good morning

Ask what students notice about the lists, using the questions as prompts.

Language note

In English, shorter expressions and contracted forms for greetings are generally considered more informal. Expressions like *Hey* or *Hiya* are considered quite informal and should only be used with friends. The longer forms are neutral, although they can be considered formal in some contexts. A lot will have to do with the intonation of the greeting, with a higher rise-fall indicating more friendliness and informality. You could point out the difference between *Nice to meet you* (suitable for first time meeting) and *Nice to see you* (suitable to greet a friend or someone you know).

1.01

1

A: Hey.

B: Oh, hiya! How's it going? What are you doing here?

A: I finished work early, so …

B: Great, well, sit down then. Would you like something to drink?

2

A: Good evening.

B: Ah, hello, Mr Sim. Mr Sim, this is Ms Parker.

A: Nice to meet you, Ms …?

C: Parker. Nice to meet you too.

3

A: Morning!

B: Hi there, Jane. How are things?

A: Oh, good. Phew. I can't believe how hot it is today.

B: I know, wonderful isn't it!

4

A: Good morning. I'm happy so many of you could make it this morning. We're already a little bit late, so I would like to start right now if possible.

Reading (SB page 6)

This is an extract from the beginning of the famous English novel *The Hobbit*, by JRR Tolkien. The encounter takes place in front of Bilbo's house.

1 Tell students to look at the image of the novel and author on page 7. Ask if they know the book and/or author. Has anyone seen the *Lord of the Rings* films or read the books (in English or their language)? You could elicit different things that students know about this book. Don't worry if students have never heard of *The Hobbit*. They don't need to know the background to understand the extract.

2 **1.02** Tell students to read the extract once through and answer the questions quickly.

1 They are talking about the uses of *Good morning*.
2 Bilbo wants to finish the conversation.

3 Ask students to read the extract again more carefully and tick the meanings of *Good morning* that are not mentioned.

2 and 8 are not mentioned as meanings of *Good morning*.

TEACH GLOBAL THINK LOCAL

Reading extra

To exploit this text further, tell students to pay close attention to all the words and phrases in the Glossary on page 7 when they read the second time. Then ask them to close their books. Write the words and the definitions from the glossary all jumbled up on the board. Students must try to match them from memory and then write an original sentence in English for each one.

Pronunciation (SB page 6)

1 **1.03** Ask students to read the instructions. Then play the recording once all the way through. Play it a second time, pausing after each utterance. Ask students if it's friendly or unfriendly.

A and D are friendly (A is very friendly); B and C are unfriendly (B is rude, C is bored).

2 Play the recording a third time and pause after each utterance. Ask the students to repeat.

3 It's best if you demonstrate this activity. For many students, the default intonation tends to be rather neutral, or even unfriendly. Read the first sentence out with completely flat and neutral intonation. Then do the same with a rise-fall intonation, sounding more polite. Finally, say it with a falling intonation and a frown, looking unfriendly. Students then practise in pairs.

Grammar (SB page 6)

1 Read the pairs of sentences out loud to the students and ask them which one sounds more correct. Elicit possible reasons why this is correct. Ask them to read the information in the grammar box after they have the answers.

1 a   2 b

2 Ask students to read through the text once quickly and ask them what it's about (the book *The Hobbit*). Then tell them to go through and decide if the underlined verbs are correct, and correct those that are incorrect.

are believing: *believe*
are understanding: *understand*
are feeling: *feel*
disagree: correct
are liking: *like*
love: correct
are now selling: correct (but *now sell* is also correct)
are coming out: correct

Language note

Verbs can refer to events (ie actions, or things that happen) or states (ie a general condition or feeling, without any action). We do not usually use 'state' verbs in continuous tenses. However, the same verb can be a state or 'action' verb. For example, in the sentence *He has brown eyes* the verb *have* is stative and cannot be in the continuous form. But in the sentence *He's having lunch right now* the verb *have* is expressing an action.

This rule is a generalisation, and not a hard-and-fast one. There are increasingly examples of state verbs being used in continuous tenses. In Indian English, for example, *I am understanding you perfectly* is quite usual. More common, and one which your students may have seen, is the advertising campaign for McDonald's™ which uses *love* in a continuous tense *I'm lovin' it*. Just so you know, this could be an area of the language which is changing!

G Grammar focus

Refer students to the language summary on state and action verbs on page 132.

You can use exercise 1 on page 133 for:

a) extra practice now
b) homework
c) review a couple of lessons from now.

The answers are on page 142 of the Teacher's Book.

Speaking (SB page 7)

Ask students to work in pairs and ask and answer the questions. This could be quite a short speaking activity if students don't like novels like *The Hobbit*. To extend it further, see below.

TEACH GLOBAL THINK LOCAL

Alternative procedure

To extend the *Speaking* activity, write these questions on the board and ask students to choose a total of four (from these and those in the book) to interview a partner:

What books did you read for school? Did you enjoy them?

Do you think it's important for young people to read classic works of literature in school?

Do you know other books that have been made into films? Were they good or bad adaptations?

If you see a film adaptation of a book, does it make you want to read the book?

What is your favourite book or story?

Alternatively you could run this as a whole-class discussion, if you have a smaller class.

Part 2

TEACH GLOBAL THINK LOCAL

Lead-in

There are two options here, depending on whether or not you are teaching in an English-speaking country. Both involve bringing in copies of the classified section of a local newspaper, one for every two students (this could be multiple originals if you have access to free newspapers, or photocopies of the jobs section).

In an English-speaking country

Distribute the copies of the classified section and ask students to find the job adverts in pairs. Ask them to go through these and answer the following questions:

Are there any jobs that specifically mention English skills?

What jobs do you think you could do, with your level of English?

What jobs would you NOT want to do?

Students then compare answers with another pair. Feed back and ask which jobs in the students' own countries require them to have good English skills.

In a country where English is not the first language

Distribute the copies of the classified section (this may be in the students' own language) and ask students to find the job adverts in pairs. Ask them to find the following:

- a job for which English would be helpful
- a job for which you don't need English at all
- a job they think they would like
- a job they think they would dislike.

Students then compare answers with another pair. They must do this in English. Feed back and ask which jobs in the students' own countries require them to have good English skills.

Vocabulary and Pronunciation (SB page 8)

If you did the *Lead-in*, go straight to exercise 2.

1 In pairs, ask students to discuss the questions. Direct them to the *Useful phrases* to help them. Feed back.

2 Students match the jobs to the types of English spoken.

1 (picture f) c	2 (picture a) f	3 (picture d) d
4 (picture b) b	5 (picture e) e	6 (picture c) a

3 1.04 Play the recording while students underline the stressed syllables. Then play the track again and ask students to listen again carefully. Which syllable is more stressed? Say one of the key words, emphasising the stressed syllable, eg *medical*. Then ask students to practise saying the words themselves, paying attention to the stressed syllable.

1.04
medical
legal
scientific
aviation
business
technical

Listening (SB page 8)

This is an interview with Henry Emery, an expert on aviation English. Here he talks about what is different about this kind of English and why it is important.

1 1.05 Tell students they are now going to listen to a specific kind of English, one of the kinds of English in Vocabulary and Pronunciation exercise 2. Play the recording once. Ask students to guess what kind of English it is. Play the recording a second time and confirm any correct guesses. You could refer students to the audioscript on page 152 and ask them to look for words that suggest the answer (*Mayday*, *position*, *see the ground*, *aircraft type*, *altitude*).

Aviation English

2 Students match words to the definitions. Make sure they know how these words are pronounced, as they will hear them during the interview.

1 emergency	3 air traffic control officer
2 engine	4 safety

3 1.06 Ask students to read the statements before they listen. Then play the recording all the way through once. Students tick the correct statement.

c

4 Tell students to read the statements and decide whether they are true or false from memory. Then play the recording through again and check answers. If you think that it still hard for them (this is the first long listening of this level of *Global*) then play it in 'chunks', pausing after each answer.

1 F (There are many types of avation English.)
2 T
3 T
4 F (There are many differences. The words and the grammar they use must be simple and easy to understand.)
5 T
6 T
7 T

5 Ask students if they had heard of this kind of English before. What information did they find most interesting? You could ask students to look at the audioscript on page 152 and find one piece of information they thought most interesting.

1.06

A: Henry Emery, you teach aviation English and at the moment you're writing a new course for pilots and air traffic control officers. Could you start by telling us what aviation English is?

B: Well, there are many types of aviation English. Because aviation is international, people who work in lots of different areas in the aviation industry have to communicate in English. Since 2008 all international pilots and air traffic control officers must have a minimum level of English so that they can communicate with each other clearly and quickly. Many more aviation professionals are taking special aviation English courses now, and this will certainly improve the safety of communications in the future.

A: What are the differences between aviation English and normal English?

B: There are many differences. Perhaps the biggest difference is that pilots and air traffic control officers can't see each other because they communicate on the radio. So the words and the grammar they use must be simple and easy to understand. Most of the time, pilots and air traffic control officers use a set of simple phrases. For example, when an air traffic control officer wants a pilot to fly higher, they say something like *Fastair 345. Climb flight level 320*.

A: So pilots and air traffic control officers don't use normal English at all?

B: Well, they also need to have a good level of plain English too. This is so they can communicate when something unusual happens, for example when there is a medical emergency on board or if there is an engine fire. One very important area for pilots and air traffic control officers is good pronunciation. If people don't understand you, then you could be in trouble! This is true for both native and non-native English speakers. I once heard an English pilot ask an American air traffic controller to repeat his message three times!

A: Why is a single language for aviation important?

B: Pilots need to talk to air traffic control officers from different countries. For example, when you are flying into a busy international airport, there are many other pilots of different nationalities who are flying in too. Pilots and air traffic control officers have to understand all of the communications on the radio so they know exactly what is happening at any time.

Grammar (SB page 9)

1 Write on the board:

Pilots learn a special English for aviation.

The pilot is learning a special English for aviation.

Elicit what the difference is between the two sentences, grammatically (the second sentence uses present continuous). Then ask students to complete the rules of use. Remind them of the difference between state and action verbs (from Part 1).

First rule: present simple

Second rule: present continuous

Third rule: present continuous

2 Ask students to find examples of each in the audioscript for track 1.06 on page 152.

Habits and routines, things that are always true: *you teach avation English*; *people who work*; *pilots and air traffic control officers use*

Things happening now: *you're writing a new course; avation professionals are taking; when you are flying*

State verbs: *they also need to have a good level of plain English; they know exactly what is happening; simple and easy to understand*

3 Ask students to read through the text once first and tell you what it is about (machine translation). Students then complete with the correct form of the verb.

Answers are numbered in the order they appear in the text.

1 communicate
2 has
3 means
4 prevents
5 are starting
6 use / are using
7 translate / are translating
8 don't understand
9 is getting
10 are developing

4 Go through the first example with the class. Tell them that there may be more than one possible answer; the important thing is to communicate the time reference correctly choosing either present simple or present continuous.

Words in italics will vary according to students' own answers.

1 I use *a Macintosh.*
2 I'm sitting on the train.
3 I'm living in *the old town centre.*
4 I prefer *coffee*, thanks.
5 I *play tennis twice a week.*

G Grammar focus

Refer students to the language summary on present simple and continuous on page 132.

You can use exercises 2 and 3 on page 133 for:

a) extra practice now
b) homework
c) review a couple of lessons from now.

The answers are on page 142 of the Teacher's Book.

Speaking (SB page 9)

1 Go through the list of languages with the class, drilling pronunciation (note especially the stress on the last syllable of languages ending in *–ese*: *Chinese*, *Portuguese* etc). Ask students to choose what they think are the top five languages. Then tell them to turn to the back of the book. Were they surprised?

2 In pairs. Students discuss the questions. The questions refer to all languages, not just the ones in exercise 1. Point out the *Useful phrases*.

Alternative procedure

Books closed after exercise 1. Write the questions on the board, or dictate them. Students then ask and answer them in pairs. Circulate and monitor. Then ask students to open their books at page 9 and look at the *Useful phrases*. Go through these, clarifying for example *to get by in a language*. Students now change partners and repeat the exercise, but this time trying to extend their English further by incorporating the expressions.

Part 3

TEACH GLOBAL THINK LOCAL Lead-in

Ask students to work in pairs and brainstorm the following questions:

Can you name a city that has a lot of culture?

Why do you think it has culture?

Feed back in open class. Build up a list of things that make a city have 'a lot of culture', eg art, museums, monuments, history, theatre.

Listening (SB page 10)

1 Read the first sentence to the students and ask the questions. Can anyone name an official Capital of Culture?

2 **1.07–1.08** Tell students they are going to hear about two cities that were named Capitals of Culture. Do students know either of these cities? Explain that the first time they listen you want them to decide which city was most affected by being Capital of Culture. Play the recording.

Sibiu

3 Ask students to try to answer the questions from memory. They then compare answers with a partner. Play the recording a second time for them to check.

1 Sibiu	4 Brasilia
2 Brasilia	5 Brasilia
3 Sibiu	6 Sibiu

1.07–1.08

Interview 1

A: Costin, you're from Sibiu. Can you tell us about the city?

B: Yes. Er … Sibiu is in Romania, in the centre of Romania, and it's a small city … about 150,000 inhabitants.

A: And your country was Capital of Culture in 2007. What was that year like?

B: It was an amazing year for Sibiu. There were three important cultural events in the city every day.

A: So how did the year change the city?

B: Well, Sibiu is a medieval city. When the communists were in power, they didn't look after the town so it was in a bad state. To prepare for 2007, the government restored many of the ancient monuments. They also improved the roads and invested money in the airport. We already had an international airport but it needed modernising.

A: What about visitors? How many visitors does Sibiu have in a normal year?

B: Before 2007, we had about 100,000 tourists a year. Sibiu has a long history – it was built by German settlers from Saxony in the 12th century and has also belonged to Turkey and Austria – and er … it's always been a city of art and culture. But not many tourists knew about the city until it became a capital of culture.

A: Has the number of tourists increased since 2007?

B: Yes, a lot. In 2007 we had about a million visitors and now more and more people are coming here.

Interview 2

A: Marina, you're from Brasilia …

B: Yes, that's right.

A: Can you tell us why Brasilia was chosen to be an American Capital of Culture?

B: Well, firstly, because of its wonderful modern architecture. Brasilia was a planned city – if you look at it from the air, you'll see it has the shape of a flying bird or a plane. The most important buildings are in the middle and there are lots of flats and hotels on the wings.

A: How long did it take to build?

B: Well, the planning started in 1956 and Brasilia officially became the capital in 1960 although it wasn't finished then, of course.

A: Still, that's very impressive. Who designed the buildings?

B: Well, Oscar Niemeyer designed most of the important buildings. He was a Brazilian architect – um … a student of Le Corbusier. Today Niemeyer's buildings are the most popular tourist attractions.

A: What about cultural events in Brasilia? What sort of things can people experience here?

B: Well, Brasilia is a very cosmopolitan city – lots of people come to Brasilia on business from around the world or just for shopping in the designer boutiques. So there are lots of different cultural events, from, er … traditional festivals to exhibitions of contemporary art and fashion shows.

4 Ask students which city would they like to visit if they had the chance: the modern Brasilia or the medieval town of Sibiu. To make this last exercise less specific about these two cities, you could ask students any of the following questions:

Do you prefer cities with old buildings or modern architecture? Why?

Can you give examples?

Have you visited any cities like either of these? Which ones?

What were they like?

Extend your vocabulary (SB page 10)

Go over the information in the box. Students complete the phrases with *look* and the correct particle. Note that these are not all phrasal verbs, which are dealt with in Unit 5.

1 look for
2 look up
3 look at
4 look after
5 look around

Grammar (SB page 11)

1 Students put the words in order to make questions.

1 Can you tell us about the city?
2 What was that year like?
3 How did the year change the city?
4 How many visitors does Sibiu have in a normal year?
5 Has the number of tourists increased since 2007?

2 Students now match the rules with the examples from exercise 1.

First rule: 2
Second rule: 3, 4
Third rule: 1, 5

3 Tell students to read through the information about Amman quickly and tell you what it's about. They then complete the questions.

1 Is Amman an old city?
2 How many inhabitants does Amman have? (*How many people live in Amman/live there?* is also possible but this kind of question will be addressed in the next lesson.)
3 What can tourists do in Amman?
4 When was it Capital of Culture?
5 What kind of things did the city do? / What kind of cultural events did Amman organise?

G Grammar focus

Refer students to the language summary on questions on page 132.

You can use exercises 4 and 5 on page 133 for:
a) extra practice now
b) homework
c) review a couple of lessons from now.

The answers are on page 142 of the Teacher's Book.

Vocabulary and Pronunciation (SB page 11)

1 **1.09** Ask students to make common phrases to talk about places with the words in the exercise. Point out that all the words were mentioned in the listening. Then play the recording for students to listen and check their answers.

1 e
2 c
3 f
4 a
5 b
6 d

2 Play the recording again for students to decide whether the stress is on the first or second word. This is often hard to hear, so do an example first and echo the phrase, giving extra prominence to the stressed word. Play the rest of the recording, then play it again (or say the phrases) and ask students to listen and repeat.

1.09
international <u>airport</u>
ancient <u>monuments</u>
<u>tourist</u> attractions
designer <u>boutiques</u>
cultural <u>events</u>
modern <u>architecture</u>

3 Ask students which of the things referred to Sibiu and which were connected to Brasilia.

Sibiu: international airport, ancient monuments
Brasilia: tourist attractions, designer boutiques, cultural events, modern architecture

TEACH GLOBAL THINK LOCAL Extra activity

You may want to check understanding of these phrases further. To do this, you could ask additional concept check questions. Here are some examples to help get you started.

Are ancient monuments old or modern?

Can you give me an example of a cultural event?

What is the difference between an international airport and another kind of airport?

Are designer boutiques the best place to get things cheap?

4 Ask students to say which things they think are important when they visit a new city. Can they add any other things to the list?

Speaking (SB page 11)

1 Explain the situation to the students. Individually, ask students to think of a town they could nominate. If you think that this is too hard for students then tell them they should talk about their own town. Direct them to the questions and tell them to make some notes. Circulate and monitor, giving help where needed.

2 Before you put students in pairs, direct them to the *Useful phrases*. Give a couple of examples yourself about a city, using the useful language. Tell students to think about how they want to start their short presentation and to mouth their first lines silently to themselves.

Now put the students in pairs. Tell them to tell each other about their choice for a city. The other student listens and asks questions.

3 Circulate and monitor the activity. After they finish, ask students to swap roles and repeat. Do some whole-class feedback on what cities were mentioned and why. Take this opportunity to correct any mistakes you overheard.

If time allows, ask students to swap partners and repeat the activity. But this time they should try to do it more quickly, and more fluently.

Part 4

TEACH GLOBAL THINK LOCAL

Lead-in

Write the following sentence on the board: *She has a lot of culture. She is a very cultured person.* Explain to the class that you want them to imagine someone said this about a teacher. What did they mean? What kinds of things do the students think this person knows? What kind of person could it be? This will begin to unwrap some of the issues surrounding a definition of *culture*.

Reading and Speaking (SB page 12)

The text is about the difficulty of defining culture and about different kinds of culture.

1 Ask students to complete the definition with their own words. This is quite a challenging task. If you think it will be too difficult to make an abstract definition of culture, give students the option of completing the sentence with examples of things that are 'cultural'. Give some examples to start them off: *Culture is classical music. Culture is literature. Culture is how people do things.* Be prepared to accept all different kinds of answers, including things like *Culture is difficult to explain* (which is true; it's the topic of the reading!). Feed back.

2 Tell students to read the text *Towards a definition of culture* and to see if there are any examples of what they said in exercise 1.

3 Ask students to read again more closely and complete the text with the missing sentences.

The correct order is a, e, f, b, d. Sentence c is the extra sentence.

4 Check that students understand what a citizenship test is (a test given to new immigrants to a country who wish to become citizens of that country). Students then read questions adapted from an Australian citizenship test and decide whether they are questions about culture with a capital *C* or with a small *c*. They can mark these with a *C* or *c*. Note that students do not have to answer these questions, only to decide what kind of culture each one addresses.

1 C
2 C
3 C
4 c
5 C
6 C
7 c
8 C
9 C

5 Ask students which kind of culture they think is more important to know about. There is no one right answer to this question, but you might want to encourage students to give reasons for their answers.

TEACH GLOBAL THINK LOCAL

Reading extra

There are several words with double consonants that students sometimes misspell. Ask students to close their books. Write the following pairs of words from the text on the board. Students have to choose the correct one.

dificult	*difficult*
literature	*litterature*
beliefs	*belieffs*
imigrants	*immigrants*
comunity	*community*

Tell them to open their books and check their answers again.

Grammar (SB page 12)

1 Students find examples of the different kinds of question in Reading and Speaking exercise 4.

2, 3 and 6 are subject questions.

2 Now direct students' attention to the second exercise. They must complete the questions given. Do an example or two to help them get started.

1 What popular sports do Australians watch on television?
2 Who lived in Australia before European settlers arrived?
3 What do Australians celebrate on 26 January?
4 How many states and territories are there in Australia?
5 What is a barbeque?
6 Which Australian city held the Summer Olympics in 2000?

3 Tell students to open their books at page 130 and read the answers to the questions from Reading and Speaking exercise 4. Without turning back to the original page, ask them to try to write the questions from memory. Check answers.

G Grammar focus

Refer students to the language summary on subject and object questions on page 132.

You can use exercises 6 and 7 on page 133 for:

a) extra practice now
b) homework
c) review a couple of lessons from now.

The answers are on page 142 of the Teacher's Book.

Writing and Speaking (SB page 13)

1 Ask students to work individually and write two to four questions about their own culture. Circulate and help students who are having trouble thinking of ideas. Give them time for this activity, and encourage students to look at the questions in Reading and Speaking exercise 4 and Grammar exercise 2 for ideas.

2 Ask students to work in groups of three or four. They should share their questions with each other, making sure that everyone gets all the answers. Now tell them that they have to choose the eight best / most interesting questions and write them on a new piece of paper.

3 Get each group to exchange their quiz with another group. One student should read out the new questions to their group and everyone tries to answer the questions. Circulate and monitor. Which group had the hardest quiz?

TEACH GLOBAL THINK LOCAL

Speaking extra

Tell students you are going to do a special dictation about culture. They will need a blank sheet of paper. Tell them to write at the top of the right corner of the page: *I AGREE*. Tell them to write in the bottom left corner: *I DON'T AGREE*.

Explain that you are going to dictate a series of statements. Students must write them on the page in the area that reflects their opinion. If they don't know or don't have an opinion on a sentence they can write the sentence in the middle of the page. Dictate the following sentences.

Citizenship tests are a good idea for new immigrants to a country.

Cultures around the world are becoming more and more the same.

It is important to know about culture.

Young people today don't know enough about their culture.

If you want to be cultured you have to have a lot of money.

Ask students to work in pairs and compare their dictations, and then to discuss where they wrote the sentences on the page. Hold a whole-class discussion at the end.

Function globally: making recommendations

These lessons in *Global* are designed to provide students with immediately useful functional language. They all follow a similar format.

Warm up (SB page 14)

Aim: to introduce the topic via a quick speaking task or picture work.

Tips:

- Do not over-correct here, especially in speaking activities.
- Encourage students to use what language they can at this stage.

Listening (SB page 14)

Aim: to present the functional language in context via a conversation or series of conversations.

Tips:

- Ask students to read the exercises first before listening.
- Play the recording all the way through for each task (there are always two tasks).
- For multiple conversations pause the recording after each one.
- If students find it very difficult, play the recording a final time and allow them to read the audioscript at the back of the book.

1 Conversation 1: what to see in the area
Conversation 2: what to do on Friday evening

2 Conversation 1: a walk to the harbour, a trip to the caves, the organised tour
Conversation 2: a concert, pubs with live music, the student union

1.10–1.11

Conversation 1

A: We'd like to get a feel for the area, you know, on our first afternoon. Can you recommend anything to see nearby?

B: Well, if you don't want to go far, I'd suggest walking down to the harbour. It's very pretty and it's a nice little walk.

C: That sounds good, thanks. Um, perhaps you can help us with something else. We were thinking of looking at the caves tomorrow. Are they worth seeing?

B: Oh, yes, you shouldn't miss the caves, they're one of the most popular tourist attractions. I can really recommend the organised tour. It's very good.

A: Mmm, I think we'll do that tomorrow then. Thanks.

B: You're welcome. Enjoy your day.

Conversation 2

A: So, did you have a good day?

B: Yes, thank you, I think I learned lots of new things. Juliette and I want to go out on Friday evening. Can you suggest anything? Juliette really likes music.

A: Well, what about a concert? There have lots of famous bands on at the Arena. I can look if there's anything on this Friday ...

B: That's a good idea but … er … it might be too expensive.

A: Yes, I suppose tickets for big bands are quite expensive … Um, well, there are lots of good pubs with live music. Or you could try the student union on Chambers Street. You can dance there and it's quite cheap.

B: That sounds great.

Language focus (SB page 14)

Aim: to draw students' attention to the items of functional language.

Tips:

- Make sure students have time to understand the form and meaning of the phrases, but you needn't translate them word for word.
- Students should be able to pronounce these phrases intelligibly, so drill them.

1

I'd suggest
1 you shouldn't miss
2 I can really recommend
3 what about
4 there are lots of good
5 you could try

2

1 a 2 a 3 b 4 b

Speaking (SB page 14)

Aim: to allow students an opportunity to use this language in a meaningful, real-world context.

Tips:

- There is sometimes a choice of tasks. Any task involving reading a script will be easier than a task involving students making their own scripts. This gives you flexibility for mixed-ability classes.
- Give students time to prepare this activity, and circulate and monitor carefully.
- Correct sensitively, paying attention to the target language especially.
- If time allows, ask students to repeat the task, but with a new partner.

Global English

These lessons in *Global* have two main goals. The first is to give you and your students interesting information about English and language in general. The second goal is to provide students with practice in different kinds of reading comprehension tasks that they are likely to encounter in future study (for example, exams).

Warm up (SB page 15)

Aim: to engage students with the topic, and highlight potentially difficult vocabulary in the text.

Tips:

- be generous in helping students here with any unknown words in the first task.
- ask students to relate this task, wherever possible, to similar events or texts in their own lives. This will help them with the reading.

1

1 barbecue
2 dollars
3 small
4 traffic lights
5 a wedding

2 Students' own answers.

Reading (SB page 15)

Aim: to provide students with interesting information about English, and reading exam practice skills; where possible to focus on interesting or useful aspects of language in the text.

Tips:

- Get students to read through the whole text once first before doing the tasks.
- Many of these texts have been graded slightly, or not at all. There is a glossary of difficult words. Get students to read that first as it will help them understand the rest.
- There are two tasks. The first is an easier task, often focusing on the gist of the passage. The second is a more difficult task, similar to reading exam questions.
- If there is a third question, the purpose is to raise student's awareness about a language feature; do not expect them to produce it immediately.
- This language is not tested or reviewed in future units, which means you have more flexibility with this material as to when and where you use it.

1

1 T
2 F
3 T
4 T
5 F
6 T

2

1 any of the following: plants and animals, customs and practices, food and drink
2 *bateria*, *lakh*
3 Nigeria

Speaking (SB page 15)

Aim: for students to relate the material in the reading to their own language, culture and experiences.

Tips:

- This is a short speaking activity and can be done in whole-class mode or in small groups.
- Wherever possible, ask students to think of and provide examples in their own language but explain them in English too.

As you go through these *Global English* lessons in the book, don't be afraid to ask students for opinions and reactions to the information in the text – not only answering the comprehension questions. Which do they find interesting? Do they know of similar experiences or facts in their own language or other languages? Some of your learners might be in your class because they are very interested in language, and these texts provide a great opportunity for you to capitalise on that motivation.

Writing: a report

These lessons in *Global* are designed to provide students with extended writing practice. They all follow a similar format.

Reading (SB page 16)

Aim: to provide a sample text for students to analyse.

Tips:

- Many of these texts deliberately contain errors which the students will be asked to focus on and correct later in the lesson.
- At this stage of the lesson merely ask them to read the text and extract the information.
- There are often two questions for these texts: one which focuses on gist and the other on specific details.
- If a student does ask a question about an error in form, praise them for noticing it, and explain that they will be correcting them shortly.

1 Students' own answers.

2

1 Persian, also called Farsi or Parsi
2 the official language, used in government, the media and education
3 parts of Afghanistan, Tajikistan and Uzbekistan
4 over 60 languages or dialects, including Turkish, Kurdish and Arabic
5 same alphabet as Arabic; written from right to left
6 French, Arabic

Language focus: making additional points (SB page 16)

Aim: to highlight and focus on a particular aspect of language that students can use to improve their writing.

Tips:

- Sometimes this section serves as revision or reinforcement of language that students have encountered passively before in the unit (for example, in the reading texts) – make this link clear where possible.
- Let students check their answers in pairs or small groups, then correct in open class.

1

It is **also** sometimes called Farsi, or Parsi.
Persian **is also** spoken in parts of Afghanistan …
We **also** have different words …
In addition, there are cities in the south …
In addition to Persian …
as well as Persian words
as well as 'tashakor' or 'motehshakeram'
… if you can use some Persian words **as well.**

2

1 Use *in addition* **at the beginning** of a sentence. Use *as well* **at the end** of a sentence.
3 Use *in addition to* or *as well as* **before** a noun.
4 Use *also* with a verb **in the middle** of a sentence.

3

Students' own answers.

Writing skills: planning (SB page 16)

Aim: to give students a chance to develop their writing through various different micro skills.

Tips:

- Sometimes this section focuses on common student errors in writing.
- Clearly explain the focus and do an example of one of the questions first with the students before asking them to continue on their own.
- Let students check their answers in pairs or small groups, then correct in open class.

1 c 2 a 3 b

Preparing to write (SB page 16)

Aim: to give students time to brainstorm ideas for the writing task.

Tips:

- Allow students to brainstorm ideas in pairs or small groups.
- At low levels, this may involve some use of L1 (the students' mother tongue); be tolerant of this, but be on hand to help with translations or English where needed.
- Ask students to make notes here, but not begin writing.

Writing (SB page 16)

Aim: to give students practice in more extended writing tasks.

Tips:

- This section can be done as homework.
- Remind students to refer back to the model text, but to be careful of the typical errors.
- Ask students to check their work carefully before they hand it in.

Global review

These lessons in *Global* are designed to provide students with an opportunity to review and consolidate the language they have studied in the unit.

Grammar and Vocabulary (SB page 17)

Aim: to give students revision of all the main grammar and vocabulary points that arose in the unit.

Tips:

- Demonstrate the activities by doing the first one as a whole class.
- Allow students time to do this, and encourage them to look back through the unit for help.
- When you come to correct this, do not simply go around the class asking for the right answer – encourage students to say *why* they think something is correct, and seek confirmation from others before moving on.

Grammar	Vocabulary
1	**1**
1 come	1 legal
2 am spending / 'm spending	2 scientific
3 am having / 'm having	3 business
4 have	4 medical
5 do not usually go / don't usually go	5 technical
6 prefer	6 aviation
7 am visiting / 'm visiting	**2**
2	1 attractions
1 is *The Hobbit*	2 boutiques
2 wrote	3 event
3 did Tolkein die	4 architecture
4 do pilots speak	
5 can I learn	

Speaking and Writing (SB page 17)

Aim: to provide extra speaking practice that will review and consolidate language presented in the unit.

Tips:

- Give the students time to read and understand the instructions.
- Circulate and monitor the students, encouraging them to use only English here.
- Make notes of any incorrect use of language, but refrain from correcting if students are in the middle of the task.

Study skills

These lessons in *Global* are designed to provide students with skills and strategies in learner training and learner autonomy. For more on learner autonomy and learner training, see the essay on page xxiii.

Understanding your learning style (SB page 17)

Tell students to read the information in the box. Do they agree? Have they ever thought about the way in which they learn things? Explain that there are different learning styles, and that they are going to do a questionnaire to help them think about their own style.

1 Go through the questions first. Tell students not to worry about the headings at the moment, just to tick the sentences that they think apply best to them.

If you like, you could also do the questionnaire at the same time.

2 Put students into small groups. Tell them to go through their questionnaires together and compare their answers. Reflecting on and talking about how they learn is arguably more important than getting the results of the questionnaire. Circulate and monitor.

When groups have finished, students check the answer key in their books to discover their learning style.

A Global: a, d, f	C Impulsive: b, d, f
Analytical: b, c, e	Reflective: a, c, e
B Visual: c, f, h	
Auditory: a, d, g	
Kinaesthetic: b, e, i	

Point out that the letters correspond to the learning styles but that most people have a mixture of styles.

At the end of this activity, tell students to reflect back on what they talked about. If they find that they learn better in a certain way then tell them to try and play to those strengths, especially when studying.

Background note

It's important for you as a teacher to vary your teaching style as well so that your class has something for different learning styles each time. It is impossible to meet every single learning style in each lesson, but teachers who vary the pace and style of activities often stand a better chance of keeping the students' attention and creating a memorable learning experience. The notes and alternative procedures in the *Global* Teacher's Book should help you do that.

UNIT 2 Lives & Legends

Coursebook

Unit 2	Language	Texts	Communicative skills
Part 1 SB page 18	Grammar Past simple and past continuous Vocabulary and Pronunciation *-ing* and *-ed* adjectives Word stress	Listening An interview with a ghostwriter	Speaking Ghostwriting Writing Ghostwriting a partner's experience
Part 2 SB page 20	Vocabulary Relationships Grammar Past perfect and past simple Pronunciation Weak forms	Reading *White Teeth*	
Part 3 SB page 22	Grammar Modifiers Vocabulary and Pronunciation Extreme adjectives Word stress	Reading and Speaking *Grimms' fairy tales*	Listening and Speaking A fairy tale
Part 4 SB page 24	Vocabulary Prepositions Extend your vocabulary Ways of talking about meaning Grammar *used to* and *would*	Reading *Legendary places – modern meanings*	Writing A mini saga
Function globally SB page 26	Generalising and giving examples Talking about philosophy Talking about likes / dislikes and family / friends		
Global voices SB page 27	Listening to people talk about influences on their lives Talking about *stuff* Talking about people who have influenced your life		
Writing SB page 28	A narrative Complex sentences Writing a story		
Global review SB page 29	Grammar and vocabulary review Extra speaking and writing practice		
Study skills SB page 29	Improving your reading skills		

Additional resources

eWorkbook	Interactive and printable grammar, vocabulary, listening and pronunciation practice Extra reading and writing practice Additional downloadable listening and audio material
Teacher's Resource Disc	Communication activity worksheets to print and photocopy
Go global: ideas for further research	**Lives** Ask students to find an American or British online genealogy or family history site and try to find anybody with the same family name as you (without registering). **Legends** Ask students to search for real places that use the name El Dorado, Atlantis or Shangri-La. What places are they? Do they refer to the legend?

Part 1

TEACH GLOBAL THINK LOCAL Lead-in

Ask students what sort of people write biographies / books about their lives. Make a list on the board together (politicians, sports stars, actors, singers, other people with interesting lives ...). Ask students if they read any of these books or if they have read an interesting biography recently.

Speaking (SB page 18)

Background note

Andrew Crofts is a British ghostwriter. He writes books for people all over the world with interesting life stories. You can find more information about him at http://www.andrewcrofts.com/.

1 **1.12** Tell students to look at the images on the page. Explain that the man in the photo is Andrew Crofts, a ghostwriter. Read definitions 1–3 with students and elicit the meaning of *pen name* if necessary. Ask students to decide on the definition they think is correct. Play the first part of an authentic interview with Andrew Crofts and ask students to check their answer.

Definition 3

1.12

A: Andrew, what exactly does a ghostwriter do?

B: A ghostwriter helps someone who has a story or an expertise that they want to put into book form but doesn't actually have the right skill to produce the book themselves. So they have the story in their head, or in their filing cabinets, or in their memory in some way, and a ghostwriter will listen to what they have to say and then will create a book from that.

2 Ask students to work in pairs and discuss the questions.

Possible answers

1 People who aren't able to write their life story themselves because they have no time or aren't good at writing or writing in English.

2 Advantages: you don't have to think of a story, you hear interesting stories.

Disadvantages: people don't know that you wrote the books.

Background note

Jimi Hendrix (1942–1970) was an American musician renowned for his skill on the electric guitar. Kathy Etchingham was the inspiration for his song 'Gypsy Eyes'.

3 Direct students to the three book covers and descriptions at the bottom of the page. Clarify any new words if necessary. Ask individual students which book they find most interesting and would perhaps like to read. Prompt them to explain why.

Listening (SB page 18)

This is the second and third part of the interview with Andrew Crofts.

1 **1.13** Explain that students are going to listen to how Andrew Crofts became a ghostwriter. Check comprehension of the two explanations before playing the interview.

Explanation 2

1.13

A: What were you doing before you became a ghostwriter?

B: Well, I – I discovered it by accident. I was interviewing a man for a business magazine, who was uh ... a thing called a business guru, who used to hold seminars for people and teach them how to improve their profits and things, and he ... at the end of the interview, he said to me, 'I've been asked to produce a series of books, which I want to do for publicity reasons, but I don't have the time to actually do it myself.' He said, 'If I give you the material, uh ... will you write the books, and I'll have the glory, and you can have the money.'

2 Direct students to the words in the box. Ask students to check the meaning of these words in a monolingual dictionary, if possible.

TEACH GLOBAL THINK LOCAL Alternative procedure

Explain or check the meaning of the the words in context.

For example: *I'm a sucker for chocolate cake. Do I like chocolate cake? What about you?*

Would you like to work in journalism – be a reporter for a newspaper or TV?

In monolingual classes, you could explain the phrases and ask students to confirm the meaning in their own language.

3 **1.14** Direct students to the possible reasons why Andrew Crofts likes being a ghostwriter. Emphasise that they should not worry if don't understand everything that is said. Play the final part of the interview.

He finds other people's lives and stories interesting.

He gets out of the house and meets lots of different people.

He likes living somebody else's life for a few months.

1.14

A: You've written many successful books as a ghostwriter. Have you been tempted to stop ghostwriting and write books under your own name?

B: I have written books under my own name as well, but if I … I'm just a sucker for a story and if somebody rings me up, particularly if they have an interesting foreign accent and I think, you know, I'm going to travel somewhere interesting and meet somebody that's had a life I've … is going to be new and interesting to me, I just can't resist.

A: What have you learned from your experiences as a ghostwriter, as a writer and as an individual?

B: I think as a writer it is the capturing other people's voices … erm and learning how to structure a story so that it works in a book form.

As an individual it has taught me a huge amount about how the rest of the world lives. Otherwise … like most writers I don't go out that much and I wouldn't go out at all if I could sit at home and write novels just from my imagination. So it has forced me to go out and meet a far more diverse … erm number of people than I would ever otherwise have come across. But at greater depth than if I'd done journalism which is the other option. As a journalist you get to do that, you get to meet a huge range of people but you're there perhaps for ten minutes interviewing a film star before you're shuffled out of the hotel room or you're there for an hour or two with somebody … erm and then you move onto the next story, which suits a lot of people. But I actually do quite like the intense couple … two or three months of being in one person's skin, erm, and I've found that … I've learnt a lot about other people.

A: Thank you, Andrew.

4 Ask students to discuss the question in pairs. Invite feedback from one or two pairs, encouraging them to tell the class the reasons for their answers.

Grammar (SB page 19)

1 Copy the example from the grammar box on the board. Check comprehension by asking: *What is the main information in this sentence?* (Kathy Etchingham became Jim Hendrix's girlfriend.) *What is the background information?* (Jimi Hendrix was just starting to become famous.) Show the two actions visually with an arrow for the action in progress and a dot for the completed action.

Jimi Hendrix was just starting to become famous when Kathy Etchingham became his girlfriend.

Ask students if they can identify the names of the two tenses (past continuous and past simple).

Ask students to mark the verbs in the other examples with an arrow or a dot in the same way and complete the rules.

discovered; were planning

what were you doing; became

First rule: completed actions

Second rule: actions in progress

Language note

Remind students that we often use the past continuous with *while*. Direct students to the *My Gorilla Journey* book summary on page 18 for an example.

Students should be familiar with the structure of the past continuous tense. Before doing the next exercise, revise the structure with the class using the examples in the grammar box. Remind students of the irregular spellings of some *–ing* forms (eg *planning*).

Point out that *was / were* are pronounced as weak forms /wəz/ and /wə/. Drill the examples in the grammar box.

2 Ask students to complete the summary of the book in pairs. Do the first one or two with the class as examples if necessary. In class feedback, elicit why each tense is used. Check pronunciation of weak forms.

Answers are numbered in the order they appear in the text.

1	was studying	5	were living
2	met	6	started
3	married	7	experienced
4	returned	8	were attacking

3 Ask students to imagine they are writing a story. Direct students to the sentences. Ask them to complete the sentences in pairs and then write two sentences of their own, making them as dramatic as possible. Point out they can do this by using lots of adjectives and adverbs to create atmosphere and add detail.

Students compare with another pair and read out their best sentence to the class.

G Grammar focus

Refer students to the language summary on past simple and past continuous on page 134.

You can use exercises 1 and 2 on page 135 for:

a) extra practice now

b) homework

c) review a couple of lessons from now.

The answers are on page 142 of the Teacher's Book.

Vocabulary and Pronunciation (SB page 19)

1 Tell students you saw a boring film at the cinema. Write *boring film* and *I was bored* on the board and point out the adjective endings. Say you went to see an amazing film and elicit the word for how you felt (amazed). Ask students which ending we use to describe feelings (*-ed*). Then ask students to work individually or in pairs and complete the two columns (see exercise 2 for answers). Take whole-class feedback. Use concept questions to check meaning. For example: *If somebody is a fascinating person what are they like? Are they interesting or boring?*

2 **1.15** Say *fascinating*, emphasising the stressed first syllable. Ask students to listen to the other words in exercise 1 and underline the stressed syllable. Check that students have heard the correct stress. Play the track again and ask students to repeat the words, paying attention to the stress.

fascinating	fascinated
confusing	confused
inspiring	inspired
shocking	shocked
embarrassing	embarrassed
disappointing	disappointed

3 Direct students attention to the example. Ask them to write six similar sentences about their lives using the adjectives in exercise 1. Give students enough time to think of ideas. Ask students to swap sentences with a partner and read their partner's work.

Writing (SB page 19)

1 Tell students to choose one of their sentences from Vocabulary exercise 3 and tell their partner more about what happened (*where*, *when*, *why*, *how*).

Alternatively if students have read each other's work, tell the partner to pick the event they would like to learn more about. The partner takes notes. Then the pairs swap roles. You might like to give each student a time limit for this.

2 Students 'ghost' their partner's experience by writing about it in their voice, starting with the structure given. Encourage students to use adjectives and adverbs to make the paragraph sound as interesting as possible.

3 Students swap paragraphs and read their ghosted experience. Ask students to give their partner feedback, focusing on factual correctness and how interesting it was to read. In class feedback, invite one or two students to rate their partner's ghostwriting skills.

Part 2

Vocabulary (SB page 20)

1 Ask students to look at the photo and illustrations and say what sort of relationship (family, friends, colleagues) they think the people in the pictures have with each other and why. Ask students if they think the people have a good or bad relationship and why.

Read out the words in the task, modelling pronunciation and word stress (*great-grandfather*, *acquaintance*, *fiancée*). In pairs students discuss the differences in the words, then discuss in full-class feedback. You can illustrate some relationships on the board with a family tree or invite students to do this.

Your *grandfather* is the father of one of your parents. Your *great-grandfather* is the *grandfather* of one your parents.

A *friend* is somebody you know well. An *acquaintance* is somebody you don't know very well.

A *colleague* is somebody you work with, in any position. A *boss* is somebody who has a higher position than you.

Your *fiancée* is a woman you are going to marry (you are engaged to her). Your *ex-wife* is a woman you used to be married to (you are divorced from her).

A *stepbrother* is the son of your stepmother or stepfather (your mother's or father's new partner) and is not related to you by blood. A *half-brother* is the son of your mother or father with another partner and is therefore related to you by blood.

Language note

The male form of *fiancée* is *fiancé* (this follows French spelling which distinguishes male and female forms).

2 Ask students to match the sentence halves so that the words in italics make common phrases. Do the first sentence as an example.

1 e 2 c 3 f 4 b 5 a 6 d

3 Give students time to think up or write sentences about people they know. Then invite them to tell the class or a partner.

Reading (SB page 20)

1 Tell students they are going to read an extract about a family dispute (argument). Ask students to discuss what often causes family disputes.

Possible answers
unfair division of household tasks
different views on upbringing of children
money
problems with other family members
spending too little time with family

2 1.16–1.17 Look at the title of the novel and the information about the author with the class. Ask if anybody has read or heard of this novel or the film adaptation.

Ask students to read the summary. Check that students understand the word *punish*.

Students read and listen to the extract and then, either individually or in pairs, write one sentence to summarise it. Students compare with a partner or another pair. Take whole-class feedback.

3 Ask students to read the sentences and see if they can answer any of them. Students then read the two texts again and check, or find the answers.

1 T	4 F (She didn't say *yes* or *no* to him.)
2 T	5 F (He forgot what those two words meant.)
3 D	

4 Students work in pairs. Ask them to read the three tasks and then choose one. Ask students to feed back to the class about each of the tasks.

Grammar (SB page 21)

1 Read out the first example sentence. Ask students which event happened first (*put*). Ask students what words in the sentence tell them this (*and then*). Students identify the tenses of both verbs (past simple).

Give students a few moments to look at the other two examples and then ask similar questions.

1 put
2 had decided
3 had changed

2 Students complete the rules by circling the correct option.

First rule: *had*
Second rule: *before*

3 Do the first sentence as an example. Write on the board *The husband moved out of the family house because …* and encourage students to complete it using the past perfect. Then students write reasons for the other events individually or in pairs. Take whole-class feedback.

G Grammar focus

Refer students to the language summary on past perfect and past simple on page 134.

You can use exercise 3 on page 135 for:

a) extra practice now
b) homework
c) review a couple of lessons from now.

The answers are on page 142 of the Teacher's Book.

Pronunciation (SB page 21)

1 Direct students to sentences 1–4. In pairs, students read out a sentence to their partner at a natural pace. The other pays attention to how the underlined word sounds.

2 1.18 Students listen to the pronunciation of the words. In class feedback establish which words are stressed (strong forms) and which words are unstressed (weak forms). Explain that we usually stress the words that carry meaning. Model the forms again and drill them with students.

Students complete the rules using the words in the box by referring back to sentences 1–4.

1 /həd/ (weak form)
2 /hædnt/ (strong form)
3 /kən/ (weak form)
4 /kɑːnt/ (strong form)
First rule: affirmative sentences
Second rule: negative sentences, questions and short answers

3 1.19 Students read, listen to and repeat the quotes, paying attention to the weak forms. Point out before listening that they are not just in auxilaries. Ask individual students to read out the sentences. Point out the weak forms and drill pronunciation.

1 *can* /kən/; *your*: /jə/	4 *the* /ðə/
2 *is* /ɪz/; *than* /ðən/	5 *of* /əv/
3 *is* /ɪz/ *a* /ə/; *her* /hɜː/	6 no weak forms

4 Look at the quotes in exercise 3 again and ask students to explain the meaning. Students then work in pairs and discuss if they agree or disagree, explaining their reasons.

In monolingual classes ask students if they can think of similar quotes in their own language. Discuss if the meaning is the same or different.

In multilingual classes invite individual students to say similar quotes in their own language and explain the meaning in English.

Part 3

TEACH GLOBAL THINK LOCAL Lead-in

Direct students' attention to the information on page 22 about fairy tales. Write the expression *fairy tale* on the board. Ask students to brainstorm things they associate with fairy tales and write them on the board. Help with vocabulary if necessary.

Possible answers: prince, princess, stepmother, tower, gold, giant, forest, witch, wolf.

Speaking and Listening (SB page 22)

Background note

The story in the listening is the story recorded by the Grimm brothers in later editions of their book *Children's and Household Tales*. The Grimms themselves changed the story from the first edition of 1812 in which the woodcutter's wife is the children's own mother and not their stepmother.

1 Direct students' attention to the picture of Hansel and Gretel on page 22. Ask students if they know the story.

2 Students work in pairs and describe the picture, using the questions and useful phrases to help them. In whole-class feedback establish that Hansel and Gretel are brother and sister.

3 Read the questions and answers with the students. Ask them which answers they think are correct but don't confirm them at this stage.

4 **1.20** Play the recording. Students check their answers to exercise 3. Encourage students to explain why the parents left the children (they were poor and didn't have enough food for the children; the stepmother didn't want the children) and why Gretel killed the witch (the witch wanted to make Hansel fat and then kill him).

1 a
2 b

1.20

Hansel and Gretel

A woodcutter lived in a big forest with his second wife and his two children, Hansel and Gretel. The woodcutter was extremely poor and the family was always hungry. The stepmother wanted to get rid of the children but the woodcutter refused to listen to her. However, one evening when the children were in bed, the woodcutter said to his wife: 'Our food is nearly all gone. How are we to feed the poor children?' She answered, 'Early tomorrow morning we will take the children out into the forest and leave them there.' The woodcutter was terribly sad but he finally agreed.

The two children were awake and they heard what their stepmother had said. The next day, the woman gave the children some bread and they all walked to the forest. While they were walking, Hansel threw little pieces of bread onto the ground, so that he could find the way home.

After a while, they came to the middle of the forest and the father lit a fire. The woman said: 'Stay by the fire, children, we will go into the forest and cut some wood.' Hansel and Gretel were quite tired and soon they fell asleep. When they woke up, it was night. Hansel looked for the pieces of bread but they had gone – the birds had eaten them. The children walked all night and all day but the forest was enormous and they couldn't find the way home. At last, they reached a little cottage made of bread and cakes. The children were very hungry and they started to eat pieces from the house. Suddenly, the door opened, and an old woman came out. Hansel and Gretel were rather frightened but the old woman was kind to them and gave them food.

However, the old woman was actually a wicked witch. When a child came to her house, she killed it, cooked it and ate it. In the morning she locked Hansel in a small room. Then she said to Gretel, 'Cook something good for your brother, he needs to get fat. When he is fat, I will eat him.'

Every morning the witch felt Hansel's finger to see if he was fat enough. But she had bad eyes and Hansel tricked her: he held out a little bone instead of his finger. However, after four weeks the old woman could not wait any longer. 'Tomorrow I will kill him and cook him,' she said to Gretel.

Early in the morning, the witch heated the oven. 'Get in,' said the witch to Gretel, 'and see if it is hot enough.' She planned to close the oven, cook Gretel and eat her too. But Gretel said: 'How do I get in?' The witch put her head and shoulders into the oven to show Gretel. Then Gretel pushed the witch into the oven and she burned to death. Gretel ran to Hansel, and cried: 'Hansel, the old witch is dead!' They searched the witch's house, and they found lots of jewels.

The children walked through the forest until they saw their house and ran inside to their father. Their father was delighted to see them. He had been miserable since he had left the children in the forest. Hansel and Gretel gave their father the jewels and they lived very happily together.

TEACH GLOBAL THINK LOCAL Extra activity

Reconstruct the whole story with the class. Prompt students to tell you what happened. Note the main events on the board. Then go back to the story and prompt students to tell you any details they can remember.

Focus on the happy ending.

5 Direct the students to the characters in the box. Make sure they understand who the woodcutter is. Play the recording again. Students pay attention to what the characters do.

Students write down adjectives to describe each character and then compare answers in pairs. Walk round and help students with vocabulary where necessary. Alternatively you could write adjectives on the board for students to choose from.

In feedback encourage students to explain their choice of adjectives and link them to events in the story.

Possible answers

Gretel: frightened, brave

Hansel: clever, inventive

the stepmother: unkind, selfish

the witch: old, wicked

the woodcutter: weak, sad/miserable

Grammar (SB page 22)

Language note

Quite usually means 'to some degree'. However, in some contexts and depending on intonation, it can mean 'very' or 'totally'. For example with extreme adjectives: It was *quite amazing* (with emphasis on *quite*) means 'it was totally amazing'.

1 Direct students' attention to the example sentences and elicit the meaning of the words in bold. Explain that these are modifiers – they 'modify', or change, the meaning of the adjective by making it weaker or stronger.

Read out the words in the box. Ask students to put them in the correct column using a dictionary if necessary. Alternatively give students example sentences and ask them to work out the meaning from context.

Stronger	Weaker
extremely	a bit
really	fairly
terribly	quite
very	rather

Background note

At the end of the Grimms' version of this story, Red Riding Hood, her grandmother and the huntsman fill the wolf with stones and he falls over and dies. In a continuation, another wolf speaks to Red Riding Hood on the way to her grandmother's house. She tells her grandmother and they lock the door and lie in wait for the wolf. When he comes, they make a trap for him and he falls into a trough of water and drowns.

2 Look at the picture and the title of the fairy tale. Ask students if they know the story and what *hood* means (a hat joined to a piece of clothing).

Ask students to complete the story with modifiers from exercise 1. Point out that several answers are possible.

Students then work in pairs and retell the story.

G Grammar focus

Refer students to the language summary on modifiers on page 134.

You can use exercises 4 and 5 on page 135 for:

a) extra practice now

b) homework

c) review a couple of lessons from now.

The answers are on page 142 of the Teacher's Book.

Vocabulary and Pronunciation (SB page 23)

1 Read out the example sentences in turn. Point out the words in bold and prompt students to explain them by completing the meaning. Drill the word stress of the three words (*enormous*, *delighted*, *miserable*).

1 very big

2 very happy

3 very sad

2 Students work in pairs and match the definitions.

1 c	4 f
2 e	5 a
3 d	6 b

3 1.21 Direct students' attention to sentences 1–3.

Play the recording and ask students to repeat the sentences. Ask students to underline the stressed words, then drill the pronunciation again.

1 big, enormous

2 pleased, delighted

3 sad, miserable

4 Students make similar sentences using the words in exercise 2. Give an example of your own if you wish (*My mobile phone isn't just old, it's ancient*). Students practise saying their sentences silently, paying attention to sentence stress. Ask each student to tell the class one of their sentences.

5 Students complete the sentences about themselves.

6 Students work in pairs. Direct students' attention to the example. Ask them to choose three of their sentences from exercise 5 and read the sentences to their partner. The partner should comment on what they have heard.

Reading and Speaking (SB page 23)

1 Elicit from students what problems Hansel and Gretel and Little Red Riding had to deal with (an unkind stepmother, being alone, a wicked witch; a wolf / stranger pretending to be somebody else) and write them on the board. Ask students what problems children today have to deal with and write them on the board. Compare the lists and ask students if they think fairy tales can help children today to deal with their problems.

2 **1.22** Direct students' attention to the text and the suggested subtitles. Students read the text and choose the best subtitle. If you think they may find the text difficult, you could play the recording for them to listen as they read. Discuss with students why they chose their answer and why the other two answers are not correct.

b Learning for life

3 Ask students to discuss the questions in pairs and then take whole-class feedback.

TEACH GLOBAL THINK LOCAL

Homework extra

Ask students to think of a fairy tale they know from childhood and write a short version of the story (similar to the *Little Red Riding Hood* text).

Ask students to include a couple of sentences at the end about the moral message of the story.

In small classes, ask students to read their story to the class. In larger classes, students can swap stories with a partner.

Part 4

TEACH GLOBAL THINK LOCAL

Lead-in

Revise the prepositions of place that students already know (*behind, in front of, next to, under, in, on*) by taking an object and asking students where it is.

Then ask students to take an object from their bag. Students work in pairs; they hide their objects without their partner seeing it. Demonstrate the task with a volunteer pair. One student asks their partner questions to find the object: *Is it in your bag? Is it under your chair? Is it behind your pencil case?* The partner answers *yes* or *no* until the object is found.

Vocabulary (SB page 24)

1 Look at the words in the box with students. Convey meaning by drawing a graphic representation of each one on the board. Read the language note with the class and ask students if they know a synonym for these words (eg *under* for *beneath* and *inside* for *within*).

Then direct students to the picture of the tower. Ask students to work in pairs and complete the description of the picture.

2 **1.23** Play the recording. Students listen and check their answers.

There is a tall, dark tower. In front of the tower is a horse. **Beside** the horse there is a man. There is a princess **within** the tower. **Beneath** the tower there is a secret tunnel.

Against the tower wall there is a ladder. **Around** the tower there is a circle of trees. **Beyond** the trees there are some mountains. **Above** the tower there is a dragon.

3 Students complete the sentences by choosing the correct word.

1 within	3 above	5 beneath
2 behind	4 beyond	

TEACH GLOBAL THINK LOCAL

Extra activity

Ask students to write a short description using five of the prepositions in the box in exercise 1 and some of the objects or people in exercises 1 and 3 (*tower*, *forest*, *prince*, *hill*, *village*, etc). They can add other people and objects if they wish.

Students work in pairs and dictate their description to their partner. Their partner draws a picture. Students then compare their drawings with the descriptions.

Reading (SB page 24)

1 Direct students' attention to the names of the three places in the box. Brainstorm what students know about these places and make notes on the board. Don't give them any extra information at this stage.

2 Divide students into groups of three and ask them to choose the place they are most interested in. Students read their text individually and answer the questions.

Text A (Atlantis)

1 It's a legendary city beneath the sea.
2 The legend comes from the ancient Greeks.
3 Today, Atlantis means any ancient, advanced and lost civilisation.

Text B (El Dorado)

1 El Dorado is a legendary golden city in South America.
2 The legend probably comes from a tradition of the Muisca people in the highlands of Columbia.
3 Today, the name El Dorado can signify any place where you can make lots of money, quickly.

Text C (Shangri-La)

1 It's an imaginary valley deep within the Himalayan mountains.
2 The legend comes from a 1933 novel called *Lost Horizon* by James Hilton.
3 Today, Shangri-La represents a hidden, perfect place or a quest for happiness.

3 Students work in groups of three and tell their partners about their place.

4 Students stay in their groups and use their information to answer the questions.

1 Atlantis	4 Shangri-La
2 Shangri-La	5 El Dorado
3 El Dorado	6 Atlantis

Extend your vocabulary (SB page 24)

The three texts contain different words to talk about meaning. Ask students to read the information. Model word stress (*represent*, *symbolise*) and then clarify the meaning of the three verbs: *Which one is used to talk about linguistic meaning? Which two verbs are used to talk about a symbol of something?*

Students discuss what the items in the list symbolise in their culture and then tell the class.

Background note

1 In many cultures green represents life and rebirth, the environment and nature. It also represents jealousy and envy.
2 The number 13 symbolises bad luck in some countries, but in certain places such as China it is a lucky number.
3 A red rose often symbolises love.
4 A snake can represent evil and cunning, but also rebirth.

Grammar (SB page 25)

1 Look at the examples and rules with the class. Alternatively, write the example sentences on the board. Ask if the sentences are in the past, present or future. Then establish which of the verbs refer to habitual actions and which to states.

Students complete the sentences with the correct form of *used to* or *would*. Point out that in some cases, more than one answer is possible. Ask students why *would* isn't possible in sentences 1 and 4 (because they are past states).

1 used to	3 used to / would
2 used to / would	4 used to

2 Direct students to the list of topics. Ask students to pick three and make notes.

3 In pairs, students tell each other about the things they wrote about in exercise 2. Demonstrate with a student: talk about a real or imaginary experience in your past.

G Grammar focus

Refer students to the language summary on *used to* and *would* on page 134.

You can use exercises 6 and 7 on page 135 for:
a) extra practice now
b) homework
c) review a couple of lessons from now.

The answers are on page 142 of the Teacher's Book.

Writing (SB page 25)

1 Students read the definition of a mini saga.

2 Explain that students are going to write a mini saga about a legendary place – real or invented. Direct students to the table with ideas. Clarify any unknown words or phrases.

3 Students write their mini sagas either in class or for homework. Then ask students to work in groups and read out their stories. Decide which is the best in each group and read this out to the class. Vote for the best mini saga in the class.

Function globally: generalising and giving examples

These lessons in *Global* are designed to provide students with immediately useful functional language. They all follow a similar format.

Warm up (SB page 26)

Aim: to introduce the topic via a quick speaking task or picture work.

Tips:

- Do not over-correct here, especially in speaking activities.
- Encourage students to use what language they can at this stage.

Listening (SB page 26)

Aim: to present the functional language in context via a conversation or series of conversations.

Tips:

- Ask students to read the exercises first before listening.
- Play the recording all the way through for each task (there are always two tasks).
- For multiple conversations pause the recording after each one.
- If students find it very difficult, play the recording a final time and allow them to read the audioscript at the back of the book.

1 The speaker is a teacher or lecturer.

2 philosophy

3

1 T

2 T

3 F (They found it difficult to live in the way that Confucius expected.)

4 T

5 F (He was a peasant from a simple background.)

1.24

As we have already seen, Confucius felt that people should live moral lives. Generally speaking he believed that people have obligations rather than rights, for example to one's family and one's elders. Confucius had many followers and he expected them to change their lives to reflect his teaching. On the whole, his students were young men from good families, such as the sons of bankers or officials. They were intelligent and skilled in communicating their ideas. Most of the time, however, these students found it difficult to live in the way that Confucius expected. For instance, Confucius thought people should always think of the interests of other people before thinking of their own personal interests. This was of course very difficult for young men who wanted to become wealthy and make a career for themselves. So perhaps it's not surprising that Confucius' favourite disciple was from a more simple background, a peasant called Yan Hui. From your reading last week, what can you tell me about Yan Hui? … The young man in the second row … yes?

Language focus (SB page 26)

Aim: to draw students' attention to the items of functional language.

Tips:

- Make sure students have time to understand the form and meaning of the phrases, but you needn't translate them word for word.
- Students should be able to pronounce these phrases intelligibly, so drill them.

1

1 c

2 a

3 b

2

General statements: *Generally speaking*, *On the whole*, *Most of the time*

Examples: *such as*, *for instance*, *for example*

Speaking (SB page 26)

Aim: to allow students an opportunity to use this language in a meaningful, real-world context.

Tips:

- There is sometimes a choice of tasks. Any task involving reading a script will be easier than a task involving students making their own scripts. This gives you flexibility for mixed-ability classes.
- Give students time to prepare this activity, and circulate and monitor carefully.
- Correct sensitively, paying attention to the target language especially.
- If time allows, ask students to repeat the task, but with a new partner.

Global voices

These lessons in *Global* are designed to provide students with exposure to authentic speakers of English from both native and non-native English backgrounds. They all follow a similar format.

Warm up (SB page 27)

Aim: to introduce the topic and highlight potentially difficult vocabulary the students will encounter.

Tips:

- Be generous in helping students with the vocabulary here, but let them try to work it out first.
- Circulate and monitor any speaking task, but be careful not to over-correct.
- Follow up any short discussion pairwork with an open class discussion, asking students to report back what they said.

Listening (SB page 27)

Aim: to expose students to English spoken with a variety of accents.

Tips:

- Students will need to hear the recording at least twice, if not more times, to understand it. There are almost always two tasks.
- The first time they listen, tell them you don't expect them to understand every word; some of it will be hard. This is because the text has not been scripted or graded in any way. It's what they would hear in 'the real world'.
- The first task is easier and focuses on gist, the second task is more detailed.
- Pause after each speaker on the second listening, and don't be afraid to replay the whole thing if students appear to need it.
- Students can read the audioscript at the back of the book if you / they wish.
- It may be tempting to hunt for specific pronunciation or language errors, but we recommend against this. In real-world communication not everyone speaks perfect English all the time, not even native speakers.

1

1 his parents	3 one of his university teachers
2 her aunt	4 a friend

2

2 She talked to her about **growing up**.

3 He encouraged him to learn more about the **practical side** of computer science.

1.25–1.28

Martin, Czech Republic

I'm going to talk about my parents who really influenced me a lot in my career, in my goals for all this stuff, what I intend to do, because they always pushed me and helped me if I had some problem or stuff. Also because they reached, I guess, really, really high goals and they are really important people in my, in my country. So … I feel like, I wanna be as them, you know …

Eva, Swizerland

Erm, my aunt I think, had an importance influence on my life because … erm, we're in some way very similar and it's very interesting to talk to her how it was to … to grow up, to go through these kind of difficult years you have growing up and it's very interesting to have a perspective of a person that's 20 years older than you, not only your friends that go through the same experience at the same time. We spent a lot of time together, just doing anything, just going out and see exhibitions and just stuff like that.

Abdul, Saudi Arabia

Er, I can remember one of my teachers at university. He pushes me to do the practical part of computer science, because my major is computer science, er, rather than focusing just on the theoretical part of the – this knowledge, so I started to program or to practise the real environment of programming.

Erica, Italy

One of the person that most influenced my life I can say was a friend of mine that I met many years ago when I was at university. And er … she's never been my best friend and definitely she's not at the moment because I haven't heard from her for ages, but she was very influential for … on my life because I think she taught me the best way to study at university.

Language focus: *stuff* (SB page 27)

Aim: to raise students' awareness of a particular piece of language present in the listening.

Tips:

- This language is not included in unit tests or reviews, it is included here to help students understand international English.
- The objective is awareness-raising, not production. Don't expect students to produce this language in an exercise or in conversation immediately.

1

1 things
2 informal
3 uncountable

2

1 Put all your stuff in the back of the car.
2 Most people have too much stuff.
3 Our supermarket sells all sorts of stuff.
4 I gave all my baby stuff to my sister.
5 Who put all this stuff on my desk?
6 There's a lot of good stuff on her website.

Speaking (SB page 27)

Aim: for students to discuss the same or similar questions as the speakers in the listening.

Tips:

- The speaking tasks here are slightly more open to allow for students to explore the subject. Give them time to do this.
- If students are working in pairs, circulate and monitor. Make notes of incorrect language use to correct afterwards (or in a future class).
- As you go through the book and the *Global voices* lessons, ask students for feedback on these listening activities and their potential use of English with other people. Are they very difficult? Have students used their English as a 'lingua franca' with other non-native English speakers? How did they find it? What tips do they have on understanding or making themselves understood in an international context?

Writing: a narrative

These lessons in *Global* are designed to provide students with extended writing practice. They all follow a similar format.

Reading (SB page 28)

Aim: to provide a sample text for students to analyse.

Tips:

- Many of these texts deliberately contain errors which the students will be asked to focus on and correct later in the lesson.
- At this stage of the lesson merely ask them to read the text and extract the information.
- There are often two questions for these texts: one which focuses on gist and the other on specific details.
- If a student does ask a question about an error in form, praise them for noticing it, and explain that they will be correcting them shortly.

1 b

2

1 both	4 N	7 N
2 N	5 both	8 N
3 H	6 H	9 H

3

Kind actions can influence and change behaviour.

Writing skills: complex sentences (SB page 28)

Aim: to give students a chance to develop their writing through various different micro skills.

Tips:

- Sometimes this section focuses on common student errors in writing.
- Clearly explain the focus and do an example of one of the questions first with the students before asking them to continue on their own.
- Let students check their answers in pairs or small groups, then correct in open class.

1

One day, **when** Hungbu was working in the fields, he found a bird …

He took the bird home **and** looked after it carefully.

The bird gradually became stronger, **and when** summer came, it flew away to a warm place. A year later, the bird flew back **and** gave Hungbu a seed. He sowed the seed **and** it soon grew …

When Hungbu opened one of the gourds, he was amazed …

The next day, he bought an enormous house **and** moved there with his family.

When he heard about his brother's good luck, Nolbu was extremely jealous **and** decided to do the same as his brother. He also found a bird, **but** he broke its leg **and** looked after it until it became strong.

… goblins immediately came out of it **and** stole all his money.

… Nolbu felt ashamed **so** he went to his brother to ask for help.

Hungbu was sorry for him **and so** he invited him to share his house.

2

1 Hungbu sold the treasure and bought an enormous house.
2 When Hungbu opened the door, the bird flew away.
3 When Hungu found the bird, he felt sorry for it, so he took it home.
4 Hungbu worked hard and gave money to his family, but his brother was lazy and never gave money to anyone.

Preparing to write (SB page 28)

Aim: to give students time to brainstorm ideas for the writing task.

Tips:

- Allow students to brainstorm ideas in pairs or small groups.
- At low levels, this may involve some use of L1 (the students' mother tongue); be tolerant of this, but be on hand to help with translations or English where needed.
- Ask students to make notes here, but not begin writing.

Writing (SB page 28)

Aim: to give students practice in more extended writing tasks.

Tips:

- This section can be done as homework.
- Remind students to refer back to the model text, but to be careful of the typical errors.
- Ask students to check their work carefully before they hand it in.

Global review

These lessons in *Global* are designed to provide students with an opportunity to review and consolidate the language they have studied in the unit.

Grammar and Vocabulary (SB page 29)

Aim: to give students revision of all the main grammar and vocabulary points that arose in the unit.

Tips:

- Demonstrate the activities by doing the first one as a whole class.
- Allow students time to do this, and encourage them to look back through the unit for help.
- When you come to correct this, do not simply go around the class asking for the right answer – encourage students to say *why* they think something is correct, and seek confirmation from others before moving on.

Grammar

1 Possible forms

1 used to love / loved
2 often told / would often tell / often used to tell
3 were / used to be
4 exchanged
5 planted
6 had grown
7 climbed
8 came
9 was sleeping
10 stole
11 woke up
12 was
13 had disappeared
14 was following
15 cut
16 died
17 lived

2

Strong: extremely, really, terribly, very

Weak: quite, fairly, rather, a bit

Vocabulary

1 *great-grandfather*: the rest are not relatives
2 *dirty*: the others are extreme adjectives
3 *inspiring*: this is positive, the rest are negative

4 *while*: prepositions of time; the rest are prepositions of place
5 *shocking*: the rest describe how someone feels, while *shocking* describes how something makes someone feel
6 *protect*: the rest are synonyms
7 *fall out*: this is negative; the rest describe good relationships
8 *grandfather*: the rest are not blood relatives

Speaking and Writing (SB page 29)

Aim: to provide extra speaking practice that will review and consolidate language presented in the unit.

Tips:

- Give the students time to read and understand the instructions.
- Circulate and monitor the students, encouraging them to use only English here.
- Make notes of any incorrect use of language, but refrain from correcting if students are in the middle of the task.

Study skills

These lessons in *Global* are designed to provide students with skills and strategies in learner training and learner autonomy. For more on learner autonomy and learner training, see the essay on page xxiii.

Improving your reading skills (SB page 29)

1 Explain that this section focuses on reading skills. Direct students to exercise 1 and ask them to discuss the questions, giving more details.

2 Read through the information in the box with students and check that they have understood. Then ask students to match the types of texts with the types of reading in sentences 1–6. Point out that there might be more than one answer, depending on different aims. When students have finished, ask them to work in pairs and compare ideas.

2

Answers depend on how interested you are, what information you need, and how important the information is.

Possible answers

a poem: 1, 2 or 6

a recipe: 2

a bill: 4

a blog: 3

a newspaper article: 3

a grammar page: 2 or 4

a holiday brochure: 5

a love letter: 1 or 2

3 Direct students to the questions and check they understood them. Students work in pairs and discuss the questions.

4 Ask students to think how they can improve their reading skills. They should think of two ideas and then compare with a partner.

Hot & Cold

Coursebook

Unit 3	Language	Texts	Communicative skills
Part 1 SB page 30	Grammar Future forms: plans and intentions Vocabulary Materials	Listening A desert survival expert	Speaking Talking about a photo from different points of view Speaking Planning a trip
Part 2 SB page 32	Extend your vocabulary Words that go with *problem* Grammar *will* and *be going to* for predictions	Reading *Endless energy?* Listening and Vocabulary Energy	Writing An online comment: giving opinions
Part 3 SB page 34	Grammar *so* and *such* Vocabulary *cold* (metaphor)	Reading *Coming in from the cold*	Speaking Talking about the cold
Part 4 SB page 36	Grammar Real conditionals Vocabulary Words to describe statistics	Reading and Pronunciation *Weather ups and downs* Intonation Listening In a department store	Writing A list poem
Function globally SB page 38	Requests and offers Listening to conversations about clothes in shops Shopping expressions		
Global English SB page 39	Caribbean English Giving a short presentation about the weather		
Writing SB page 40	A formal letter Rules for writing formal letters Writing a job application		
Global review SB page 41	Grammar and vocabulary review Extra speaking and writing practice		
Study skills SB page 41	Writing a learner diary		

Additional resources

eWorkbook	Interactive and printable grammar, vocabulary, listening and pronunciation practice Extra reading and writing practice Additional downloadable listening and audio material
Teacher's Resource Disc	Communication activity worksheets to print and photocopy
Go global: ideas for further research	**Hot** Ask students to find out more about one of the sources of alternative energy – are there many websites that talk about this? **Cold** Ask students to find one of the blogs of the Alaskan bloggers and read their latest entry.

Part 1

TEACH GLOBAL THINK LOCAL Lead-in

Write the words *the desert* on the board and elicit words students associate with this. Examples could be *hot*, *sun*, *sand*, *dry*, *cold at night*. Ask if any students have been to a desert, and if so which one. If you are teaching in a desert country, then ask students what the advantages and disadvantages are of living in such a place.

Speaking (SB page 30)

1 Direct students' attention to the picture of the desert on page 30 and ask them to ask and answer the questions in exercise 1. Feed back as a whole class. Possible vocabulary that might emerge from this picture could be: *rock*, *grass*, *sky*, *desert*, *rain clouds …*

2 This activity encourages the students to think critically about how different points of view can affect one's opinion about a particular place. Put the students into groups of three and ask each to choose one of the roles A, B or C in exercise 2. Allow them some time to make notes about their reaction to the situation. When they are ready, they tell the others in the group their feelings in role. Circulate and monitor, encouraging the students to give as many details as possible. If you have time, ask the students to change groups and change roles. They then repeat the activity.

TEACH GLOBAL THINK LOCAL Mixed ability

To provide more support for weaker students or classes, dictate the following sentence stems for them to complete, or write them on the board.

This place makes me feel …

When I see this I get … because …

It's… and … and … and I really think it's …

Listening (SB page 30)

This is an interview with Tony Nestor, an American expert on deserts who runs courses on survival. He has a company based in Arizona called Ancient Pathways.

1 Explain what the students are going to hear and ask them to read the information about Tony Nester. Ask them to brainstorm a list of things that he might take with him on a trip into the desert. Write these on the board and ask students to copy it down.

2 **1.29** Play the recording once. Students tick the words on their list that he mentions.

3 Ask students to look at the information in the box and try to complete what they can from memory. Then play the recording again and ask them to check their answers.

1 between 20 and 25
2 knife-only
3 three
4 how to find water
5 how to signal for help
6 how to start a fire with only one match
7 get lost
8 24
9 72

1.29

Well, our company is called Ancient Pathways and every year we run between 20 and 25 courses. Around two courses a month. Next week I'm taking a group on one of our most popular courses. It's a knife-only survival course. We're going to be in the desert for three days, and we're taking the following things: a hat; sunscreen; a water bottle; a T-shirt and pants (but not cotton, better a mix of materials); a wool sweater for the night (it gets really cold); a knife, and that's it.

We're going to learn the three things that are most important to know if you want to survive in the desert: how to find shelter, how to find water and how to signal for help. We're also going to learn other survival techniques, like how to start a fire with only one match. We'll probably have six people on the course, but we are still waiting for more.

For this trip, we're going to the Painted Desert. It's around 30 minutes away. It's a beautiful area, but it's common for people to get lost there. People get lost in the deserts around here every month. They think they're going for a walk for just an hour or so and then they can't find their way back. The idea behind this course is to give people the tools to survive for 24 to 72 hours if they're lost in the desert.

I haven't decided yet where to take the next group. I think I'll take the next group to the Mojave Desert, as this is also a fascinating place.

4 Ask students to look at the questions and choose one that they would like to answer. Give them some time to think of what they want to say, then tell them to work in pairs and answer their questions. Check back with the whole class what different people talked about. If stronger students finish early, ask them to discuss another one of the questions.

Grammar (SB page 31)

1 Ask students to turn to the audioscript on page 153 and find the sentences. Then ask them to complete the grammar rules with *be going to + infinitive*, *present continuous* or *will*.

First rule: *be going to* + infinitive
Second rule: present continuous
Third rule: *will*

Language note

All three of these forms can be used to talk about future arrangements. *Going to* is more frequent in spoken and informal contexts. Both *be going to* and the present continuous indicate that a decision has been made, but the present continuous indicates that arrangements are in place or have been made – in the Student's Book this is explained by specific references to times or places. Be aware that a common mistake for students is to use present simple for this kind of future: ~~Tomorrow I go to the dentist.~~

2 Ask students to look at the sentences and complete them with the verb in brackets. Tell them that for some, more than one answer is possible, but they should try to use the present continuous if they can.

1	are / 're leaving
2	aren't going
3	are / 're going to walk
4	will / 'll take
5	are / 're going to learn
6	are / 're going to learn

TEACH GLOBAL THINK LOCAL Alternative procedure

To check answers you could ask students to listen as you read them out. Tell them to imagine you are all going on a trip into the desert together. Read out the sentences in a conversational way, at normal speed. Include the answer in the gap so that students can check if they have it right. Add your own details if you want to elaborate the story further! When you have finished, students check again with a partner. Then go through the answers in your usual way.

3 Ask students to choose three sentences from the list to complete with their own ideas. To help them get started do one or two yourself and read them to the class. Circulate and monitor, helping students where needed. Then ask students to work in pairs and complete their sentences. Ask different students to read out their sentences.

G Grammar focus

Refer students to the language summary on future forms on page 136.

You can use exercise 1 on page 137 for:

a) extra practice now
b) homework
c) review a couple of lessons from now.

The answers are on page 142 of the Teacher's Book.

Vocabulary (SB page 31)

1 **1.30** Let students read the introduction and look at the photos. They should read the words quietly to themselves first. Clarify any words that are unclear. Then play the recording and let students listen and repeat the words.

2 Give a couple of examples yourself as in the book, showing the items as you do so. Then ask students to work in pairs make as many true sentences as they can in two minutes of things they have that are made of those materials.

3 Draw students' attention to the list of items and go through the example. Then ask them to think of their own examples individually. Ask students to compare their answers in pairs. Feed back. Note that the exercise calls for likely and unlikely combinations, not possible and impossible ones. Answers will vary, but use your judgement. A cotton scarf or a wool scarf is more likely. A rubber scarf is unlikely, but not impossible!

Point out the *Language note*, and drill the pronunciation of *woollen* /ˈwʊlən/ and *wooden* /ˈwʊdən/.

Speaking (SB page 31)

1 Explain the situation to the students. Make sure that they understand they already have a map, bottle of water and knife with them. They must decide on what other three objects they want to take on their trip.

Give the students the following instructions for the activity:

You must do this only in English.

You must take turns talking to each other about the items.

You must give reasons for your choices.

Make sure students understand words like *compass* and *matches*. Circulate and monitor the task.

2 Ask pairs to work with other pairs. They now compare their answers. Feed back on any interesting language or persistent errors that came up.

Note: this task is very similar to pairwork speaking tasks for international exams. If your students are preparing for such an exam it may be worth pointing this out.

Part 2

TEACH GLOBAL THINK LOCAL **Lead-in**

Ask students to look around the room and write the word for anything connected to electricity they see. If they don't know the word in English, they can write it in their own language to look up later. Give them a minute or so, then ask them to compare and check answers in pairs. Conduct whole-class feedback, writing any new words up on the board. Typical answers may be the appliances or devices in the room (eg *CD player*, *computer*, *light*) but also try to elicit/teach words such as *socket* (or *plug* in US English), *cable*, *switch* and *bulb*. Do this before Listening exercise 1.

Listening and Vocabulary (SB page 32)

This is a short lecture about renewable and non-renewable sources of energy on the planet.

1 Ask students to think individually for a minute about the answer to this question. The more they think about it, the more things they can probably come up with. Tell them to write down the first five things they can think of. Check back in open class, and try to push them a bit further than typical, easy answers such as *lights*, *car*, *television*.

2 **1.31** Ask students to read and listen to the words, which are all sources of energy. Clarify any difficult words yourself, or by getting a student to check them in the dictionary. Then play the recording again and ask students to repeat the words.

3 **1.32** Tell students to put the words into two categories: *renewable energy sources* or *non-renewable energy*. Clarify the meaning of the categories (*renewable* means that the energy can be renewed; it is not a finite amount). Let students try to categorise the words first, but don't help them or go over answers. Explain that they are going to hear a lecture on energy sources and they must listen and check their answers. Play the recording.

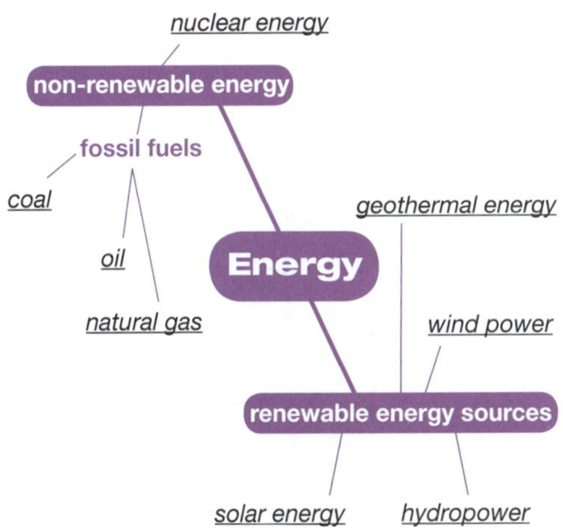

1.32

The most important energy sources today are non-renewable energy sources, that is sources which we won't be able to use at some point in the future. Non-renewable energy sources include all fossil fuels – that's coal, natural gas and, of course, oil. From oil we get petrol and diesel which most of the world's cars run on. When we burn fossil fuels they produce carbon dioxide which many people believe contributes to global warming.

Non-renewable energy sources also include nuclear energy which is produced using the metal uranium. Nuclear energy is a clean source of energy that does not cause global warming but can be very dangerous.

Renewable energy sources include all energy sources that are produced more quickly than we use them. For example, solar energy from the sun, wind power, hydropower using water, waves and tides, and geothermal power which uses underground heat. These energy sources are clean sources of energy which do not cause wide-scale global warming. At the moment they do not supply a large amount of energy but in the future renewable sources will definitely play a much bigger role.

4 Students listen again and make notes of the answers. Play the recording a second time. Feed back.

1 fossil fuels: coal, natural gas and oil
2 nuclear energy
3 solar energy, wind power, hydropower and geothermal energy

5 Ask the last question in open class. Depending on your students, they may not know the answer to this! If they don't, you could make it a homework task to find out. However, typical answers will be oil, nuclear energy, hydropower and natural gas (although there may be more and more solar energy and wind power in some countries these days).

Reading (SB page 32)

This is a text about alternative sources of energy that have been suggested to alleviate a future energy crisis.

1 Ask students to look at the photos and speculate how these things (sugar cane, nappies and human movement) could be used to create energy. Elicit a few answers, but do not say if they are correct or not.

2 **1.33** Play the recording for students to listen and check their answers. Feed back.

Biomass is produced from plants, eg sugar cane, to create heat, electricity or biofuel.

Human waste, eg from nappies, is heated to create oil.

Crowd farms create energy from people walking on a special floor.

3 Ask students to make a list of the different kinds of energy, and to read the text a second time. Play the recording for them to listen as they read and check. They should note what are the main arguments in favour and main arguments against each one. Point out that these texts are written in the point of view of someone in favour of each energy source, so the disadvantages may be harder to spot (because they are downplayed).

Biomass

+ possible to store it, cheaper in future, renewable
- requires lots of land, water and energy itself to grow it, which may be needed for growing food

Human waste

+ environmentally friendly process, large supplies of nappies available
- difficult to produce large amounts of energy

Crowd Farm

+ human movement is an abundant and cheap source
- expensive to produce

4 Remind students of the word diagram about energy they filled in for Listening and Vocabulary exercise 3. Ask them to find words in the text for energy sources and verbs in the text that go with *energy*.

energy sources: biomass, heat, biofuel, electricity, (household) waste

verbs that go with *energy*: *produce*, *use*, *take*, *make*

TEACH GLOBAL THINK LOCAL

Reading extra

Divide the students into three groups, A, B and C. Assign each group one of the energy sources in the text. The group has to prepare a short speech to 'sell' the energy idea to others. They cannot read the text out loud; they have to explain it in their own words. Once groups are ready, reorganise the class into ABC groups of three. If you have extra students then make one or two groups bigger. Each student in the new groups takes a turn 'selling' their form of energy to the others. Circulate and monitor. At the end, ask which energy source was most effectively 'sold'.

Extend your vocabulary (SB page 32)

Point out that the text is about solutions to energy problems. Ask students to read the information in the box about other words that commonly occur with *problem*. To help concept-check the meaning of these words, ask them to choose one of the short speaking tasks and do it with a partner.

Grammar (SB page 33)

1 Ask students to find examples of the two different kinds of future in the text.

1 More land for fuel *will* unfortunately mean less land for growing food.

The one drawback is that it *will* probably be difficult to produce large amounts of fuel.

2 Crowd Farms *aren't going to be* practical in the next few years …

… using biomass *is* definitely *going to be* cheaper and more efficient in the future.

2 Students complete the rules for the tenses.

Second rule: *going to*

Third rule: *will*, *going to*

Language note

Will and *going to* are both used to make future predictions. *Going to* tends to be used when the prediction is based on strong evidence. *Will* is often used when evidence is not so obvious. For decisions and plans we prefer to use *going to*.

3 Ask students to look at the charts and answer the questions in pairs.

1 The most important energy sources will be: oil, gas, coal / peat.
2 We will use less oil. (15% less)
3 We will still use nuclear power.
4 We will use 4.5% more renewable energy. (1.1% more hydro; 3.4% more combustables, renewables and waste – referred to as 'other' in the 2030 pie chart)

TEACH GLOBAL THINK LOCAL

Mixed ability

Ask stronger students to prepare a short oral presentation on the charts. Their presentation should address all the questions, but not just list the answers one after another.

4 Explain the information about *going to*. Ask students to complete the sentences with their own ideas.

1 The ball is going to hit him / her.
2 It's going to bite him / her.
3 The car isn't going to stop.
4 She's going to take his / her bag.
5 He's / She's going to walk into a lamp post.

Grammar focus

Refer students to the language summary on *will* and *going to* on page 136.

You can use exercise 2 on page 137 for:

a) extra practice now
b) homework
c) review a couple of lessons from now.

The answers are on page 142 of the Teacher's Book.

Writing (SB page 33)

1 Explain what a blog is. Ask if any students ever read blogs or articles online. Do they comment on them? Tell them that they are going to write a comment about one or all of these texts.

2 Students write their comment on a piece of paper (give them some time for this). If you are worried that they won't write much, assign a minimum of three sentences and show them the *Useful phrases*.

3 Students exchange their comments and read the new ones. Ask them to decide if they agree or not. Feed back. Note that this is an example of quick writing for fluency. Do not demand that the comments all be in correct English at this point; they can be corrected later.

If you think students would benefit from a model for the writing, give them the following:

> I don't quite understand how biomass is made into biofuel. But until now I thought biomass was an environmentally friendly alternative to fossil fuels. Reading this article, I realised that renewable sources of energy can still harm the environment. In my opinion, we need to make sure that all future sources of energy won't cause new environmental problems.

TEACH GLOBAL THINK LOCAL

Alternative procedure

For this activity you need large copies of the three texts in *Endless Energy?* and a series of sticky labels. Pin the texts on the wall. Explain what a comment on an online site or blog is. Give each student a label. They write their comment and stick it under the text on the wall. Once all students have finished, give them another label. Ask them to read the comments on the wall, to choose one and write a second comment addressing something the first person said. Repeat the process a third time. You can collect the labels to use later on for error correction or further study.

Part 3

TEACH GLOBAL THINK LOCAL

Lead-in

Before the class, choose two or three of the questions from Speaking exercise 1 below. Do an informal survey of 5–10 people at your school, asking the questions and making notes of the answers. Use these answers as part of the feedback on exercise 1 – say *I did a survey of people around the school using these questions. Here's what they told me …* Students can compare their answers to those that people at the school said.

Speaking (SB page 34)

1 Ask students to read through the questions silently (you could write these on the board so the students do this with books closed) and choose four of them. They should then note their answers. Students should do all this without speaking.

2 Pairwork. Explain what students have to do, going through the instructions with them. Demonstrate with a student. Say the number of a question. The student asks you the question and you answer. Then swap roles. Once students have understood, they continue in pairs. Monitor and give feedback at the end (incorporating your own survey results if you did the *Lead-in* above)

Reading (SB page 34)

The text on page 35 is a series of short extracts about living in Alaska, from the point of view of Alaskan bloggers. All the blogs were active and real at the time of writing.

1 Ask students to tell you what they know about Alaska and write this on the board. Then ask them to read the information on page 34. Did they know any of this before? Ask them to read the information again. Ask: *Which are facts and which are opinions about Alaska?*

> The 3rd, 5th, 7th and 9th sentences are all opinions.

2 Ask students to read *Coming in from the cold* on page 35 and to identify the topics mentioned.

> Friendly people, sports, tourists and the weather are mentioned.

3 Students read the text a second time and put the sentences back where they belong.

> 1 Jillian Rogers' blog
> 2 Ian Herriott's blog, second gap
> 3 Jean McDermott's blog, second gap
> 4 Jean McDermott's blog, first gap
> 5 Stefan Milkowski's blog
> 6 Ian Herriott's blog, first gap

4 Pairwork. Students ask and answer the two questions. Feed back, encouraging them to give reasons for their answers.

TEACH GLOBAL THINK LOCAL

Reading extra

As these are texts taken from blogs, the style is a bit more informal. Ask students to find examples of this in the texts. If they are having difficulty, give them the following characteristics to look for:

- Use of CAPITAL letters to emphasise something
- Use of exclamation marks (!) more than in formal writing
- Use of discourse markers like *well*
- Several clauses linked with commas.

Grammar (SB page 34)

Ask students to read information in the grammar box. Alternatively, ask them to close their books. Write the two example sentences and leave gaps for *so* or *such*. Ask them to suggest which words go in the gaps.

1 Ask students to combine the two sentences to make one sentence. Do one as an example to help them get started.

1. Alaska is such a cold place that people use electric heaters to keep their cars warm at night.
2. The temperature is so low in winter that rubber tyres freeze.
3. It's such a cold day that the hairs in your nose freeze when you breathe.
4. It's so cold in Alaska that even dogs wear snow boots.

TEACH GLOBAL THINK LOCAL

Extra activity

In some exams, sentence transformation exercises are common. If you think your students would benefit from this, ask them to try to transform the sentences in exercise 1 so they have a similar meaning, but changing *so* for *such*. The transformations should then be the following:

1. Alaska is so cold that people use electric heaters to keep their cars warm at night.
2. There are such low temperatures in winter that rubber tyres freeze.
3. It's so cold that the hairs in your nose freeze when you breathe.
4. Alaska is such a cold place that even dogs wear snow boots.

Warning: this is quite a challenging task at this level!

2 Ask students to choose three adjectives and use their adjectives to complete the sentences with their own ideas. Do the same yourself, then circulate and monitor. Feed back in open class, including your own examples.

G Grammar focus

Refer students to the language summary on *so* and *such* on page 136.

You can use exercise 3 on page 137 for:

a) extra practice now

b) homework

c) review a couple of lessons from now.

The answers are on page 142 of the Teacher's Book.

Vocabulary (SB page 35)

1 Explain that in English the word *cold* is sometimes used as a metaphor for unfriendliness or loneliness. To clarify, do the first question as an example with the class (*He's not talking to me. Is he giving me the cold shoulder?*) and explain that this means he is ignoring the person. Students complete the exercise. Check answers.

1. shoulder
2. blood
3. icy
4. ice
5. in the cold
6. reception

Language note

In cold blood means in a cruel, calm way without showing any emotion.

If you are left *in the cold*, you are not included in a group.

2 Ask students if they have any similar expressions in their language.

Part 4

TEACH GLOBAL THINK LOCAL Lead-in

Before the class comes in, write the letters from the following words in one corner of the board, jumbled up: *spring*, *summer*, *autumn*, *winter*. As a warm-up activity before you start the lesson, ask students to make as many words as they can with three or more letters using the letters on the board. Explain that all these letters will spell four words that are connected to today's lesson, but don't say what they are. Praise any correctly spelt words that the students produce.

Reading and Pronunciation (SB page 36)

This is a text about how the weather affects sales of certain products in the USA.

1 In pairs. Students ask and answer the questions from exercise 1. Feed back on answers to the second question.

2 **1.34** Students read and listen to the text *Weather ups and downs*. Ask them to compare their lists to the products mentioned in the text. Use this time to check any unknown words.

3 **1.35** Ask students to focus on the three sentences in exercise 3 and to read them to themselves quietly. Then play the recording. What do they notice about them? Play the recording a second time and ask them to mark where the voice goes up and where it goes down.

↘ ↘ ↗
1 In a good sales year in the US, there is a warm, sunny
↘ ↗ ↘ ↘ ↗ ↘
spring, a hot and dry summer, a cool autumn and a
↗ ↘
cold winter.

↗ ↘
2 People wait to buy warm winter clothing like wool
↘ ↘ ↘ ↘
jumpers, warm coats, gloves and hats.

↘ ↘
3 Other typical items sold in winter are hot-water bottles,
↗ ↘ ↘ ↘
medicines against colds and flu, car batteries and
↘ ↘
heating appliances.

Language note

In English pronunciation of lists, the intonation of the speaker tends to rise on individual items in the list and then fall on the last item, to indicate that the list is finished. While this is not always the case, it is a useful rule of thumb to help students be more aware of the discourse function and importance of intonation.

4 In pairs. Students take turns reading out their lists. Circulate and monitor, checking intonation. Feed back and ask students which things they usually buy on their list. Do they think that weather plays a role in how they buy things?

TEACH GLOBAL THINK LOCAL Mixed ability

If you have early finishers, refer them to the letters on the board (from the *Lead-in* activity). Can they find other words using these letters? Do they know yet what words they spell?

Vocabulary (page 36)

1 Ask students to find the verbs in the text. To help them, you could give the first letter of each word.

go up: *increase*, *rise*, *grow*
go down: *decline*, *decrease*, *fall*

2 **1.36** Ask students to make two columns, one for verbs and one for nouns. They copy the verbs from exercise 1 into one column and then complete the second column with nouns. Encourage them to use dictionaries if they have them.

verb	noun	
increase	increase	go up
grow	growth	
rise	rise	
decline	decline	go down
decrease	decrease	
fall	fall	

1 grow/growth 2 increase, decrease

Go over the answers, drawing the students' attention to the words which have the same form. Play the recording. Students listen and repeat the words. Point out the difference in stress between the noun and verb forms of *increase* and *decrease*, shown in the table above.

3 Explain that many of these verbs are useful ones to talk about graphs or figures, and that they go with certain prepositions. Let students try to complete the exercise first on their own, but allow them to use a dictionary to check. Check the answers and drill the pronunciation of the words in sentences.

1 by 2 of 3 to 4 in

4 Students now put all the language work together and try to complete the sales presentation of the graph with words from exercises 1–3. Ask students to read their presentation to each other, then feed back.

1	rise / increase / grow
2	one hundred and fifty thousand
3	rise / increase / grow
4	three hundred thousand
5	increase
6	two hundred thousand
7	fall / decrease / decline
8	fifty
9	fall / decrease / decline
10	two hundred and fifty thousand

Listening (SB page 36)

This is a series of three conversations in between customers and sales assistants.

1 **1.37–1.39** Clarify what a *department store* is (a large shop divided into different sections, each section selling a different kind of thing). Explain that the students are going to hear conversations in a department store. Students listen and say which products the customers are going to buy.

1 g 2 c 3 b

2 Ask students to listen again and to make a note of the words or phrases that helped them decide (in bold in the audioscript below). If you have time and think the students will benefit from it, play the listening a final time but let them read along with the audioscript in the back of the book.

1.37–1.39

(1)

A: Everybody's wearing these now. They look fantastic with a casual jacket or coat. And the **wool** is lovely and soft. Let me show you … If you look in the mirror, you'll see what I mean.

B: Hmm, I don't know … I don't usually wear **hats** … but it is nice and **warm**. Er … if I change my mind, can I get my money back?

A: Yes, of course. Just keep your receipt.

(2)

A: … so if you want to **program it to make coffee** for when you wake up, just do this … It's so simple, and it's extremely energy efficient. I have one of these machines myself and I'm delighted with it – it's great when you have to get up early on a cold, dark morning at this time of year. What do you think? I know it's a bit more expensive than the others but if you take it, you won't regret it, I promise. In fact, you'll wonder what you did without it!

B: OK, OK, you've convinced me. I'll take it.

(3)

A: Can I help you?

B: Oh, thanks, I'm just looking at these …

A: Yes, terrible weather at the moment, isn't it? I have to **scrape the ice off my car** every morning before I come to work. Those are very good, the **plastic** doesn't break as easily as some of them. And, er … we have a special offer in the store today – if you buy anything over five dollars, we'll put your name in a prize draw. If you're one of the ten winners, you'll get six bottles of wine.

B: Oh, OK, that sounds good. I think I'll take two of these, then.

Grammar (SB page 37)

1 Draw students' attention to the sample sentences from the listening and reading texts. Ask them to read these and complete the rules.

First rule: present simple
Second rule: present simple, *will*

Language note

The zero and first conditionals are sometimes called 'real' (as opposed to hypothetical) conditionals. In real conditionals, the present tense is used to talk about present and future events. The meaning of these conditional sentences is not hard to understand, but students most often make a mistake by using *will* + verb in the *if* clause (*if I ~~will~~ have time I will call you*).

2 Students read the sentences and decide which ones are false. Note that they should be reading these for meaning, and not grammatical correctness (all the sentences are grammatically correct!).

1 c
2 b

3 Point out the structure of the sentences that the students read in exercise 2 (present simple + present simple). In pairs, students make their own three sentences, two true and one false. Circulate and monitor. Then ask each pair to read their sentences to another pair. Can they guess which ones are true and which one is false?

4 Tell students to complete the sentences using the first conditional. Check answers. Point out that these sentences are all examples of weather proverbs. You may need to clarify certain words, eg *thunder*, *wonder*, *crow* and the concept of the wind *dying* (the wind stops).

1 If it *is* a year of snow, fruit *will* grow.
2 If the sun *sets* in grey, the next *will be* a rainy day.
3 In February if you *hear* thunder, you *will see* a summer wonder.
4 If crows *fly* low, the wind *will blow*, if crows *fly* high, the wind *will die*.

5 Ask students if they have any similar proverbs in their language to the ones in exercise 4. Are there any other weather sayings or proverbs from their language that they can translate? Accept any answers here; they do not have to be in the target language.

G Grammar focus

Refer students to the language summary on real conditionals on page 136.

You can use exercises 4 and 5 on page 137 for:

a) extra practice now
b) homework
c) review a couple of lessons from now.

The answers are on page 142 of the Teacher's Book.

Writing (SB page 37)

1 Ask students to brainstorm a list of things that they associate with hot or cold. Do a few examples yourself to help them get started. These could be a mixture of literal and figurative things, eg HOT: *fire*, *sun*, *desert*, *stove*, *summer*, *passion*, *love*, *sunglasses*. COLD: *ice*, *snow*, *freeze*, *scarf*, *gloves*, *loneliness*. Circulate and monitor.

2 Students turn to page 130 and follow the instructions. Go over these with the students. Emphasise that the poem does not need to rhyme, but it will sound better if they include extra details.

Allow students some time to do this. Circulate and monitor. At the end, invite students to read their poems out to the class.

TEACH GLOBAL THINK LOCAL **Homework extra**

For homework ask the students to find a poem or quote about either *hot* or *cold* in English that they like. They should bring it, and the source they found it from, to the next class.

Function globally: requests and offers

These lessons in *Global* are designed to provide students with immediately useful functional language. They all follow a similar format.

Warm up (SB page 38)

Aim: to introduce the topic via a quick speaking task or picture work.

Tips:

- Do not over-correct here, especially in speaking activities.
- Encourage students to use what language they can at this stage.

Listening (SB page 38)

Aim: to present the functional language in context via a conversation or series of conversations.

Tips:

- Ask students to read the exercises first before listening.
- Play the recording all the way through for each task (there are always two tasks).
- For multiple conversations pause the recording after each one.
- If students find it very difficult, play the recording a final time and allow them to read the audioscript at the back of the book.

1
1 a 2 b 3 b 4 a 5 a
2
Conversation 1: the changing room
Conversation 2: the price
Conversation 3: a different size
Conversation 4: a different colour
Conversation 5: a refund

1.40–1.44

1
A: I'd like to try this on, please.
B: The changing room is just over there.
A: Erm … where?
B: At the back of the shop. Shall I show you where it is?

2
A: Could you tell me how much these jeans are?
B: Erm, I think that's the last pair in that style … I'll let you have them for £25.
A: OK, great. I'll take them.

3

A: I can't find my size in these jeans. Would you mind helping me find a size 8?

B: Sure, let me have a look. I think I've got a pair at the back of the stall … Here you go.

A: Thanks.

4

A: Could I try these shoes in black, please? I'm not so keen on the brown.

B: In black?

A: Yes, please.

B: OK, I'll get them from the storeroom.

5

A: Hi, I bought this leather jacket last week and I don't think it suits me. I wonder if I could get a refund?

B: Do you have your receipt?

A: No, sorry.

B: Erm … Usually you need your receipt. I'll ask the manager.

Language focus (SB page 38)

Aim: to draw students' attention to the items of functional language.

Tips:

- Make sure students have time to understand the form and meaning of the phrases, but you needn't translate them word for word.
- Students should be able to pronounce these phrases intelligibly, so drill them.

1 e 2 b 3 a 4 d 5 c

Speaking (SB page 38)

Aim: to allow students an opportunity to use this language in a meaningful, real-world context.

Tips:

- There is sometimes a choice of tasks. Any task involving reading a script will be easier than a task involving students making their own scripts. This gives you flexibility for mixed-ability classes.
- Give students time to prepare this activity, and circulate and monitor carefully.
- Correct sensitively, paying attention to the target language especially.
- If time allows, ask students to repeat the task, but with a new partner.

Global English

These lessons in *Global* have two main goals. The first is to give you and your students interesting information about English and language in general. The second goal is to provide students with practice in different kinds of reading comprehension tasks that they are likely to encounter in future study (for example, exams).

Warm up (SB page 39)

Aim: to engage students with the topic, and highlight potentially difficult vocabulary in the text.

Tips:

- be generous in helping students here with any unknown words in the first task.
- ask students to relate this task, wherever possible, to similar events or texts in their own lives. This will help them with the reading.

Reading (SB page 39)

Aim: to provide students with interesting information about English, and reading exam practice skills; where possible to focus on interesting or useful aspects of language in the text.

Tips:

- Get students to read through the whole text once first before doing the tasks.
- Many of these texts have been graded slightly, or not at all. There is a glossary of difficult words. Get students to read that first as it will help them understand the rest.
- There are two tasks. The first is an easier task, often focusing on the gist of the passage. The second is a more difficult task, similar to reading exam questions.
- If there is a third question the purpose is to raise students' awareness about a language feature; do not expect them to produce it immediately.
- This language is not tested or reviewed in future units, which means you have more flexibility with this material as to when and where you use it.

1

a 4

b 1

c 3

d 2

2

1 does not stay dry

2 going for a walk

3 it's very hot today

4 any hot drink

Speaking (SB page 39)

Aim: for students to relate the material in the reading to their own language, culture and experiences.

Tips:

- This is a short speaking activity and can be done in whole-class mode or in small groups.
- Wherever possible, ask students to think of and provide examples in their own language but explain them in English too.

As you go through these *Global English* lessons in the book, don't be afraid to ask students for opinions and reactions to the information in the text – not only answering the comprehension questions. Which do they find interesting? Do they know of similar experiences or facts in their own language or other languages? Some of your learners might be in your class because they are very interested in language, and these texts provide a great opportunity for you to capitalise on that motivation.

Writing: a formal letter

These lessons in *Global* are designed to provide students with extended writing practice. They all follow a similar format.

Reading (SB page 40)

Aim: to provide a sample text for students to analyse.

Tips:

- Many of these texts deliberately contain errors which the students will be asked to focus on and correct later in the lesson.
- At this stage of the lesson merely ask them to read the text and extract the information.
- There are often two questions for these texts: one which focuses on gist and the other on specific details.
- If a student does ask a question about an error in form, praise them for noticing it, and explain that they will be correcting them shortly.

1 Voluntary work teaching sports in a community school in Tanzania.

2

Name	Stefanie Jucker
Nationality	Swiss
Teaching experience	Training to be a primary school teacher. Taught the staff of a sports shop about sports equipment.
Sports played:	Tennis, athletics, basketball and swimming.
Personal qualities	Friendly and empathic, likes children and can work well in a team.
Reason for applying	Wants to do something useful after she graduates. Wants to learn about other cultures and to gain more experience of teaching.
Availability for interview	Any time.

Writing skills: a formal letter (SB page 40)

Aim: to give students a chance to develop their writing through various different micro skills.

Tips:

- Sometimes this section focuses on common student errors in writing.
- Clearly explain the focus and do an example of one of the questions first with the students before asking them to continue on their own.
- Let students check their answers in pairs or small groups, then correct in open class.

1

She has broken rules 2, 4, 5, 7, 8.

2

Address: place Stefanie's address top right of the letter with the date below the address. Place the recipient's address on the left starting on the line below the date.

Body of letter: expand contracted forms *I'm*, *I'd*, *it'll* to *I am*, *I would*, *it will*.

Final paragraph: add *I look forward to hearing from you.*

Closing: amend *Yours faithfully* to *Yours sincerely.*

Preparing to write (SB page 40)

Aim: to give students time to brainstorm ideas for the writing task.

Tips:

- Allow students to brainstorm ideas in pairs or small groups.
- At low levels, this may involve some use of L1 (the students' mother tongue); be tolerant of this, but be on hand to help with translations or English where needed.
- Ask students to make notes here, but not begin writing.

Writing (SB page 40)

Aim: to give students practice in more extended writing tasks.

Tips:

- This section can be done as homework.
- Remind students to refer back to the model text, but to be careful of the typical errors.
- Ask students to check their work carefully before they hand it in.

Global review

These lessons in *Global* are designed to provide students with an opportunity to review and consolidate the language they have studied in the unit.

Grammar and Vocabulary (SB page 41)

Aim: to give students revision of all the main grammar and vocabulary points that arose in the unit.

Tips:

- Demonstrate the activities by doing the first one as a whole class.
- Allow students time to do this, and encourage them to look back through the unit for help.
- When you come to correct this, do not simply go around the class asking for the right answer – encourage students to say *why* they think something is correct, and seek confirmation from others before moving on.

Grammar

1

1 If the weather **is** cold, I generally **prefer** to stay indoors.

2 If we **continue** to use non-renewable energy sources, **we'll face** big problems in the next few years.

3 I**'ll probably stop** using my car if the price of petrol **doesn't go down** soon.

4 It's raining outside. You**'ll get wet** if you **don't take** an umbrella.

5 Tomorrow I**'m going** to the city centre to look for some clothes for my holiday in Alaska. I**'m going to buy** some warm gloves and a wool hat, and I think I**'ll get** a new coat, too.

2

1 The jeans were so expensive that I didn't buy them.

2 It was such a hot day that sales of fans went up.

3 The Sahara desert is such a dry place that few plants grow there.

4 It's so cold in winter that car tyres freeze.

Vocabulary

1

cold: mood

energy: environmental

a problem: supply

toy: icy

jacket: wooden

2

1 by

2 in

3 of

Speaking (SB page 41)

Aim: to provide extra speaking practice that will review and consolidate language presented in the unit.

Tips:

- Give the students time to read and understand the instructions.
- Circulate and monitor the students, encouraging them to use only English here.
- Make notes of any incorrect use of language, but refrain from correcting if students are in the middle of the task.

Study skills

These lessons in *Global* are designed to provide students with skills and strategies in learner training and learner autonomy. For more on learner autonomy and learner training, see the essay on page xxiii.

Writing a learner diary (SB page 41)

1 Ask students to think back on the last lessons they have done with you in the book. What things do they remember? Elicit a couple of answers in open class. Then tell students to open their books at page 41 and look at the questions in exercise 1. They should read these quietly on their own and make notes of things they remember.

Feed back on this in open class, asking students some of the questions. Then read them the information about learner diaries in the box.

Students' own answers.

2 Now direct students to exercise 2 and tell them these are examples of things that learners could write in their learner diary. Students read and match each sentence to one of the questions in exercise 1. Feed back.

1 b 2 f 3 d 4 c 5 a 6 e 7 g 8 h

3 Tell students you would like them to try keeping a learner diary for a little while. Ask them to look at the questions in exercise 3. These will help them plan for their diary.

Students' own answers.

Background note

At Intermediate level, students have enough English to be able to do an activity such as this. They needn't write a lot in their diary, and they should ideally be the ones controlling how, when and where they record things. While we recommend that all students try to keep a learner diary, we also recognise that this does not suit everybody's learning style (see *Study skills*, Unit 1) as it is a rather reflective activity. We also recommend you don't collect these diaries to read or correct, unless the students ask you to. It should be a student-driven activity.

UNIT 4 Friends & Strangers

Coursebook

Unit 4	Language	Texts	Communicative skills
Part 1 SB page 42	Grammar Present perfect and past simple Vocabulary and Speaking Adjective suffixes: *-ive*, *-ful*, *-ous*	Reading *A creative friendship*	Speaking and Pronunciation Comparing two paintings Contrastive stress
Part 2 SB page 44	Vocabulary Expressions with *what* Grammar Present perfect with *yet* and *already*	Reading *Guardians of the Kingdom*	Speaking Telling a friend your news
Part 3 SB page 46	Vocabulary Crime Extend your vocabulary *stranger* and *foreigner* Grammar Modals of deduction	Listening and Reading *Strangers on a Train*	Speaking Making predictions about a film
Part 4 SB page 48	Speaking and Vocabulary Usual and unusual Grammar *somebody*, *anybody*, *nobody*, *everybody*	Listening and Reading Who is Average Man?	Speaking The class Average Man or Woman
Function globally SB page 50	Starting a conversation Listening to people starting conversations in different settings Using positive and negative question tags		
Global voices SB page 51	Listening to people talking about what makes a good friend Describing positive characteristics Discussing personal qualities		
Writing SB page 52	Giving your news Punctuation Describing experiences		
Global review SB page 53	Grammar and vocabulary review Extra speaking and writing practice		
Study skills SB page 53	Working with mistakes		

Additional resources

eWorkbook	Interactive and printable grammar, vocabulary, listening and pronunciation practice Extra reading and writing practice Additional downloadable listening and audio material
Teacher's Resource Disc	Communication activity worksheets to print and photocopy
Go global: ideas for further research	**Friends** Ask students to find an online museum with Picasso or Matisse paintings and choose a painting they like to describe to the rest of the class. **Strangers** Ask students to find a report or statistics about the average man or woman in your country and prepare a short presentation about him or her.

Part 1

TEACH GLOBAL THINK LOCAL Lead-in

Before class, make a list of famous 'pairs' of friends that your students will know. Some famous English 'pairs' you could include are Batman and Robin, Tarzan and Jane, Mickey Mouse and Minnie Mouse, Tweedledum and Tweedledee (from *Alice in Wonderland*), Sherlock Holmes and Watson.

Make sure you include some local examples too, or ones from your students' cultural background. You will need enough for the whole class. Write each name on a separate piece of paper and mix them up. When students arrive, give each person a paper with a name on it. They must then find their partner, using only English. When they have found their partner, tell them to sit down together and start the lesson.

If you have an odd number, include the following group of three: Athos, Porthos and Aramis (the three musketeers!)

Speaking and Pronunciation (SB page 42)

1 Direct students' attention to the two paintings. Ask them if they recognise the artist (they are both paintings by Picasso: *Portrait of Gertrude Stein*, 1906 and *Dora Maar*, 1937). Do the first question in open class. Encourage people to say more than *It's a woman*.

Possible answers

She is sitting. She isn't smiling. She has dark hair. She looks serious. She is on a chair. She is posing for the painting.

2 **1.45** Explain that students will now hear someone explaining two differences between the paintings. Play the recording once and ask what differences the speaker mentions. Then play it again and ask students if they can hear the stressed words (in bold in the audioscript below). Note: this is difficult, especially from a recording, so play the recording again if necessary, or say the sentences yourself with exaggerated stress on the words.

1.45

In the first picture the woman looks quite **old**, but in the second picture the woman looks quite **young**.

In the first picture the woman has **one** nose, but in the second picture the woman has **two** noses.

3 Play the recording again and ask students to listen and repeat. Make sure they are putting more stress on the key words.

Language note

This activity is to practise a feature of stress and intonation, how English uses both of these to emphasise key information in a sentence. In this case, the key information the speaker wants to communicate is the difference between the images, so she stresses the words that are different in each one. Working on stress in the context of describing differences is a useful skill for students to practise, especially as these tasks are common in English speaking tests and international exams.

4 Go through the *Useful phrases* with the class, drilling them for pronunciation and clarifying anything that they don't understand (eg *harmonious*). Students now discuss the other differences between the pictures in more detail. Circulate and monitor, making sure that they are stressing the key words to show the differences.

5 Ask students to answer the questions and tell you what they know about the artist. This will probably go quite quickly, but that's OK! They will find out more in the *Reading*.

Reading (SB page 42)

This is a text about the friendship that developed between the artists Pablo Picasso and Henri Matisse.

1 Ask students to read the text once through quickly. When they have finished, tell them to cover up the text and try to do exercise 1 with a partner from memory. They then refer back to the text and check their answers. Feed back.

	Matisse	Picasso
Nationality	French	Spanish
Born	1869	1881
Died	1954	1973
Personality	self-assured, reserved	passionate, decisive, ambitious

2 **1.46** Play the recording for students to listen as they read the text again, making notes about the questions. They then check in pairs.

1 They met in Paris in 1906 when Matisse was already a successful artist and Picasso was at the start of his career.
2 Matisse inspired Picasso to use colour. Picasso inspired Matisse to experiment with style.
3 Special and creative; people thought they were rivals but they said their disagreements were friendly.
4 He continued to refer back to Matisse in his work.

TEACH GLOBAL THINK LOCAL Mixed ability

To make exercise 2 more challenging, divide the class into two groups, A and B. Ask group A to close their books. Group B do exercise 2 in their books, but turn away from the board so they cannot see it. Write the answers on the board for group A to see. Group A write questions for the answers. When they have finished, remove the questions. Form AB pairs to check their answers.

Note: group A has the more difficult task. Make sure that your weaker students are in group B.

Grammar (SB page 42)

1 As this will not be the first time students encounter these tenses, you could do more testing of them on the forms and uses of these two tenses. Ask students to close their books. Write the three sample sentences on the board. Ask students to identify the verbs and tense in each case. Then ask students to tell you rules that differentiate the two verb forms in their use. To help them, write *specific time*, *unspecific time*, *up to now* and *in the past* on the board.

Feed back on answers, then ask students to check in the book and circle the correct words.

First rule: an unspecific time in the past
Second rule: continues up to the present
Third rule: a specific time in the past

2 Ask students to read through the text quickly first. Ask *Who is in the painting? What is the meaning of the pink faces?* Students then complete the text with the correct form of the verbs.

Answers are numbered in the order they appear in the text.

1 lived
2 worked
3 have become (became is also possible here, if the meaning is that the artists are no longer alive)
4 has exhibited
5 has painted
6 sold

3 Do this as an example first. Get a student to ask you one or two of the questions. Give slightly fuller answers (not just *Yes* or *No*). Tell students you want them to do the same (ie give longer answers). Students then ask and answer the questions in pairs. Feed back on these in whole-class format.

Language note

Present perfect and past simple are difficult for students to use correctly.

The rules of use given in exercise 1 are useful rules of thumb, but be aware that:

- present perfect can be used with a specific time, as long as it is not stated, eg *I have visited the United States, but only once*.
- the past simple can be used to refer to a specific time that is not stated, eg *We saw it*.
- it's also possible, and common, in spoken English to begin with present perfect only to add a specific time afterwards, eg *Oh, I've seen that film. Last summer.*
- in American English, the expressions *yet* and *already* are often used with the past simple, which would be considered incorrect in British English, eg *Did you do it yet? I ate already.*

G Grammar focus

Refer students to the language summary on present perfect and past simple on page 138.

You can use exercises 1 and 2 on page 139 for:

a) extra practice now
b) homework
c) review a couple of lessons from now.

The answers are on page 142 of the Teacher's Book.

Vocabulary and Speaking (SB page 43)

1 Ask students to find the adjectives in the text. Do not check answers with them, as this is done in exercise 2.

2 **1.47** Play the recording for students to check their answers. Ask students to mark the main stressed syllable on the words (underlined in the audioscript below). Then play the recording again for students to listen and repeat.

decisive	successful
creative	powerful
famous	ambitious
jealous	

Language note

One useful rule of thumb you can point out to students here is that the suffixes here are not stressed (ie do not stress *-ive*, *-ous* or *-ful*) and the final vowel sound will be an unstressed /ə/ or /ɪ/ sound.

3 Students now match the adjectives to their meanings. Many of these adjectives should be familiar to students already, and the text should help, but allow them to use dictionaries if necessary.

1 jealous	5 creative
2 powerful	6 ambitious
3 decisive	7 famous
4 successful	

4 Students now try to make adjectives from the words in exercise 4, using the same endings as in exercise 1. Let them try to do this by instinct first, before allowing them to check in a dictionary. Check answers and drill pronunciation of the new adjectives.

religious, attractive, forgetful, humorous, mysterious, competitive, helpful, imaginative, faithful

TEACH GLOBAL THINK LOCAL

Extra activity

If you are working in a class where all the students speak the same language it may be worth doing contrastive analysis of the adjective endings. The endings *-ive* and *-ful* often have a similar equivalent in other languages.

5 Ask students to read the two expressions and their meanings. Ask them to think of examples of relationships like these, and whether or not they agree with one or both of the sayings.

6 Explain that you now want students to talk about a friend of theirs. To help them gather their thoughts, tell them to read through the questions and think of what they want to say. Give them a couple of minutes for this. Tell them they don't have to answer all the questions.

Put students in pairs. Give them the following instructions:

Tell your partner about the friendship you were thinking about.

Don't just answer each of the questions, try to link your ideas together naturally.

Use only English.

Help your partner by asking questions or asking for clarification.

Circulate and monitor.

TEACH GLOBAL THINK LOCAL

Homework extra

Ask students to research a famous friendship between two other well-known people. This could be actors, authors, musicians, politicians or historical figures. The people can be from any country. Students prepare a short written account of the friendship. They have to think of an adjective to describe the friendship and give their text the title *A … friendship.*

Part 2

TEACH GLOBAL THINK LOCAL

Lead-in

For this lead-in you will need a few local newspapers with comics inside them. It doesn't matter whether these are in English or not. These could come from the comics section or the editorial page of each newspaper (political comics work well). Put these up around the room before students arrive. When you start the class, invite the students to walk around in pairs and look at the comics. They must try to say something in English about each one (their reaction, what they think it means, etc).

Reading (SB page 44)

The reading in this lesson is from a graphic novel called *Guardians of the Kingdom* about two guards on an endless wall. It is not a long text, but the students are asked to analyse the language used (both the vocabulary and the grammar) of this authentic extract quite intensively.

1 Ask students the questions in open class. Elicit the names of popular graphic novels or comics in their country. Do students think these are only for young people?

2 Students read the extract from *Guardians of the Kingdom* and answer the questions.

1 The men are guards / soldiers.
2 They are friends.
3 One guard has forgotten which side they are supposed to be guarding.

3 Ask students to read the text again more carefully and find the words or expressions.

1 glorious
2 barbaric
3 What d'you mean 'now'?
4 You've what?
5 Some soldier you are!

4 Ask students the questions in open class. Give them time to think about what point the author could be trying to make.

Answers could vary. It could be that guarding the wall is a pointless exercise. Or that the guardians come from a militaristic and patriotic country, given the references to the barbaric wastes and glorious homeland. It is essentially a comment on how most of a soldier's life probably is spent sitting around and not realising why they are there.

Background note

Guardians of the Kingdom author and illustrator Tom Gauld is quite well known for his work which has appeared in British newspapers such as the *Guardian*.

Vocabulary (SB page 44)

1 Students match the sentences with the most likely response. Tell them to underline the expressions with *what* in the exercise.

1 f	2 g	3 b	4 a	5 c	6 d	7 e

2 **1.48** Play the recording for students to listen and check. In pairs, students then read the exchanges together. Circulate and monitor, correcting pronunciation as necessary. Then ask students to answer the questions about the conversations. If you do not have enough time, ask them to choose three of the exchanges and create the next two lines.

Answers will vary, but the relationship between all the speakers is quite close and informal.

TEACH GLOBAL THINK LOCAL

Extra activity

Tell students to create two similar exchanges using a different expression with *what* in each one. This is a useful task for early finishers. Ask the students to read out their conversations and have others guess what the relationship between the speakers could be.

Grammar (SB page 44)

1 Ask students to study the two sentences. Ask *What tense is in each one? How do we form this tense?* Then ask them to choose which explanation is the best for both sentences. Go over the rules for using *yet* and *already*.

Sentence 2 best describes their use.

Language note

As mentioned in Part 1, *already* and *yet* are often used with the past simple in American English.

2 Students read the imagined exchanges between the two guards and complete B's answers. Check answers and pronunciation.

1 Sorry, I haven't finished it yet.
2 We've already had coffee!
3 Have you broken it again?
4 They've already gone home.
5 Sorry, I've eaten it.

3 This activity is for students to personalise the target grammar. Do an example of one of each first about you. Write them on the board and tell the students about them, eg:

I haven't passed my driving test yet, but I want to.

I've already marked your exams this week, which I'm pretty happy about!

I've read several English books. That has helped me improve my English.

Students now do the same. Circulate and monitor. Feed back by asking volunteers to read their sentences aloud.

G Grammar focus

Refer students to the language summary on present perfect with *yet* and *already* on page 138.

You can use exercises 3 and 4 on page 139 for:

a) extra practice now
b) homework
c) review a couple of lessons from now.

The answers are on pages 142 and 143 of the Teacher's Book.

Speaking (SB page 45)

Ask students to form AB pairs and turn to page 126 or page 128. Give them time to read the instructions on their page. Circulate and make sure that everyone is on the right page. Allow them time to think of things to say. Then students roleplay the conversation.

You could ask one pair to perform their roleplay in front of the class.

Part 3

TEACH GLOBAL THINK LOCAL

Lead-in

Conduct a brainstorm of names of crimes. Students may not know the words for these in English, so ask them to use their dictionaries or be prepared to help and translate if necessary. Write these up on the board. Make sure you include serious and less serious crimes. Once you have a list of ten, ask students to work in pairs and rank them in order of seriousness.

Here are some crimes you could add to the list:

arson, assault, bike theft, blackmail, burglary, car theft, forgery, murder, rape, smuggling

Note that many of these words are rather low frequency (thankfully!). This activity should be viewed as a warmer only to introduce the topic of crime. The vocabulary in exercise 1 is more generative (collocations and word combinations) and allows students to talk about a wider range of things within the topic.

Vocabulary (SB page 46)

1 Students match the words in the box to the word groups to make common collocations. Allow them use of the dictionary to help them. Check answers. To clarify meaning further, ask students to explain the difference between each phrase in the pairs.

1 be
2 evidence
3 commit
4 prison
5 have
6 a suspect

2 Ask students to complete the text with the phrases.

1 commit	6 suspect
2 murder	7 guilty / innocent
3 have	8 innocent / guilty
4 motive	9 prison
5 arrest	

Language note

Another word for prison is *jail*. In British English *jail* is sometimes written as *gaol*.

3 Ask students which facts in the text surprised them. If you want to structure this task a bit more, tell them to mark each fact as follows: for every fact they knew already they put a tick; for every fact they didn't know they put a question mark (?); for every fact they thought was surprising they put an exclamation mark (!). Students then compare what they wrote next to the facts. Do they think these facts would be the same in their country?

Listening and Reading (SB page 46)

This is an extract from the screenplay to *Strangers on a Train*, written by crime novelist Patricia Highsmith and made into a famous thriller film by Alfred Hitchcock in 1951.

1 Ask students to think of any famous crime novels or television shows they know and make a note of these. Elicit different examples, providing some of your own as well (television shows are more likely to work here; they do not have to be American or British shows). Ask students how realistic they think they are, given the facts they read about crime before.

2 Direct students' attention to the photo and tell them it's from a film called *Strangers on a Train*. In pairs, students discuss the questions. Emphasise that the students should imagine what *they* think the scene should say. If some students know the film, tell them to keep quiet about it for now!

3 **1.49** Now play the recording and let the students listen. The answer to the question is in the final sentence.

He means that they should 'cross' or swap murders, so that he kills Guy's wife and Guy kills his father.

4 Tell students to turn to the film script on page 131. Play the recording again, letting them read along. Then students turn back to page 46 and complete the summary of the conversation.

1 crimes / murders
2 Miriam / Guy's wife
3 Bruno's father
4 they are complete strangers and they don't have a motive

1.49

A: Want me to tell you one of my ideas for murdering my father?

B: You've been reading too many of these.

A: You want to hear about the busted light socket in the bathroom, or the carbon monoxide in the garage?

B: No. I may be old fashioned, but I thought murder was against the law.

A: But not against the law of nature. My theory is that everybody is a potential murderer. Didn't you ever want to kill somebody? Say one of those useless fellows Miriam was running around with?

B: You can't go around killing people just because you think they're useless.

A: Oh, what's a life or two? Some people are better off dead, Guy. Take your wife and my father, for instance. It reminds me of a wonderful idea I had once. I used to put myself to sleep at night figuring it out. Now, let's say you want to get rid of your wife.

B: Why?

A: Well, let's say she refuses to give you a divorce. Let's say. You'd be afraid to kill her because you'd get caught. And what would trip you up? Motive. Now, here's the plan ...

B: I'm afraid I haven't time to listen.

A: It's so simple, too. A couple of fellows meet accidentally, like you and me. No connection between them at all. Never saw each other before. Each of them has somebody he'd like to get rid of, but he can't murder the person he wants to get rid of. He'll get caught. So they swap murders.

B: Swap murders?

A: Each fellow does the other fellow's murder. Then there is nothing to connect them. The one who had the motive isn't there. Each fellow murders a total stranger. Like you do my murder and I do yours.

B: We're coming into my station.

A: For example, your wife, my father. Criss-cross.

5 Pairwork. Students read and discuss the questions. They can refer back to the film script to read the text again if there is still anything they did not understand. Circulate and monitor, helping where necessary. Feed back.

Background note

Alfred Hitchcock (1899–1980) was an English filmmaker and producer. He has been called 'The Master of Suspense' for the more than 60 films he made, many of which were in the thriller genre. *Strangers on a Train* was released in 1951. Patricia Highsmith (1921–1995) was an American novelist most famous for her books *Strangers on a Train* and *The Talented Mr Ripley*, both of which have been adapted for film. The screenplay for *Strangers on a Train* was adapted by Raymond Chandler, who students will learn more about in *Global* Upper Intermediate.

Strangers on a Train has been referred to numerous times in popular American and British culture, especially in other thriller films and television shows.

Extend your vocabulary (SB page 47)

Write the words *stranger* and *foreigner* on the board. Explain that these two words are often confused by language learners. Ask if anyone can explain the difference. Then go over the information in the box. Students then discuss the questions in pairs.

TEACH GLOBAL THINK LOCAL Alternative procedure

As an alternative to pairwork, put students into groups of three and assign one the role of interviewer. He/She has to interview the other two using the questions. At the end, ask the interviewers to report back.

Grammar (SB page 47)

1 Students read the sentences and complete the rules of use of the different modals. This should not be too difficult as they will have already encountered these in their language learning. Go over the answers, checking the pronunciation of all the modal verbs (especially *could* and *can't* which can often be mispronounced.

First rule: *must* /mʌst/

Second rule: *can't* /kɑːnt/

Third rule: *might* /maɪt/, *may* /meɪ/

2 Working individually, students complete the sentences with the correct modal verbs. Check back answers on this first, then ask them to decide who could say each sentence, Guy or Bruno (this makes students think harder about the meaning of the sentences).

1 must
2 might
3 must
4 can't
5 could
6 can't

G Grammar focus

Refer students to the language summary on modals of deduction on page 138.

You can use exercise 5 on page 139 for:

a) extra practice now
b) homework
c) review a couple of lessons from now.

The answers are on page 143 of the Teacher's Book.

Speaking (SB page 47)

1 Pairwork. Make sure students understand all the phrases (point out that some of these are recycled from *Vocabulary* on page 46). Tell students they are going to speculate about how the film ends. They should read the sentences individually and then discuss with their partner how likely they think each sentence is.

Circulate and monitor, listening out for use of the target language but not correcting at this stage. Feed back and reformulate phrases to encourage them to use the modal verbs.

2 **1.50** Students listen to the summary of the film at the end and check their guesses from exercise 1.

1.50

In the 1951 film *Strangers on a Train*, Bruno Anthony meets Guy Haines on a train. Bruno suggests to Guy that Guy should kill his father and he himself will kill Guy's wife.

Guy forgets the conversation but Bruno thinks that the two have made a deal. Bruno kills Guy's wife Miriam while she is at an amusement park. The police think that Guy is the murderer because he had a motive and no alibi.

Bruno finds Guy and tells him it is now his turn to kill Bruno's father. Guy refuses and Bruno gets angry. Bruno has Guy's gold lighter which Guy left on the train. He threatens to plant the lighter as evidence at the murder scene.

Guy and Bruno get into a fight on a carousel at the amusement park. The police come to arrest Guy but there is an accident and Bruno is thrown to the ground. He dies holding the lighter and the police realise that Bruno was the murderer. Guy and Anne are free to start a new life together.

TEACH GLOBAL THINK LOCAL

Homework extra

Here are three possible homework ideas that follow on from this lesson:

- Ask students to watch the film, if possible.
- Ask students to find or create a tense dialogue from another thriller film. They bring their dialogue to class to read aloud.
- Ask students to research more about Alfred Hitchcock's films. What are some of the most famous Hitchcock thrillers? Who had a cameo role in many of Hitchcock's films? (Himself.) Which ones would they like to see?

Part 4

TEACH GLOBAL THINK LOCAL

Lead-in

Instead of doing a different lead-in, use the Speaking and Vocabulary exercise 1 to localise the material. To do this, adapt the sentences in exercise 1 so that the words in *italics* are about local or familiar people or things to your students. Start the class by dictating the sentences and then ask a student to write them up on the board. Make sure everyone has got the correct spelling, then ask them to underline the adjectives. Then ask if the underlined words describe something usual or unusual.

Speaking and Vocabulary (SB page 48)

1 Students read the sentences and decide if the adjectives are about something usual or unusual. Do the first example with them. Check back and drill the pronunciation of the adjectives.

1	usual	5	unusual
2	unusual	6	unusual
3	usual	7	unusual
4	usual	8	unusual

2 Pairwork. Students to read the questions and select three questions to ask their partner. Alternatively, you could ask them to choose three questions *they* feel able to answer. In pairs, students indicate the questions they wish to answer and the other asks these. Circulate and monitor. Feed back by asking a few students to read a question and answer aloud.

Listening and Reading (SB page 48)

This is a lecture about Adolphe Quetelet, a Belgian mathematician who invented the statistical concept of the average man. The reading text is a series of characteristics of the Average Man in the UK, according to a television show that tried to discover this.

1 Ask students the question in open class. Elicit possible answers for *average* being a good thing and being a bad thing. Write these as *pros* or *cons* on the board. Give them an example to start with, eg:

Pros: having a quiet life, not attracting attention

Cons: not feeling special or wanting to achieve anything

2 **1.51** Tell students they are going to listen to a lecture about the concept of Average Man. Play the recording once.

Sentence 2

3 Play the recording again. Students decide whether the statements are true or false.

1	F (He was Belgian.)
2	T
3	F (He has an average chance of being a criminal.)
4	T
5	T

1.51 Who is Average Man?

Adolphe Quetelet was a Belgian mathematician in the 19th century who was especially interested in statistics and the human population. His work was very influential in the world of statistics.

In 1835 Quetelet invented *l'homme moyen*, which is French for 'the average man'. Average man is very boring: he has exactly average height and weight, an average life, an average chance of being a criminal and an average number of children.

However, Quetelet believed that Average Man symbolised a perfect individual. If somebody had all those characteristics they would be ideal. Anybody who didn't have all those average characteristics was an error, according to his theory.

Of course, Average Man doesn't really exist. But, this hasn't stopped people from looking for the 'perfectly average' person though – in 2007, a television programme in the UK looked for the average Briton, and they put together the characteristics of what was, at the time, the perfectly average British man.

4 Direct students' attention to the text on page 49. Ask them to read it through quickly once, then ask for a general impression. Do they think it's interesting?

Then ask them to read again and mark the facts in the following way: put an exclamation mark (!) if they think it's interesting and a tick (✓)if they think the fact would be the same for men in their country. They then compare notes, and answer the third question (What things do you think would be different for women?). Circulate and monitor. Feed back.

Background note

The British television show to find the UK's Average Man was called *In Search of Mr Average* and aired in 2007. The show's producers claimed to have found a man who represented the perfect average for the country, an office worker in Swindon, a town in the south of England.

Grammar (SB page 49)

You could do this as a test-teach-test activity. Books closed. Dictate the four sentences from the grammar box. Students check their dictation in pairs.

Then read out the rules one by one, but elicit the pronouns, eg *Which pronouns do we use when we don't want to refer to a specific person or when we do not know who the person is? Which pronoun do we use in affirmative sentences and questions when we expect a particular answer?*

1 Students choose the correct option to complete the sentences. When you go through the exercise, ask students to explain why they made their choices, grammatically (ask them to refer back to the rules).

1	Everybody	4	Is
2	Nobody	5	somebody
3	anybody		

2 Now ask students to complete the sentences with their own ideas. Do one or two examples yourself. Afterwards, ask students to work in small groups.

Language note

These words are also called 'indefinite' pronouns, and refer to things in a general and open way. While the examples (and rules) here refer to people, the same rules apply to pronouns formed in this way with *-thing*, or *-one*. There is no difference in meaning between pronouns ending in *-body* and pronouns ending in *-one*.

These pronouns also follow similar rules as to the use of *some* and *any*. For example *somebody / someone* can be used in questions in which the speaker expects a specific answer (*Did someone eat the last piece of cake?)* whereas *anybody / anyone* is more open ended (*Has anyone got a copy of today's newspaper?)*

TEACH GLOBAL THINK LOCAL

Extra activity

You could extend this grammar work to do more practice of the indefinite pronouns with *-where* and *-thing*. Write the following on the board: *nobody, nowhere, nothing*. Then do a question and answer drill. Ask individual students the following questions. They must answer using one of the words on the board:

T: *What did you do last night?*

S1: *Nothing!*

T: *Where did you go last weekend?*

S2: *Nowhere!*

T: *Who did you talk to yesterday?*

S3: *Nobody!*

Do this around the class. Then write *anybody, anywhere, anything* on the board and repeat. This time the students must give a longer, but still negative answer, eg:

T: *What did you do last night?*

S1: *I didn't do anything!*

Grammar focus

Refer students to the language summary on *somebody*, *anybody*, *nobody* and *everybody* on page 138.

You can use exercise 6 on page 139 for:

a) extra practice now

b) homework

c) review a couple of lessons from now.

The answers are on page 143 of the Teacher's Book.

Speaking (SB page 49)

1 Divide the class into two groups. Explain the task and assign each group a group leader. One group is to do a report on 'Class Average Man' and the other on 'Class Average Woman'. (if you have a lot of women in the class then the report could be for the whole group, entitled simply 'Class Average Person').

2 The group leader should elicit the questions for the prompts in the box, and then ask for two other questions. When they have finished, each person in the group is assigned a question or two to ask the others. Circulate and help.

3 Now students get up and ask their question(s) to every other student in the class. They should make a note of their answers, and then calculate the average answer.

4 Students get back into groups and report their answers to the group leader. The group leader puts all the answers together to prepare a report on Class Average Man or Woman. The group leader reports back to the teacher and the class.

Function globally: starting a conversation

These lessons in *Global* are designed to provide students with immediately useful functional language. They all follow a similar format.

Warm up (SB page 50)

Aim: to introduce the topic via a quick speaking task or picture work.

Tips:

- Do not over-correct, especially in speaking activities.
- Encourage students to use what language they can at this stage.

Listening (SB page 50)

Aim: to present the functional language in context via a conversation or series of conversations.

Tips:

- Ask students to read the exercises first before listening.
- Play the recording all the way through for each task (there are always two tasks).
- For multiple conversations pause the recording after each one.
- If students find it very difficult, play the recording a final time and allow them to read the audioscript.

1

1 Conversation 1 goes with picture b (they are waiting to pay for something)

2 Conversation 2 goes with picture c or d (they are colleagues talking about work)

2

Conversation 1: the woman's job, waiting

Conversation 2: changes at work, somebody else's health

1.52–1.53

Conversation 1

A: Sorry, but er … do I know you from somewhere?

B: Erm … I don't think …

A: Oh, I know. You work at the supermarket don't you? Quick Shop?

B: Yes, that's right.

A: Sorry, I'm sure you can't remember all your customers, I just thought you looked familiar. It's always very busy in there, isn't it?

B: It certainly is. Always a queue at the till.

A: Well … I hope this queue goes a bit quicker.

B: Mmm, yes, slow, aren't they?

Conversation 2

A: So, how was your meeting?

B: It was fine. I've just come out. Have you heard that they're going to reorganise our office?

A: Yes, I've … Well, I've heard something about it.

B: Mmm, I wonder when the boss is going to tell us what's happening.

A: Well, you know what it's like here. They always tell us after they've decided.

B: I just hope they don't move me to a different department.

A: Yes … I think we all work well together … Oh, I wanted to ask you about your father … How is he now?

B: Oh much better, thanks. He's coming out of hospital soon.

A: Well, that's good news … I'm glad about that. Now, do you want to go and get some lunch? We could try that new sandwich shop round the corner.

B: Mmm, good idea.

Language focus (SB page 50)

Aim: to draw students' attention to the items of functional language.

Tips:

- Make sure students have time to understand the form and meaning of the phrases, but you needn't translate them word for word.
- Students should be able to pronounce these phrases intelligibly, so drill them.

1.54

1 complete strangers: 2, 5, 7, 9, 10
people you think you know: 3, 6, 7, 8, 9
friends: 1, 4, 7, 9

2 don't you; do you; isn't it; aren't you

3 1 negative 2 positive

Speaking (SB page 50)

Aim: to allow students an opportunity to use this language in a meaningful, real-world context.

Tips:

- There is sometimes a choice of tasks. Any task involving reading a script will be easier than a task involving students making their own scripts. This gives you flexibility for mixed-ability classes.
- Give students time to prepare this activity, and circulate and monitor carefully.
- Correct sensitively, paying attention to the target language especially.
- If time allows, ask students to repeat the task, but with a new partner.

Global voices

These lessons in *Global* are designed to provide students with exposure to authentic speakers of English from both native and non-native English backgrounds. They all follow a similar format.

Warm up (SB page 51)

Aim: to introduce the topic and highlight potentially difficult vocabulary the students will encounter.

Tips:

- Be generous in helping students with the vocabulary here, but let them try to work it out first.
- Circulate and monitor any speaking task, but be careful not to over-correct.
- Follow up any short discussion pairwork with an open class discussion, asking students to report back what they said.

Listening (SB page 51)

Aim: to expose students to English spoken with a variety of accents.

Tips:

- Students will need to hear the recording at least twice, if not more times, to understand it. There are almost always two tasks.
- The first time they listen, tell them you don't expect them to understand every word; some of it will be hard. This is because the text has not been scripted or graded in any way. It's what they would hear in 'the real world'.
- The first task is easier and focuses on gist, the second task is more detailed.
- Pause after each speaker on the second listening, and don't be afraid to replay the whole thing if students appear to need it.
- Students can read the audioscript at the back of the book if you / they wish.
- It may be tempting to hunt for specific pronunciation or language errors, but we recommend against this. In real-world communication not everyone speaks perfect English all the time, not even native speakers.

1 Students' own answers.

2

1 a 2 f 3 e 4 c 5 d 6 b

1.55–1.60

Anna, Russia

A good friend is a person who can help you in any situation you have in your life, who can understand you. And a good friend for me is my mother because I can tell her everything and she will understand me even if I will not be right.

Sofia, Argentina

I don't know, you feel a friend. I don't know how to explain how you have a relationship with a friend. You feel is your friend or not.

Elodie, Switzerland

So, a good friend for me is somebody that you can trust in – uh, somebody who is nice with you, somebody who makes you laugh. And with um, yeah, and if you can have fun with this person, so I think it will be a friend.

Sara, Italy

You have to divide friends and people you meet because friends you can really count them on your fingers. For me, two or three friends, good, good friends you really count them because it is not easy to find.

Alena, Czech Republic

OK so, a good friend is, well is a person, uh, who is kind to me and who who behaves, uh, in a good way, I mean, who will take care of me if I need and if I need any help he will, he will or she will, provide it for me and will be, you know, like my second hand.

Matt, US

A good friend is someone who I can trust and someone who's honest with me and someone who will be there despite hard times.

Language focus: describing positive characteristics (SB page 51)

Aim: to raise students' awareness of a particular piece of language present in the listening.

Tips:

- This language is not included in unit tests or reviews; it is included here to help students understand international English.
- The objective is awareness-raising, not production. Don't expect students to produce this language in an exercise or in conversation immediately.

1

1 count
2 take care
3 trust
4 kind
5 make
6 honest

2, 3 Students' own answers.

Speaking (SB page 51)

Aim: for students to discuss the same or similar questions as the speakers in the listening.

Tips:

- The speaking tasks here are slightly more open to allow for students to explore the subject. Give them time to do this.
- If students are working in pairs, circulate and monitor. Make notes of incorrect language use to correct afterwards (or in a future class).
- As you go through the book and the *Global voices* lessons, ask students for feedback on these listening activities and their potential use of English with other people. Are they very difficult? Have students used their English as a 'lingua franca' with other non-native English speakers? How did they find it? What tips do they have on understanding or making themselves understood in an international context?

Writing: giving your news

These lessons in *Global* are designed to provide students with extended writing practice. They all follow a similar format.

Reading (SB page 52)

Aim: to provide a sample text for students to analyse.

Tips:

- Many of these texts deliberately contain errors which the students will be asked to focus on and correct later in the lesson.
- At this stage of the lesson merely ask them to read the text and extract the information.
- There are often two questions for these texts: one which focuses on gist and the other on specific details.
- If a student does ask a question about an error in form, praise them for noticing it, and explain that they will be correcting them shortly.

1

Paragraph 1: b
Paragraph 2: a
Paragraph 3: d
Paragraph 4: c

2

1 T (Life is so hectic!)
2 F (It was a good job and I was happy with my life …)
3 T (I decided to go back to university and study Humanities. At the same time I continued working …)
4 F (… in the end it was worth it.)
5 T (After finishing my studies, I got a grant to do a Masters …)
6 F (… the grant allows me to travel abroad … It's a wonderful opportunity …)
7 F (Right now I'm living in Malaysia and it's really fascinating getting to know a different way of life.)
8 T (I can't wait to have him in my arms.)

Writing skills: punctuation (SB page 52)

Aim: to give students a chance to develop their writing through various different micro skills.

Tips:

- Sometimes this section focuses on common student errors in writing.
- Clearly explain the focus and do an example of one of the questions first with the students before asking them to continue on their own.
- Let students check their answers in pairs or small groups, then correct in open class.

1

1 .   2 ,   3 ?   4 :-)   5 !   6 :   7 ;

2

1 full stop
2 semi-colon / comma
3 question mark
4 exclamation mark
5 emoticon

3

full stop: job.
semi-colon: Netherlands;
colon: main news:
exclamation mark: baby!
question mark: it?
commas: baby, a boy,
emoticon: arms :-)

4

1 a   2 d   3 c   4 b

5

As most of you know, after leaving San Miguel College I went to Madrid to study physiotherapy. After that, I was lucky enough to find a job as a physiotherapist in a healthcare centre, where I stayed for ten years. It was a good job and I was happy with my life, but I wanted to broaden my horizons, so I decided to go back to university and study humanities. At the same time I continued working, which was quite stressful: university in the morning, lunch in my car, work in the afternoon and evening, and then housework at the end of the day! I was exhausted, but it in the end it was worth it. At university I met my husband Rafael, and we got married two years later.

Preparing to write (SB page 52)

Aim: to give students time to brainstorm ideas for the writing task.

Tips:

- Allow students to brainstorm ideas in pairs or small groups.
- At low levels, this may involve some use of L1 (the students' mother tongue); be tolerant of this, but be on hand to help with translations or English where needed.
- Ask students to make notes here, but not begin writing.

Writing (SB page 52)

Aim: to give students practice in more extended writing tasks.

Tips:

- This section can be done as homework.
- Remind students to refer back to the model text, but to be careful of the typical errors.
- Ask students to check their work carefully before they hand it in.

Global review

These lessons in *Global* are designed to provide students with an opportunity to review and consolidate the language they have studied in the unit.

Grammar and Vocabulary (SB page 53)

Aim: to give students revision of all the main grammar and vocabulary points that arose in the unit.

Tips:

- Demonstrate the activities by doing the first one as a whole class.
- Allow students time to do this, and encourage them to look back through the unit for help.
- When you come to correct this, do not simply go around the class asking for the right answer – encourage students to say *why* they think something is correct, and seek confirmation from others before moving on.

Grammar

1 When **did you buy** your jacket?
2 I don't know **anybody** …
3 Everybody in this class **has studied** …
4 correct
5 … so he **can't** be her best friend.
6 **I saw** an interesting film …
7 correct
8 I haven't finished my homework **yet**.
9 **Nobody** in my family …
10 … it **may / might / could** rain later.

Vocabulary

1

1 weird
2 uncommon
3 bizarre
4 successful
5 decisive
6 mysterious

2

The man had a motive.
The man committed a crime.
The police found evidence.
The police caught the suspect.
The man went to prison.

Speaking and Writing (SB page 53)

Aim: to provide extra speaking practice that will review and consolidate language presented in the unit.

Tips:

- Give the students time to read and understand the instructions.
- Circulate and monitor the students, encouraging them to use only English here.
- Make notes of any incorrect use of language, but refrain from correcting if students are in the middle of the task.

Study skills

These lessons in *Global* are designed to provide students with skills and strategies in learner training and learner autonomy. For more on learner autonomy and learner training, see the essay on page xxiii.

Working with mistakes (SB page 53)

1 Write the first sentence on the board: *I hate making mistakes when I speak English.* Ask students to decide whether they agree, disagree or aren't sure. Do not comment on what students say at this point. Tell them that in this activity you want them to think a bit more about the mistakes they make when they speak English.

Go through the questionnaire first to make sure students understand, then let them complete it individually. When they finish, ask them to compare answers with a partner.

2 Reproduce the diagram in exercise 2 on the board. Explain the terms *accurate* (not making mistakes) and *fluent* (able to speak a language well without pauses or hesitation). Explain that a person can be very accurate – they never make mistakes – but not very fluent because they speak slowly, hesitate a lot or don't say much. Others can be very fluent – they speak English without hesitating and easily – but make a lot of mistakes and so are not accurate. Some are in the middle. Ask students to put a cross on the line where they think they are.

At this point you could say what you believe in terms of error correction.

Background note

The authors of *Global* believe that errors are a natural part of language learning. For this reason we include a balance of accuracy-type exercises (usually the exercises in the Grammar or Vocabulary sections) and fluency-type exercises (the Speaking and Writing exercises at the end of individual lessons). For fluency-type exercises we recommend not correcting everything the student produces as it could eventually hamper their fluency. However, some correction is important. It is also worth distinguishing between an error that the student makes because he / she doesn't know the correct form and an error that the student makes because he / she was not really paying attention (but does know the correct form). The latter is sometimes called a 'slip', and the student can be encouraged to self-correct these with a simple gesture from the teacher.

It is important for students to strike a balance between trying to be overly accurate and overly fluent. The tips in exercise 3 should help raise awareness about this.

3 Go over the tips for dealing with errors. Ask students to tick the tips they would like to try. Encourage them to try at least one of the tips that week and follow up on this by asking them how it went later.

UNIT 5

Law & Order

Coursebook

Unit 5	Language	Texts	Communicative skills
Part 1 SB page 54	Extend your vocabulary *-ics* and *-ology* Grammar Modals of obligation and permission	Reading *Asimov's laws of robotics*	Writing Cartoon captions
Part 2 SB page 56	Vocabulary and Speaking Government collocations Grammar Past modals of obligation	Listening Laws of bureaucracy	Speaking Bureaucratic situations
Part 3 SB page 58	Vocabulary and Pronunciation Education compound nouns Grammar Present perfect simple and continuous *for* and *since* Extend your vocabulary *control*	Reading *I'm a teacher, Get Me Out of Here!*	Writing My school years
Part 4 SB page 60	Grammar Separable phrasal verbs Pronunciation Phrasal verbs Sentence stress	Listening An orderly lunch	Speaking and Vocabulary Order in the kitchen Phrasal verbs with *up*
Function globally SB page 62	Giving advice and warnings Asking for and giving directions Reporting a crime		
Global English SB page 63	Legal protection for languages Majority and minority languages Agreeing and disagreeing with statements about language		
Writing SB page 64	Giving instructions Making instructions more polite Semi-formal language		
Global review SB page 65	Grammar and vocabulary review Extra speaking and writing practice		
Study skills SB page 65	Using your dictionary: phrasal verbs		

Additional resources

eWorkbook	Interactive and printable grammar, vocabulary, listening and pronunciation practice Extra reading and writing practice Additional downloadable listening and audio material
Teacher's Resource Disc	Communication activity worksheets to print and photocopy
Go global: ideas for further research	**Law** Ask students to find a website with Murphy's Laws; choose the three funniest / strangest ones to talk about in class. **Order** Ask students to find the names of five films about classrooms or education and watch the trailers in English, then write a one-line summary of each trailer.

Part 1

TEACH GLOBAL THINK LOCAL Lead-in

Play this version of '20 Questions'. Draw a simple image of a robot on the board. Think of an object. Tell students that they have to guess the mystery object. They can ask the robot questions, but it will answer *Yes* or *No* only! They can ask up to 20 questions maximum. Every time a student asks a question, answer either *Yes* or *No*, in a robot-like voice. Can students guess the mystery object?

For an even more local version of this game, decide on a local place or landmark. Students have 20 questions to guess where it is. Good for practising prepositions!

Reading (SB page 54)

This is a text about the term 'robotics' (invented by the science fiction writer Isaac Asimov) and the Three Laws of Robotics.

Background note

Isaac Asimov is considered one of the original masters of the science fiction genre of writing and one of the most prolific writers of the 20th century. In total he wrote or edited over 500 books. The majority of these were indeed science fiction stories, but he also wrote mysteries and non-fiction books (often about science). His most famous writing on robots was in the form of short stories which often turned on logical problems associated with the 'Three Laws'. They inspired many films, most recently being a 2004 adaptation of certain elements of the robot stories and starring the actor Will Smith.

1 Ask students if they know of any famous stories or films about robots and what they think of them. Some examples of films with famous robots in them, if students are drawing a complete blank, are:

Metropolis (the female robot figure Maschinenmensch)
2001: A Space Odyssey (the robot computer Hal controls the ship)
Terminator films (killer robots disguised as humans)
WALL-E (animated garbage collecting robot)
Forbidden Planet (Robby the Robot)
Robocop (robot police officer)
Transformers (good and evil robots fighting for planet Earth)
I, Robot (the movie based on the Asimov robot stories)

2 **1.61** Explain that the students are going to read a text about the science of robotics. Ask them to read the text once through and answer the questions.

1 So that robots do not attack the humans that created them, a constant fear used in robot fiction.
2 No robots are programmed yet to follow all Three Laws.

3 Ask the students to read the text again. This task focuses more on a critical reading of the text by asking students to read between the lines. It might help to do the first question as an example with the students.

1 T (*although I did it unknowingly*)
2 T (*I am not going to let anyone in the world forget it*)
3 F (we read about *unique features of these stories* being *robot laws* but we cannot infer that there weren't other robot stories)
4 F (*Some scientists view the Three Laws as an ideal*)
5 T (*the military is one of the biggest financial donors for robotic research*)
6 F (*it is very unlikely that an attempt to follow these rules will happen*)

TEACH GLOBAL THINK LOCAL Reading extra

For a fun activity using some of the text, tell the students they are going to do a 'cough' dictation. They close their books. Say that you will read to them from the text, and every time you cough, they must write down the missing word. They only write the words for the coughs. When students are ready, read the text about the Three Laws, coughing at the following places:

The First Law: A robot must not hurt a human *cough*, or through inaction, allow a human *cough* to be hurt. (being)

The Second Law: A robot must obey *cough* by human beings unless these orders conflict with the *cough cough.* (orders, First Law)

The Third Law: A robot must protect *cough* unless this conflicts with the *cough* or *cough cough.* (itself, First, Second Law)

Extend your vocabulary (SB page 54)

Write the word *robotics* on the board. Ask students to identify the root (*robot*) and the suffix (*-ics*). Ask students to read the information about suffixes in the box. Students then complete the exercise and translate the words into their language.

electronics
psychology (*psychics* works, but it's a different kind of word!)
politics
anthropology
mythology
physics (add an *i* and you can also make *physiology*)

Other examples could be *sociology*, *biology*, *aeronautics*, *genetics* …

Grammar (SB page 55)

Ask students to read the information in the grammar box.

Language note

The whole area of modals and modality may be one that does not exist in the students' language. Although the form of modals is relatively easy to understand, one common problem is avoidance of modals. Students may tend to try and use longer structures, eg *it is permitted to walk on the grass* or *It is prohibited to smoke here*. Also, the area of *must*, *mustn't*, *need to* and *needn't* (or *have to* and *don't have to*) can cause problems as in some languages *don't have to* could have the same translation as *mustn't* in English.

The structures *have to* and *need to* are sometimes called 'semi-modals', as the negative and question forms of these structures take the auxiliary *do / don't*, unlike pure modals.

1 Students match the sentences to the meanings. Make sure they understand the difference between *necessary* and *permitted*.

1 b 2 d 3 a 4 a 5 c 6 b 7 a 8 c

2 Students circle the correct modal verb to complete the sentences.

1 mustn't
2 can
3 needn't
4 may
5 can't

3 Ask students to read the text about possible domestic robots. Do they think such a thing may be possible? Would they like to have a robot in the home? Tell them to answer the questions in exercise 3 with their own ideas.

TEACH GLOBAL THINK LOCAL

Mixed ability

Do not force students to use the target language to answer the questions. Instead just let them come up with their own answers. When you check answers, respond to the students' ideas but don't correct the grammar just yet. Once the ideas are out, ask them to try to reformulate them using the modal verbs they have looked at in the previous exercises.

G Grammar focus

Refer students to the language summary on modals of obligation and permission on page 140.

You can use exercise 1 on page 141 for:

a) extra practice now
b) homework
c) review a couple of lessons from now.

The answers are on page 143 of the Teacher's Book.

Writing (SB page 55)

Ask students to look at the cartoons on the page. Tell them that they should write a caption for each one. To make it a bit harder, tell them to try to include some of the language they have studied in this unit. Circulate and monitor.

Ask students to work in small groups and compare their captions. As an optional follow-up you could ask students to read their caption out loud and the rest of the class guesses which cartoon it goes with.

Background note

The original captions for the cartoons were:

I find it difficult to switch off. (robot on couch)

Get back in here and finish your lunch. (mother and child robot)

TEACH GLOBAL THINK LOCAL

Homework extra

Ask students to find and watch a video clip of any of the English films mentioned above about robots. They should watch and listen, making note of an interesting phrase or expression they hear and reporting back on this the next day in class.

Part 2

TEACH GLOBAL THINK LOCAL Lead-in

Before the class, find the names and addresses of several big government buildings locally and make a note of them (this works best if you are teaching in an area where you and all the students live in the same city). Write the addresses on the board and ask students what they have in common. If they can't guess, start writing up the names of the buildings (eg Department of Transport, Department of Justice, Parliament, etc). Use this information to ask students some questions about local government buildings. Have any of the students been inside one? What do they think of them? What are some common situations that they encounter with local government? Do they know anyone who works for the government? What does he / she do?

Vocabulary and Speaking (SB page 56)

1 Students complete the sentences with the words in the box. Check answers and drill pronunciation.

1 civil servant
2 town hall
3 Red tape
4 government department
5 political party
6 prime minister
7 pay a fine
8 complete a form

2 Pairwork. Students choose and discuss three of the questions. This gives them a chance to put the vocabulary to meaningful use. Circulate and monitor. Feed back by asking a few students to present their answers to the whole class.

Listening (SB page 56)

This is a series of four conversations set in bureaucratic situations.

1 Write the word *bureaucracy* on the board and clarify its meaning. You could point out that in English *bureaucracy* has two main meanings: the first is 'a complicated and annoying system of rules and processes', while the second is 'the people employed to run government organisations'. The ironic 'laws' below refer more to the second meaning. Ask students to read about the three 'laws' that relate to bureaucracies and match each one to its explanation.

1 The Peter Principle
2 Parkinson's Law
3 Acheson's Rule of the Bureaucracy

Background note

All these 'laws' are intended to be satirical. They poke fun at realities of British and American bureaucracy but are easily applicable elsewhere. Another famous 'law' that is used for humourous purposes (although not only about bureaucracies) is Murphy's Law: 'If something can go wrong, it will.'

2 **1.62–1.65** Explain that the students are now going to hear four conversations about bureaucracies. Ask them to listen and make a note of the problem in each one (they will answer this in exercise 3). Which conversation refers to one of the laws in exercise 1?

Conversation 4 is an example of the Peter Principle.

3 Play the recording again for students to answer the questions.

Conversation 1: his birth certificate
Conversation 2: he couldn't get away from work
Conversation 3: he had to write letters rather than emails; he had to come to the office; he had to wait a long time; he has been told to come back next week
Conversation 4: no

1.62–1.65

Conversation 1

A: Next, please!
B: Hi. Yes, I'm here for a copy of my birth certificate.
A: Have you completed the form?
B: Which form?
A: Form number BC 342. This one, here.
B: Oh, yes, that one. That one. Yes, here it is.
A: OK. Two weeks.
B: Two weeks? I need it now.
A: Sorry. You should have come earlier. We can't give it to you for another two weeks.

Conversation 2

A: Hello.
B: Good morning.
A: Yes, I have a meeting with Mr … Mr Green.
B: Hold on a minute please. Sorry, your name?
A: Mr Patel.
B: Ah yes, Mr Patel. Your meeting was yesterday.
A: Yes, I know. But yesterday was impossible. I wasn't allowed to leave work, you see.
B: Well, I'm sorry …
A: That's okay, I can see Mr Green over there, he doesn't look busy.
B: I know, but you need an appointment.
A: But I only need to talk to him for two minutes!
B: Well … OK then. Mr Green?

Conversation 3

A: Ah, finally.

B: Yes, is there a problem?

A: Yes, there is a problem. A big problem.

B: Please calm down.

A: Calm down? I had to write three letters to three different departments. I couldn't send emails – I had to write letters. Then I had to come down here. Then I had to wait for four hours in the queue with all these people. And now somebody has told me to come back next week!

B: I'm sorry, we have a lot of work. And this is the busiest time – you should have phoned first.

A: I pay my taxes!

B: Listen! I didn't have to come over here to talk to you, but I did. I'm trying to help you, so please, calm down.

Conversation 4

A: And it's been terrible. Really just terrible.

B: Why?

A: Well, Graham was a great colleague. He really knew everything about the system and was fun to work with.

B: So, what happened?

A: Two months ago Graham got a new job as a manager. He didn't want to leave our office, but he had to go.

B: But that sounds great. What's the matter?

A: He's not a good manager! The whole department is disorganised now. And I don't think Graham's very happy in the new job.

B: Maybe he shouldn't have taken the job.

A: I know. You're right.

4 Ask students if they can identify with any of the situations in the listening. Have they ever had a similar problem? Note that dealing with red tape and governmental bureaucracy is not always a laughing matter. If you think that this might raise potentially very sensitive issues with your students then don't force them to share these in the class.

Grammar (SB page 57)

Ask students to read the information in the box and clarify terms like *obligation* and *lack of obligation* (having to do something and not having to do it).

1 Students complete the sentences with the correct words.

1 had to
2 had to
3 didn't have to
4 couldn't
5 weren't allowed to

2 Students complete the sentences with their own ideas. To help them, do a couple of examples yourself first, eg:

In the summer when I was a child …

I didn't have to go to bed early.
I could watch all the television I wanted.
I had to spend two weeks with my grandparents.

Language note

Past modals are less difficult to understand for students, especially if they have already seen the concept of present modals. It's important to point out that the past form of *must* and *have to* is the same (ie *had to*) but there is no real past of *mustn't* – the closest in meaning being *couldn't* or *wasn't allowed to*. *Had to* and *was / were allowed to* are sometimes referred to as semi-modals.

TEACH GLOBAL THINK LOCAL

Extra activity

Dictate the following adapted sentences from exercise 1.

He was allowed to leave his job.

You couldn't buy me a present.

I didn't have to understand the headmaster.

We wanted to complain but we didn't have to speak to the manager.

Ask students to think of a context (no matter how strange!) in which these sentences would make sense. This more difficult exercise forces them to focus on the meaning of the modal verbs.

G Grammar focus

Refer students to the language summary on past modals of obligation on page 140.

You can use exercise 2 on page 141 for:

a) extra practice now
b) homework
c) review a couple of lessons from now.

The answers are on page 143 of the Teacher's Book.

Speaking (SB page 57)

1 Pairwork. Students choose one of the situations to roleplay. Some tips on doing a roleplay in class:

Give students time to think about what they want to say. At this level they needn't script the whole conversation but it might help to get the first two lines down.

Let students practise once or twice in pairs on their own first. Circulate and monitor discreetly.

Save correction of any language mistakes until after the students have finished the activity.

If the classroom furniture is moveable, set up the activity so that one student is standing front of the desk of the other (the student sitting is the bureaucrat). This will help the students get into 'role' better.

If you have time, ask students to swap partners and repeat the roleplay but improvising this time.

If your students like acting in public, then get one of the better pairs to present their roleplay to the class.

TEACH GLOBAL THINK LOCAL

Homework extra

As a follow up to the roleplay, ask students to write a letter or email based on one of the following options:

- as the customer, writing to complain about the service
- as the bureaucrat, writing a memo about the incident to his / her supervisor.

Part 3

TEACH GLOBAL THINK LOCAL

Lead-in

Tell students you are going to ask them to visualise their school days. Ask students to close their eyes. They can put their heads down on their desks. Tell them to imagine they are going to the first school they attended. Ask the following questions:

You are going to school. How are you getting there? On foot? In a bus? In a car?

You arrive at school. What does the building look like? What does the entrance look like?

You are in front of the school doors. What can you see? What can you hear? What can you smell?

Ask students to open their eyes and give them a moment to 'come back' to the room. Then tell them to tell a partner what they saw and heard.

Note: This is a short version of a guided visualisation. Some students (and teachers!) feel uncomfortable doing these, especially closing their eyes in class. Others really enjoy it. This kind of activity works best if the students and teacher are all comfortable with each other.

Writing (SB page 58)

1 Ask students to choose one of the topics and think about their answer before they start writing. Give them a moment to do this, then tell them to start. This is an unplanned piece of writing, so tell them just to write what comes into their heads.

2 After five minutes or so, tell students to stop. In pairs, students swap papers. They should now read their partner's paragraph and think of two questions to write about the text. They write the questions on the paper. Students return the papers to each other. They should then rewrite the paragraph, answering their partner's questions.

Allow more time for this second stage of writing. Ask them to check their first paragraph for language errors too, and to try to address these when rewriting. Circulate and monitor. Follow up by collecting in the second pieces of writing. Use these to diagnose common or recurring errors in student writing.

Vocabulary and Pronuciation (SB page 58)

1 Students match the compound nouns to their definitions. Allow them to use a dictionary, if they need to.

1 d	2 a	3 f	4 e	5 c	6 b

Language note

There are some differences in terms used in education between American and British English. In the UK, a *college* is a place that gives diplomas below university level, often vocational qualifications. In the US, *college* is another word for *university*.

In the US, a *state school* is called a *public school*. In the UK a *public school* is the name for a *private school,* where students or their parents pay *fees*, which can be very high.

2 1.66 Play the recording and ask students to listen and repeat the words. Once you have finished, ask students which word in each compound is stressed. Play the recording again so that students can listen out for it.

The first word is usually slightly more stressed than the second (this is a tendency, not a hard and fast rule!).

3 Ask students to read the statements to themselves. They then choose four and decide how much they agree with them by giving each statement a grade from 1 to 4. In pairs, students then discuss the statements they chose and why they agree / disagree with them.

Reading (SB page 58)

This is an excerpt from a novel about a schoolteacher's problems in keeping order in the classroom.

1 Pairwork. Ask students to look at the cover of the book and to speculate how the teacher is feeling and why he might be feeling this way. If you think the students need support, write the following sentence stems on the board to help them.

He probably feels …

He can't feel …

I think he could be …

The students must be …

The class could be …

2 1.67 Students read and listen to the extract and answer the questions.

Possible answers

1 His class 9A was not improving and he was losing control.

2 He asks a senior colleague to come in and discipline the class.

3 The pupils have now lost respect for the teacher as they think he cannot keep control of the class by himself.

Background note

Frances Gilbert taught for many years in inner-city schools in England, including one school labelled 'the worst school in the country'. Based on his experiences there he wrote *I'm a Teacher, Get Me Out of Here!* which was published in 2004. Many educators in Britain say that lack of discipline, lack of respect for the teacher and classroom management problems have been rising in recent years.

3 Ask students to read again and find the words for the definitions.

1 probationary

2 beat

3 mess around

4 stunned silence

5 mates

6 grin

4 Pairwork. Students discuss the questions. Feed back on this in open class.

5 Students complete the sentences with their own ideas. Feed back by asking one or two students to read their ideas to the whole class.

TEACH GLOBAL THINK LOCAL

Extra activity

If you have been having some difficulties with your class in terms of classroom management or discipline, you could use this lesson as a springboard to discuss them and set up a 'class contract' to try to resolve any problems. In a class contract both the students and the teacher jointly draw up a list of things they expect from each other (eg the teacher will hand back homework on time; the students will not answer their mobile phones in class) and then sign it and put it on the wall.

Extend your vocabulary (SB page 58)

Approach this as a test-teach exercise. Books closed. Write *in control, out of control, under control, lose control, beyond someone's control* on the board. Read out the sentences in the box. Students write down the missing words in each case.

Students read the explanation in the section and amend their answer accordingly, before checking as a whole class.

1 lost control

2 beyond my control

3 out of control

4 in control

5 under control

Grammar (SB page 59)

Go over the rules and examples together, clarifying the meaning of the example sentences and referring to the rules.

1 Ask the students to read through the text before doing the exercise. Ask *What is* The Class*? Has anyone seen it? Do you know of any other films about schools and classrooms? What are they?* Go over the first answer with the students, clarifying why it must be *for* (because *generations* is a period of time). Students do the rest of the exercise.

Answers are numbered in the order they appear in the text.

1 for
2 Since
3 for
4 Since

2 **1.68–1.71** Explain that students are going to hear short extracts of conversations in schools. Play the recording, pausing after each clip to give students time to answer using the present perfect continuous.

Possible answers

1 They have been fighting.
They have been doing something they shouldn't.
2 She has been making a presentation.
The class has been applauding.
3 They've been writing a test.
They've been doing an exam.
4 She's been seeing a boy.
They've been sharing secrets.

1.68–1.71

1

A: I'm sorry, Sir.

B: Yeah, sorry.

C: Well, OK, boys, I think you know you shouldn't have done it. But if I hear that you've been doing it again, you'll be in trouble. Is that clear?

2

Thank you, Julia, that sounded amazing … absolutely fantastic … well done.

3

Right, put your pens down everybody … OK, I'll come round and collect your papers now.

4

A: You won't tell, will you?

B: Of course not.

A: If my mum finds out that I've been meeting him, she'll go mad.

B: Well, I won't say anything about him.

A: Thanks, Kate.

3 Pairwork. Students ask and answer the questions. This is a short oral follow-up to the grammar exercises.

G Grammar focus

Refer students to the language summary on present perfect simple and continuous, and *for* and *since*, on page 140.

You can use exercise 3 on page 141 for:

a) extra practice now
b) homework
c) review a couple of lessons from now.

The answers are on page 143 of the Teacher's Book.

TEACH GLOBAL THINK LOCAL

Homework extra

For homework, ask students to bring in an old photo of their old school or of them when they were a student. In the next class ask students to work in small groups. Each student shows his/her photo to the others and says some words about it: when it was taken, where it was taken … The other students in the group must ask at least two questions.

Part 4

TEACH GLOBAL THINK LOCAL Lead-in

Draw a very simple floor plan of your kitchen on the board and elicit some of the words for typical things in a kitchen in the country where you are teaching (eg *stove*, *cupboards*). Write these on the board. Then ask students to make their own floor plan of their kitchen and describe it to a partner.

Speaking and Vocabulary (SB page 60)

1 Ask students to read the questions about keeping order in the kitchen and make sure they understand the words *annoyed*, *crockery*, *cutlery* and *boards*. If you have students who never work in the kitchen, then tell them they should try to answer for someone (a friend or family member) they know who does spend time in the kitchen.

2 Pairwork. Students compare their answers to exercise 1 and decide how much their partner likes order in the kitchen.

3 Individually, students match the verbs to the items. Point out that in some cases more than one answer is possible. You may have to explain what a *whisk* is – this is perhaps best done by miming or drawing a simple picture.

1 heat up (although you could *wash up* a saucepan or frying pan, and *clean up/mess up* a microwave!)
2 wash up (*clean up* if you were actually cleaning the sink or bowl)
3 chop up
4 mix up
5 eat up
6 clean up

Language note

To *clean* something is to remove the dirt from it. *Wash* is to clean something usually with soap and water. You *clean* the house or your room, but you *wash* your hands or your hair.

TEACH GLOBAL THINK LOCAL Extra activity

Once students have done exercise 3, play a miming game. Mime one of the actions, and students tell you what you are doing (eg *You are washing up*). Students then continue in pairs.

4 Pairwork. Students choose two sentences and create a mini dialogue around each sentence. Read out the example to show them. Circulate and monitor. Ask students to read their dialogues aloud in pairs.

Listening (SB page 60)

This is part of a lecture about two ways of organising lunch food, from India and Japan.

1 Ask students to look at and describe the photos on page 61. Have they ever seen food prepared in this way? Would they like to eat any of these dishes?

2 **1.72** Tell students they are going to hear part of a lecture about these two dishes. Play the recording for students to answer the questions.

1 B 2 T 3 T 4 B 5 T 6 B 7 B

3 Students complete the text about tiffin wallahs and bento boxes. Play the recording again and ask them to check their answers. Feed back.

1 4,000	5 six million
2 160,000	6 love
3 colours	7 ready-made
4 organisation	8 bread

1.72

Tiffin is an Indian home-cooked lunch which is eaten at work or school. Wives, mothers or servants cook the food at home each morning and pack it in metal tiffin boxes. The boxes have different parts and have a handle to carry it with. Each part contains a different food: rice, stew, bread, vegetable dishes and a sweet dish. Messenger boys called *tiffin wallahs* pick up the lunches and take them to offices or schools by bicycle, by cart or on their heads in baskets. After lunch, the tiffin wallahs pick the tiffin boxes up again and take them back to their owners. People don't take their own boxes in the morning because they are too big and on crowded trains there isn't enough space.

The city of Mumbai has a famous tiffin delivery system. Four thousand tiffin wallahs collect up to 160,000 lunch boxes and transport them on local trains to office workers. Many tiffin wallahs can't read so the boxes have codes made up of different colours. Business schools around the world have studied the system because of its efficient organisation – on average only one tiffin box in six million doesn't arrive.

Bento is a Japanese packed lunch. It consists of two parts: rice and side dishes such as meat, fish and vegetables. Bento is a good way to use up leftovers, so families often make up their lunch from dinner the night before.

It is very important that the food looks attractive. People who prepare bento often spend a long time forming rice into special shapes like bears or hearts and chopping up vegetables or sausages so that they look like flowers, stars or fish. The food is arranged carefully in a bento box. This is made of wood, metal or plastic. Today many people prefer plastic so that they can heat up food at work. The different parts of the meal are kept in order in the different parts of the box. Parts of the meal can also be wrapped up in paper or salad leaves. In the past Japanese housewives packed bento lunch boxes as a symbol of love – for their husband or children. Today, as many women work in Japan, bento boxes can also be bought ready-made. Bento is now also popular in Western countries where bread sometimes replaces the rice.

4 Students ask and answer the questions in pairs. Feed back as a whole class.

Grammar (SB page 61)

1 You could do this as a books-closed activity. Write the example sentences on the board. Ask students to:

- identify the phrasal verbs and indicate which is the verb and which is the particle (*pick up*, *take back*; *pick*, *take*; *up*, *back*)
- identify the objects and say which are nouns and which one is a pronoun (*the lunches*, *the tiffin boxes*, *them*; *lunches*, *boxes*; *them*)
- formulate a rule about objects, pronouns and phrasal verbs.

Students then open their books and complete exercise 1.

Second rule: *take them back*

Third rule: *pick up the lunches*; *pick the tiffin boxes up*

2 Check that students understand the phrasal verbs (using a dictionary if they have one). Ask them to read the text before they do the exercise. Do they agree with the authors about the importance of mess? Students then complete the text with the missing particles.

tidy it up

put up a barrier

mixes up parts / mixes parts up

put them together

try out new combintations / try new combinations out

make up new recipes / make new recipes up

G Grammar focus

Refer students to the language summary on separable phrasal verbs on page 140.

You can use exercise 4 on page 141 for:

a) extra practice now

b) homework

c) review a couple of lessons from now.

The answers are on page 143 of the Teacher's Book.

Language note

Phrasal verbs have different grammatical patterns. Here is a summary of the main ones.

Separable transitive phrasal verbs (ie that take an object): the object can go between the verb and particle or after the particle. If the object is a pronoun then it has to come between the verb and particle, eg *Pick up the boxes*. *Pick the boxes up*. *Pick them up*. The majority of transitive phrasal verbs are like this.

Inseparable transitive phrasal verbs: the object has to come after the particle, eg *Look after the children*. *Look after them*.

Intransitive phrasal verbs: these do not take an object, eg *Stand up*.

This should not be the first time students have encountered phrasal verbs, although in earlier units of *Global* they are usually taught as lexical items. In this lesson the grammatical feature of separable transitive phrasal verbs is taught, because this one of the most common grammatical errors students make.

Pronunciation (SB page 61)

1 **1.73** Ask students to say the phrasal verbs to themselves first. Can they decide which word to stress? Play the recording and ask them to listen and repeat, then underline the stressed word.

The particle *up* is more stressed in the phrasal verbs.

Pronunciation note

The stress in phrasal verbs depends on how the sentence is structured.

The main stress usually falls on the particle when it comes after a pronoun, eg *You always mix them <u>up</u>*.

The main stress usually falls on the noun when it is between the verb and particle, eg *You always mix the <u>dishes</u> up*, or after the verb and particle, eg *You always mix up the <u>dishes</u>*.

Note that in nouns derived from phrasal verbs, the stress is on the verb stem of the derived word:

There has been a <u>mix</u>-up. (noun: *mix* is slightly more stressed)

2 **1.74** Students listen and underline the stressed words in the sentences.

1 up 2 up 3 onions, garlic 4 saucepan

3 Students now pay attention to word stress and phrasal verbs over a longer utterance. Ask them to say the sentences first to themselves. Ask a couple of students to read the sentences out loud, paying attention to pronunciation. Students then read the sentences to each other and say whether they agree or disagree, and how much.

Function globally: giving advice and warnings

These lessons in *Global* are designed to provide students with immediately useful functional language. They all follow a similar format.

Warm up (SB page 62)

Aim: to introduce the topic via a quick speaking task or picture work.

Tips:

- Do not over-correct here, especially in speaking activities.
- Encourage students to use what language they can at this stage.

Listening (SB page 62)

Aim: to present the functional language in context via a conversation or series of conversations.

Tips:

- Ask students to read the exercises first before listening.
- Play the recording all the way through for each task (there are always two tasks).
- For multiple conversations pause the recording after each one.
- If students find it very difficult, play the recording a final time and allow them to read the audioscript at the back of the book.

1

Conversation 1: picture a

Conversation 2: picture b

2

1 b 2 a 3 c 4 b 5 c 6 b

1.75–1.76

Conversation 1

A: Excuse me, could you tell me how I get to Oxford Street? Should I take a taxi?

B: No, not at this time of day; the traffic is terrible. The best thing is to go on the underground – you should take the Victoria Line to Oxford Circus.

A: OK, thank you.

B: Watch out for pickpockets on the underground, though – be careful with your bag.

A: Oh, right, thank you.

B: You're welcome.

Conversation 2

A: Good afternoon. How can I help you, sir?

B: I'd like to report a mugging … they took my mobile and … oh dear …

A: I think you ought to sit down. Here … Is that better? … Right, who mugged you?

B: Two kids … well, teenagers, I suppose, a boy and a girl. I was just walking down the street, talking to my wife on the phone, and … the boy pushed me and the girl took my mobile.

A: All right, you'd better fill out a report form. If you'd come this way, sir … just mind your head there – and take care on the steps.

Language focus (SB page 62)

Aim: to draw students' attention to the items of functional language.

Tips:

- Make sure students have time to understand the form and meaning of the phrases, but you needn't translate them word for word.
- Students should be able to pronounce these phrases intelligibly, so drill them.

1 c, d, g, h

2 a, b, e, f

Speaking (SB page 62)

Aim: to allow students an opportunity to use this language in a meaningful, real-world context.

Tips:

- There is sometimes a choice of tasks. Any task involving reading a script will be easier than a task involving students making their own scripts. This gives you flexibility for mixed-ability classes.
- Give students time to prepare this activity, and circulate and monitor carefully.
- Correct sensitively, paying attention to the target language especially.
- If time allows, ask students to repeat the task, but with a new partner.

Global English

These lessons in *Global* have two main goals. The first is to give you and your students interesting information about English and language in general. The second goal is to provide students with practice in different kinds of reading comprehension tasks that they are likely to encounter in future study (for example, exams).

Warm up (SB page 63)

Aim: to engage students with the topic, and highlight potentially difficult vocabulary in the text.

Tips:

- be generous in helping students here with any unknown words in the first task.
- ask students to relate this task, wherever possible, to similar events or texts in their own lives. This will help them with the reading.

Reading (SB page 63)

Aim: to provide students with interesting information about English, and reading exam practice skills; where possible to focus on interesting or useful aspects of language in the text.

Tips:

- Get students to read through the whole text once first before doing the tasks.
- Many of these texts have been graded slightly, or not at all. There is a glossary of difficult words. Get students to read that first as it will help them understand the rest.
- There are two tasks. The first is an easier task, often focusing on the gist of the passage. The second is a more difficult task, similar to reading exam questions.
- If there is a third question the purpose is to raise students' awareness about a language feature; do not expect them to produce it immediately.
- This language is not tested or reviewed in future units, which means you have more flexibility with this material as to when and where you use it.

1

Paragraph 1: e

Paragraph 2: a

Paragraph 3: b

Paragraph 4: d

Heading c is not needed.

2

Statements 1, 2 and 4 are true, according to the text.

5 and 6 may be inferred from the text.

Speaking (SB page 63)

Aim: for students to relate the material in the reading to their own language, culture and experiences.

Tips:

- This is a short speaking activity and can be done in whole-class mode or in small groups.
- Wherever possible, ask students to think of and provide examples in their own language but explain them in English too.

As you go through these *Global English* lessons in the book, don't be afraid to ask students for opinions and reactions to the information in the text – not only answering the comprehension questions. Which do they find interesting? Do they know of similar experiences or facts in their own language or other languages? Some of your learners might be in your class because they are very interested in language, and these texts provide a great opportunity for you to capitalise on that motivation.

Writing: giving instructions

These lessons in *Global* are designed to provide students with extended writing practice. They all follow a similar format.

Reading (SB page 64)

Aim: to provide a sample text for students to analyse.

Tips:

- Many of these texts deliberately contain errors which the students will be asked to focus on and correct later in the lesson.
- At this stage of the lesson merely ask them to read the text and extract the information.
- There are often two questions for these texts: one which focuses on gist and the other on specific details.
- If a student does ask a question about an error in form, praise them for noticing it, and explain that they will be correcting them shortly.

1 She is Katie's future employer (Katie will be her au pair).
2 do the cleaning, tidy the kitchen, take the children to school, load the dishwasher, pick up the children from school, do the cooking

Language focus: giving polite instructions (SB page 64)

Aim: to highlight and focus on a particular aspect of language that students can use to improve their writing.

Tips:

- Sometimes this section serves as revision or reinforcement of language that students have encountered passively before in the unit (for example, in the reading texts) – make this link clear where possible.
- Let students check their answers in pairs or small groups, then correct in open class.

Possible answers

I'd like you to start working … and **finish** on Friday.
It's important not to arrive late because …
When you get back, **please** clean the house first of all.
You will need to start by tidying the kitchen …
Please try not to overload the dishwasher otherwise …
After that, **I'd like you to** clean the bedrooms …
When you have finished … **I'd like you to** get supper ready.
Finally, **could you please** pick up the children …
You will need to help them with their homework …
Please don't let them watch too much TV!

Writing skills: semi-formal language (SB page 64)

Aim: to give students a chance to develop their writing through various different micro skills.

Tips:

- Sometimes this section focuses on common student errors in writing.
- Clearly explain the focus and do an example of one of the questions first with the students before asking them to continue on their own.
- Let students check their answers in pairs or small groups, then correct in open class.

1

1 c 2 b

2

1 Thank you **for** your letter.
2 **I'm** glad you can baby-sit for us next week.
3 Here **are** instructions for how to find our house.
4 Here **is** some information about the house.
5 Do get in touch **if** you have any queries.
6 I look forward **to** hearing from you soon.

Preparing to write (SB page 64)

Aim: to give students time to brainstorm ideas for the writing task.

Tips:

- Allow students to brainstorm ideas in pairs or small groups.
- At low levels, this may involve some use of L1 (the students' mother tongue); be tolerant of this, but be on hand to help with translations or English where needed.
- Ask students to make notes here, but not begin writing.

Writing (SB page 64)

Aim: to give students practice in more extended writing tasks.

Tips:

- This section can be done as homework.
- Remind students to refer back to the model text, but to be careful of the typical errors.
- Ask students to check their work carefully before they hand it in.

Global review

These lessons in *Global* are designed to provide students with an opportunity to review and consolidate the language they have studied in the unit.

Grammar and Vocabulary (SB page 65)

Aim: to give students revision of all the main grammar and vocabulary points that arose in the unit.

Tips:

- Demonstrate the activities by doing the first one as a whole class.
- Allow students time to do this, and encourage them to look back through the unit for help.
- When you come to correct this, do not simply go around the class asking for the right answer – encourage students to say *why* they think something is correct, and seek confirmation from others before moving on.

Grammar	Vocabulary
1 have to	1 c
2 wasn't allowed to	2 d
3 don't have to	3 b
4 for	4 e
5 pick it up	5 a
6 mustn't	6 h
7 been working	7 j
8 wasn't allowed to	8 g
9 taken	9 f
10 had to	10 i
	11 m
	12 k
	13 o
	14 l
	15 n

Speaking and Writing (SB page 65)

Aim: to provide extra speaking practice that will review and consolidate language presented in the unit.

Tips:

- Give the students time to read and understand the instructions.
- Circulate and monitor the students, encouraging them to use only English here.
- Make notes of any incorrect use of language, but refrain from correcting if students are in the middle of the task.

Study skills

These lessons in *Global* are designed to provide students with skills and strategies in learner training and learner autonomy. For more on learner autonomy and learner training, see the essay on page xxiii.

Using your dictionary: phrasal verbs (SB page 65)

1 Ask students the question in open class and elicit a few answers. If none are forthcoming, you could suggest the following ways: making a list by verb, making a list by particle, creating sentences containing the phrasal verb.

Background note

Many students get very nervous about phrasal verbs, which are sometimes seen as a great mystery in English. The approach in *Global* is to introduce these very frequent items from an early level as simple lexical items. At Intermediate level, students can begin to learn the grammar of phrasal verbs. Students should be encouraged to think of phrasal verbs as just another kind of verb they have to learn, and nothing more sinister.

Students' own answers.

2 Go over the two study tips on phrasal verbs and how they are organised in the dictionary. Then direct them to the different phrasal verbs entries for the verb *take* and ask them to answer the question. Do the first one with them.

1 something
2 a
3 b, d
4 *land* (first sense), *put something on* (first sense)

3 Once students have clarified the meaning of each of the forms of *take* in exercise 2, they match each sentence with one of the definitions.

1 d
2 a (1)
3 c
4 b (2)
5 a (3)

4 Students' own answers.

UNIT 6 Seen & Heard

Coursebook

Unit 6	Language	Texts	Communicative skills
Part 1 SB page 66	Vocabulary *take* Grammar Passive voice	Reading *Now you see it … now you don't*	Speaking Photography
Part 2 SB page 68	Grammar Articles Pronunciation *the* Vocabulary and Speaking Colours and shapes	Reading and Listening *Optical illusions*	
Part 3 SB page 70	Vocabulary and Listening Ways of speaking Extend your vocabulary *listen* and *hear* Grammar Reported statements and questions	Reading *Overheard in New York*	Listening and Speaking What did she say?
Part 4 SB page 72	Vocabulary Electronic equipment Grammar Reported requests and commands	Listening An interview about the Stasi	Speaking Describing equipment
Function globally SB page 74	Asking for and giving opinions Listening to conversations about pictures Expressing uncertainty		
Global voices SB page 75	Listening to people talking about good news *indeed* and *at all* Talking about good news		
Writing SB page 76	A description of a place Avoiding repetition Expressing purpose		
Global review SB page 77	Grammar and vocabulary review Extra speaking practice		
Study skills SB page 77	Developing fluency in speaking		

Additional resources

eWorkbook	Interactive and printable grammar, vocabulary, listening and pronunciation practice Extra reading and writing practice Additional downloadable listening and audio material
Teacher's Resource Disc	Communication activity worksheets to print and photocopy
Go global: ideas for further research	**Seen** Ask students to find a photo on the internet that they find interesting and present it to the class. **Heard** Ask students to find an amusing overheard conversation on the 'Overheard' websites and report it to a partner.

Part 1

TEACH GLOBAL THINK LOCAL

Lead-in

Write the following on the board:

Is photography an art or a science?

Invite students to give opinions and comments.

Speaking (SB page 66)

Direct students to the questions. Clarify the meaning of *manipulate* (to change or correct something, often in a dishonest way). Students work in pairs and ask and answer the questions. You could also ask students to show each other the latest photos they have taken on their phones, if applicable.

Reading (SB page 66)

Background note

Manipulated photographs include photos which have details changed, removed or added, and photomontages or composite photos. Photographs are manipulated for various reasons. Perhaps the primary reason today is to make photos aesthetically more pleasing – particularly celebrities in magazines, or for advertising purposes. Doctored photos are also used for political purposes or propaganda, as well as in journalism. Ethical questions arise when manipulated photos are used in a deliberate attempt to deceive viewers.

1 Read out the subtitle of the text on page 67. Point out or elicit from students that *doctored* means the same as *manipulated* (changed). Students work in pairs and describe the pairs of photos.

2 2.01 Play the recording for students to listen as they read the text. In pairs, students discuss how and why each photo was changed.

Abraham Lincoln's head was put on the body of another policitian. The text does not say why (many historians believe it was because there were no studio photographs of Lincoln).

A military leader was removed from a group picture with Stalin, probably because Stalin disliked him.

The Pyramids were moved closer together so that the picture would fit the format of a magazine.

French President Sarkozy's photo was altered to make him look slimmer.

3 Look at the questions with students. Ask students to read the text again, paying special attention to the four highlighted words. Students pick the best meaning using the context to help them.

1 a 2 b 3 b 4 c

4 Students work in pairs and discuss the questions. Then discuss as a class.

TEACH GLOBAL THINK LOCAL

Extra activity

Ask students to find other manipulated photos on the internet and in magazines. They can bring them to the next lesson and tell the class about what has been manipulated and why. Students discuss the ethical implications or consequences of the changes.

Vocabulary (SB page 66)

1 Point out to students that we *take* photos and that the verb *take* is used in collocations with lots of other nouns. Ask students to make phrases with *take* using the words in the box and put them in the correct list.

Check the answers and then ask questions to consolidate comprehension: *Do you take the bus to work? Do you take sugar in coffee? Do you ever take a nap at lunch time?*

transport: *take the bus*, *take the metro*, *take a train*

food or medicine: *take milk*, *take a pill*, *take drugs*

activities: *take a nap*, *take a walk*

exams: *take a test*

control: *take power*, *take responsibility*

images: *take a picture*

TEACH GLOBAL THINK LOCAL

Mixed ability

Ask early finishers to think of or use their dictionaries to find more collocations with *take* and put them in the correct categories. For example: *take a plane* (transport), *take antibiotics* (medicine), *take exercise* (activity), *take action* (control).

2 Look at the sentence beginnings with students. Ask them to choose four and complete them. Encourage them to add extra details.

3 Students work in pairs and read out their sentences. Ask students to tell the class one of their sentences.

Grammar (SB page 67)

Look at the example sentences with the class. Ask students who took the photo or changed parts of the photo. Elicit the answer that we don't know and that it isn't important.

Look at the structure of the examples and elicit how the passive is formed and the tense of each example. Check that students understand the difference between the active and the passive and elicit examples of the active. Ask students to read the rules to consolidate.

1 Students find seven examples of the passive in the text.

photographs were changed
Lincoln's head was put
People were often eliminated
Semyon Budyonny was probably removed
the Great Pyramids of Giza were 'squeezed' together
the cover was manipulated
The correction was exaggerated
Past simple has been used.

TEACH GLOBAL THINK LOCAL Extra activity

Ask students to find five examples of the active in the text. *(Photography **lost** its innocence, the manipulation of photos **is becoming** more and more common, Tom Kennedy **stated** that …,* Paris Match ***altered** a photograph, it **had tried** changing the lighting).*

2 Complete the first gap as an example with the class. Students complete the rest of the text with the correct passive or active form.

Answers are numbered in the order they appear in the text.

1 was given	5 was given
2 produced	6 was made
3 showed / shows	7 published
4 received	8 wrote

3 Explain that the passive is sometimes used to put distance between the speaker or writer and the listener, or to avoid taking responsibility. Ask students to rewrite the letter using the passive so that it sounds more distant. Direct students to the example. Remind them to use the same tense in the passive.

We're sorry, your photographs **have been lost**. They **are usually kept** in a box on the table. The other day the shop **was being cleaned**. The box **was moved**. I'm afraid the photos **can't be found** now. A new set of photographs **will be sent** to your home address.

G Grammar focus

Refer students to the language summary on the passive on page 142.

You can use exercises 1 and 2 on page 143 for:
a) extra practice now
b) homework
c) review a couple of lessons from now.

The answers are on page 143 of the Teacher's Book.

Part 2

TEACH GLOBAL THINK LOCAL Lead-in

Close books. Find a picture of a classic illusion such as the vase / faces illusion or the young woman / old woman illusion. Print it out, project it on the whiteboard or draw it on the board. Tell students that this is an example of an illusion (/ɪluːʒən/), something that is not what it seems at first sight. Ask students if they can see the two pictures and to describe them.

Alternatively lead in to the topic with the first question in exercise 1 on page 68.

Reading and Listening (SB page 68)

1 Students work in pairs and look at the illusions in the four pictures. Ask them if they can see the illusion in each one. Ask students to feed back but don't give them further information at this stage – they will hear an explanation of the illusions in the listening.

Background note

Optical illusions work by tricking the mind and the eye into seeing something which is not actually there. Our brain processes images automatically: it tries to relate what the eyes see to things that have already been seen or experienced. In optical illusion images, the brain has difficulty in identifying distance, depth, colour or space.

2 **2.02** Ask students if they know how an optical illusion is created. Then direct students to the text on optical illusions. Students read and answer the questions. Play the recording for them to listen as they read.

An optical illusion is created by the eyes or our mind or both together.

Mathematicians, physicists and scientists have been interested in optical illusions.

3 Direct students to the words and phrases in the box. Read out each phrase in turn and ask students in which picture they can see this (or think they can!). If students have no idea, draw the pattern or objects on the board first.

a black background, criss-crossed lines, spots, straight lines
b criss-crossed lines, parallel lines, straight lines
c parallel lines, a staircase, straight lines
d curvy lines, a rod, straight lines, towers

TEACH GLOBAL THINK LOCAL Alternative procedure

Ask students to look up the words and phrases that they don't understand in their dictionary. Then invite students to the board to draw them.

4 2.03 Explain that students are going to listen to an explanation of how the four illusions (a–d) work. Read out the four names (pronunciation: Schroeder /ˈʃrɜːdə(r)/, Zöllner /ˈzɜːlnə(r)/). Students listen and match the names to the correct illusions.

1 c (Schroeder's staircase)	3 b (Zöllner's illusion)
2 d (The impossible object)	4 a (Hermann Grid)

2.03

1 This is one of the most interesting illusions. It is an example of an oscillating, or moving, illusion. The mind at first sees an object one way, and after a certain amount of time has passed, it will change its point of view. In this illusion the staircase will appear to turn upside down.

2 If you look at the two parts of this illusion separately they look completely normal. The top part is an image of three towers, and the bottom part is a picture of a rod in the shape of a U. If, however, the lines are connected an impossible object appears.

3 This optical illusion was discovered in 1860 by a German astrophysicist. It is a series of parallel lines, criss-crossed by short lines. This makes the parallel lines look as if they are moving away from each other.

4 This grid was discovered in 1870 by a physiologist. It's a series of white lines on a black background. If you look at the image, you will notice light grey spots at the intersections of the white lines.

5 Students listen again carefully to the descriptions. Then ask them to work in pairs and take it in turns to explain how each illusion works. Check students have understood each illusion. Ask if there is anybody who still can't see one of the illusions. Explain that some people simply can't see them.

Grammar (SB page 69)

Look at the example sentences with the class. Ask students to match each article in bold with the correct rule.

An optical illusion: something mentioned for the first time

a series of parallel lines: one of a group of things

The Hermann Grid: one of a kind

The lines: referred to before

the most interesting: superlative phrase

Background note

Maurits Cornelis Escher (1898–1972) was a famous graphic artist from the Netherlands. His work played with architecture, perspective and impossible spaces.

Ask students if they know this picture or other work by the artist. Ask students to complete the text with the correct articles and then compare their text with a partner. In full-class feedback ask students to explain why they chose *the* or *a*.

Answers are numbered in the order they appear in the text.

1 The	4 a	7 a	10 the
2 a	5 a	8 the	11 a
3 the	6 The	9 the	

TEACH GLOBAL THINK LOCAL **Extra activity**

Play 'Simon Says' with articles. Prepare a list of instructions with articles. Some should be grammatically incorrect or illogical. For example:

Point to the door.

Smile at the teacher.

Look at a floor. (incorrect – only one floor)

Pick up a pencil.

Find out who has got the biggest feet in the class.

Sit on the chair. (incorrect – which one?)

Wave at the student next to you.

Give the instructions. Students should only do the actions if the articles are used correctly in the sentence and situation.

G Grammar focus

Refer students to the language summary on articles on page 142.

You can use exercises 3 and 4 on page 143 for:

a) extra practice now

b) homework

c) review a couple of lessons from now.

The answers are on page 143 of the Teacher's Book.

Pronunciation (SB page 69)

1 2.04 Ask students to look at the sentences and listen carefully to the pronunciation of *the*. Play the recording, then ask students to repeat the sentences. Write the phonetics of the two variants on the board. Ask why the pronunciation is different (before a vowel in the first sentence).

1 The illusion /ðiː ɪˈluːʒən/	2 The colours /ðə ˈkʌləz/

Write a list of nouns (*artist*, *picture*, *colour*, *image*, *light*, *impression*, etc) on the board and drill the pronunciation of *the* + noun.

2 Ask students to read the rules and decide on the pronunciation of *the* in sentences 1–3. Students compare their answers with a partner.

3 2.05 Students listen and check their answers, then practise reading out the sentences to a partner.

1	/ðiː/ artist
2	/ðə/ top; /ðə/ picture; /ðiː/ other
3	/ðiː/ Escher

Language note

The /iː/ sound in *the* before a vowel is generally not as long as when *the* is pronounced /ðiː/ for emphasis, and is more like the /i/ sound at the end of a word such as *happy*.

Vocabulary and Speaking (SB page 69)

1 Point to items in the classroom (walls, objects, clothes) and ask *Is this dark or light (blue)? Is this bright (green) or pale (green)?* until you have established the meaning of *dark, light, pale and bright.*

Ask students to identify the colour in the boxes on the right of the page (from the top: brown, green, red, blue, grey, orange, blue, yellow).

Then ask individual students to describe the clothing, bag, shoes, etc of the student next to them using the words in the box.

a	dark red	e	light grey
b	dark green	f	dark orange
c	bright red	g	pale blue
d	dark blue	h	pale yellow

2 Point to the shapes in turn and ask students to name them. Direct them to the names of the shapes in the bulleted list for support.

Ask questions about the shapes to introduce vocabulary for the definition exercise: *How many sides does a triangle have? Is a cube one dimensional, two dimensional or three dimensional?*

Then ask students to work in pairs and explain the differences between the shapes.

A triangle has three sides and a rectangle has four sides.

A cube is solid and a square is flat; a cube is three dimensional and a square is two dimensional.

A circle is round and an oval is like a long narrow circle.

A pyramid is a shape with three or four triangles which make a point at the top; a cylinder is round and the same size at both ends.

A star has five points and a diamond has four points.

3 Students form AB pairs and turn to page 126 or page 128. Students take it in turns to dictate their picture to their partner. Their partner should listen carefully and draw the picture. Ask students to pay attention to the correct use of articles.

Part 3

TEACH GLOBAL THINK LOCAL Lead-in

Ask students if they would say they are more of a talker or a listener. Ask if there are situations where they talk more or less or where they prefer just to listen (with friends/strangers; at home/work, etc).

Vocabulary and Listening (SB page 70)

1 2.06 Check students understand the ways of saying something. Choose a sentence, eg *I can't hear you*, and say it as a shout, a whisper, etc. Ask students to identify the correct verb. Then play the recording. Students listen and match the way of speaking to the correct speaker.

1	groaning	3	shouting	5	sighing
2	whispering	4	mumbling		

2.06

1 No, not more bad news … oh, no … what next?

2 I heard something really interesting today but you mustn't tell anybody else …

3 Turn that music down! I said, turn that music down!

4 A: What's the matter?

B: I'm tired.

A: What? Can you speak more clearly?

5 Yes. Well. At our age, what can you expect?

TEACH GLOBAL THINK LOCAL Extra activity

Ask students to think of a sentence or choose one from the book. Students work in pairs and take it in turns to say their sentence in different ways. Their partner identifies the verb.

2 Direct students to sentences 1–6. When they are finished, ask students to compare their answers with a partner.

1	chatting	3	demand	5	beg
2	discuss	4	argue	6	eavesdropping

3 Ask students to choose three of the rewritten sentences in exercise 2 and change details so that they are true for them. Ask students to compare answers and explain their sentences.

Reading (SB page 70)

1 Students work in pairs and discuss the questions. In whole-class feedback, ask individual students for their answers. If you have a class with different ages, find out if older and younger people have different attitudes to the questions.

2 Ask students to read the information in the circle on page 71. Ask if they have ever come across these sites on the internet. Then students read the text and say which conversation they found funniest or strangest. Why?

3 Pairwork. Ask students to work out the context for each conversation using the questions given, paying attention to what the people say and how they say it. Feed back.

Possible answers

Astor Place: Two men, friends, talking about someone they know.

57th Street: A customer and a shop assistant or a waiter in a food shop or restaurant. They are talking about the food the girl is ordering.

55th Street and 5th: Two girls, two friends, talking about a phone call.

Washington Square Park South: A woman talking to a man working in a park. They are talking about a dead squirrel.

M4 Bus: A bus driver is talking to his passengers. He is talking about being late.

University Place and 14th Street: A man and a woman, arguing about their relationship and that the man lied.

44th Street and 9th: A man is talking about getting paid. We don't know who he is talking to.

6 train: A man, probably talking to a friend. He is talking about a girl he wanted to get to know.

Extend your vocabulary (SB page70)

Listen and *hear* are often confused. Ask students to read the definitions for the verbs. Do they have words with similar meanings in their language? Students read the sentences and pick the best words to complete them.

1 heard	4 heard
2 listen to	5 overheard
3 listens	

Grammar (SB page 71)

1 Ask a student *What did you do yesterday evening?* Ask another student what he / she said. Correct the reported version if necessary and write both versions on the board. Ask students what has changed in the two versions. Focus on the reporting phrase, changes in pronouns and times references and the tense but don't go into the rules for tenses at this stage. Ask students to complete the sentences and then compare with another pair.

1 There's a dead squirrel around there.
2 I ordered coffee.
3 Where are you from?
4 We don't have a pay check for you this week but we can pay you in cheese.
5 I'll get you a cab.
6 Do you want to dance?
7 I don't eat meat.
8 I love you.

TEACH GLOBAL THINK LOCAL Mixed ability

Ask early finishers to find more examples of reported speech in the text and decide what the people actually said.

2 Ask students to look back at the examples of direct speech and reported speech in exercise 1 and complete the rules. In full class feedback go through each question in turn and refer back to (or ask students to refer to) an appropriate example sentence for each rule.

First rule: the past simple; the past perfect; *would*
Fifth rule: *there*; *that*

Language note

In reported speech, time references may depend on the time that has elapsed between the action and the reporting of it. In the example *They said that they didn't have a pay check for me this week ...*, the man is describing something that has just happened and so it is still *this week. That week* would describe something further back in time, eg *They told me the job would be finished that day but it took several days longer.*

3 Direct students to the overheard conversations. Ask students to read them and then report the conversations in an email to a friend. Ask them to compare their emails with a partner. Then they feed back to the class.

Possible answers

1 I was at the taxi rank and this woman said that she wanted to go to Rivington and Ludlow. The taxi driver said he didn't know where that was, so the woman said she would show him how to get there. Then the taxi driver asked how he would get back! It was really funny!

2 I was on the bus and I heard a funny conversation. A woman said she hates (hated) it when it rains (rained) because there is (was) water and you get (got) wet. Her friend said he knew exactly what she meant!

3 I was at the station and this woman said to her daughter that they had missed the train. Her daughter said that it wasn't her fault, it was her mum's. So her mum said of course, everything is (was) her fault. And the little girl said especially global warming!

4 I was standing at the station and I heard two tourists. One asked the other if they were in New York. And the other said he hoped they were!

TEACH GLOBAL THINK LOCAL Mixed ability

You could ask weaker students to do only one or two of the texts or pair weaker students with stronger students and ask them to work together. Alternatively you could set this task for homework to allow students to work at their own pace.

G Grammar focus

Refer students to the language summary on reported statements and questions on page 142.

You can use exercises 5 and 6 on page 143 for:

a) extra practice now

b) homework

c) review a couple of lessons from now.

The answers are on page 143 of the Teacher's Book.

Listening and Speaking (SB page 71)

1 **2.07** Explain that often it isn't important to report exactly what somebody said or to include all the details. Tell students to note down the main details from each conversation. Emphasise that they shouldn't try to write down everything they hear.

2 Students work in pairs and tell their partner what they think the people said.

3 Students listen again and check.

Possible answers

1 He said he wanted two loaves of brown bread. / He asked for two loaves of brown bread.

2 She said it was nice to see her (friend) because it had been such a long time.

3 He was lost. He asked if Jack's café was near there.

4 She wanted to know how much a ring cost.

5 He said he'd gone jogging and broken his ankle.

6 She said they'd be on holiday the week after / soon.

2.07

1 Good morning. I'd like two loaves of bread – brown bread, please.

2 It's so nice to see you again! It's been such a long time – it must be over a year.

3 Oh, hello, I'm a bit lost. Is Jack's café near here? I just can't find it.

4 This is really nice, how much is it? The silver ring there … yes, that one.

5 And so I went jogging last week and what happened? I fell over and broke my stupid ankle!

6 So, just think, this time next week, we'll be on holiday! I can't wait!

Part 4

TEACH GLOBAL THINK LOCAL Lead-in

Ask students to describe the man in the picture and what he is doing. Elicit or give the word *spy*. Brainstorm with the class what they understand by a spy – who they work for, the activities they do and why they do this.

Ask students if they read spy novels or enjoy spy films. How 'real' do they think they are?

Background note

The photo is taken from the German film *The Lives of Others*. The film is about an agent of the secret police who is ordered to listen in to a playwright and his actress girlfriend. He becomes emotionally involved in their lives which leads to him withholding evidence against them. If some of your students have seen this film, ask them what they thought of it.

Vocabulary (SB page 72)

Language note

Headphones cover the ears. Many people today use a smaller piece of equipment to listen to music which fits inside the ears. These are called 'earbuds' or 'earphones'.

A combination of headphones / earphones and a microphone (used for example to phone over the internet) is a 'headset'.

1 Ask students to match the words to the uses, using a dictionary if necessary. Alternatively bring in pictures of these things and use them to introduce the vocabulary.

Ask students if they enjoy listening to music or podcasts, if they mostly do this at home or while on the move, and what sort of equipment they use.

to record: a microphone

to listen: headphones

to power equipment: a battery

to play recordings: speakers

to connect equipment: a cable

2 Read out the first sentence of the text and check comprehension of *audio surveillance*, *listen in to* and *wireless transmitter*. Ask students to complete the text with the words from exercise 1.

Answers are numbered in the order they appear in the text.

1 a microphone

2 a cable

3 headphones/speakers

4 speakers/headphones

5 a battery

Speaking (SB page 72)

Ask students what they know about the history of Germany after the Second World War and if they have heard of the Stasi. Then ask them to read the information about the Stasi.

Background note

The GDR (the German Democratic Republic), also known as East Germany, was created in 1949. The most important political party was the Communist Party.

The Berlin Wall was built in 1961 between the GDR and the Federal Republic of Germany to stop citizens leaving East Germany. GDR soldiers were told to shoot anybody who tried to get across the wall and leave the GDR.

The secret service of the GDR was the Ministry of State Security, also called the 'Stasi' (short for the German *Staatssicherheit*). The Stasi was responsible for the surveillance of its own citizens and of Western secret services.

In 1989 peaceful demonstrations by citizens of the GDR led to the collapse of the GDR and the fall of the Berlin Wall. In 1990 the two parts of Germany were reunited.

TEACH GLOBAL THINK LOCAL Alternative procedure

If you are teaching in Germany, ask students – either in pairs or as a class – to produce a short timeline showing important dates in post-German history, giving help with vocabulary as necessary. Ask them to produce a definition of the Stasi.

Students look at the photos of equipment used by the Stasi. They discuss what each was used for and how it might work, using the *Useful phrases*.

In whole-class feedback, ask students to present their ideas. Give them information about the items using the background note above.

Possible answers

red torch: I think this piece of equipment was used to record details of meetings. The equipment consists of a camera and a microphone. It's hidden in a torch.

black box with bug: I think these pieces of equipment were used to record phonecalls. The bug is hidden in a telephone and the battery is connected to the telephone cable outside the building.

pen: I think the pen contains a hidden camera and microphone. The listener wears the pen in a shirt or jacket pocket.

Listening (SB page 73)

The listening text is an interview with historian Dr Paul Maddrell. As it is authentic language, it is complex in places. Point out that students do not need to understand every word to do the tasks.

1 Direct students to the list of methods used by the Stasi. Clarify the meaning of any unknown words using concept questions. For example, to elicit the meaning of the word *informers*: *What does the verb 'inform' mean? Does it mean to get or give information? So what are informers? People who … Is it a good or bad thing to be an informer?*

Focus on the words in the box and ask them to look up those they are unfamiliar with. Then look at each word or phrase in turn with students, establish the meaning and ask which method of surveillance the word could be connected to.

recording of telephone conversations: intercept information, tap a phone

informers: source of information

agents in disguise: source of information

hidden cameras: source of information

controlling the post: intercept information, invisible ink, secret messages

listening in to radio transmission: intercept information

2 2.08 Direct students to the photo and information about Paul Maddrell and explain that students are going to listen to an interview with him. Play the recording. Students listen and tick the methods in exercise 1 that he mentions.

recording of telephone conversations

informers

hidden cameras

controlling the post

listening in to radio transmisions

2.08

A: Dr Maddrell, can you tell us more about the Stasi's surveillance methods?

B: An enormous amount of information was collected on East Germans, using many different methods. The Stasi intercepted post, recorded telephone conversations, listened in to radio transmissions and took photos of people using hidden cameras. But the most important source of information was the human informer. The Stasi asked informers to report on particular people or groups, or the places in which they worked.

A: Why were human informers so important?

B: The Stasi's aim was to watch and listen to the whole of GDR society: that means the activities of East Germans and their contacts with the outside world. The human informer was the most important source of information because the Stasi needed to know what people thought.

A: Can you give us some other examples of the surveillance methods used by the Stasi?

B: Stasi officers listened in to telephone conversations between the GDR and foreign countries, and listened in to many telephone calls in the GDR as well. In Leipzig, in the 1980s, 1,000 phones were tapped every day. The Stasi also intercepted telecommunications in West Germany and Western Europe.

A: You mentioned that the Stasi intercepted post. Can you tell us more about that?

B: Post control helped the Stasi to find spies. Western secret services told their spies to send their information to the West using invisible ink in letters, postcards and magazines. The Stasi's post control found many of these secret messages. Officers were told to look for addresses which were written very clearly: the spies wanted their letters to be delivered to the right address and so they wrote the address very neatly and clearly – but most people do not do that.

3 Ask students to read the sentences. The students listen and decide if the sentences are true or false.

In feedback, try to establish further details or reactions to the information (if appropriate).

1 F (It was human informers.) 2 T
3 F (They also listened to phone calls to foreign countries.)
4 T 5 T
6 F (They tried to write neatly and clearly so the letters reached the right address.)

Grammar (SB page 73)

Ask students to read the example sentences and the rules. Ask *What did I just ask you to do?* to elicit the answer *You asked us to read the rules.*

1 Direct students to the photo of Stella Rimington. Ask students to skim-read the text and find out who Stella Rimington is. Then ask students to read the text again and complete it with reported commands and requests using the words in brackets.

1 asked her to do
2 asked MI5 to give
3 asked newspaper editors to meet
4 asked her not to write
5 told to change

TEACH GLOBAL THINK LOCAL Extra activity

Prepare a list of quirky or humorous requests and commands on pieces of paper. For example:

Can you lend me €20? *Help me with my homework.*
Will you marry me? *Give me your mobile.*
Can you look after my pet rat?

Give one student a piece of paper and indicate another student. The student reads out the request or command. Then pretend you haven't heard and ask the other student: *What did he / she say?* The student reports the request or command. Give help where necessary. Continue with another pair.

2 Explain that Stella Rimington has also written a series of spy novels. Ask three students to read out the extract: one as narrator, one as the man on the phone, one as the woman. After reading, ask who the characters are or might be and what is happening.

Then students work alone or in pairs and put the commands and requests in bold into reported speech. Check the answers with the class and clarify any difficulties.

Answers are numbered in the order they appear in the text.
1 She told him to keep calm.
2 She asked him to tell her what had happened.
3 She asked him when he could meet.
4 He said to come to his flat.
5 She told him to give her the address.
6 He ordered her to come at eight.

3 Ask students what sort of life they think secret agents have. Is it hard? Glamorous? In pairs, they should think of the things secret agents are told to do or not do. Then they compare their ideas with another pair and tell the class some of their ideas.

Ask students if they think countries should have secret agents. Is it more or less important now than in the past?

Possible answers

to stay alert	not to give away information
to observe details	not to trust people
to keep physically fit	not to drink too much

G Grammar focus

Refer students to the language summary on reported requests and commands on page 142.

You can use exercise 7 on page 143 for:
a) extra practice now
b) homework
c) review a couple of lessons from now.

The answers are on page 143 of the Teacher's Book.

Function globally: asking for and giving opinions

These lessons in *Global* are designed to provide students with immediately useful functional language. They all follow a similar format.

Warm up (SB page 74)

Aim: to introduce the topic via a quick speaking task or picture work.

Tips:

- Do not over-correct here, especially in speaking activities.
- Encourage students to use what language they can at this stage.

Listening (SB page 74)

Aim: to present the functional language in context via a conversation or series of conversations.

Tips:

- Ask students to read the exercises first before listening.
- Play the recording all the way through for each task (there are always two tasks).
- For multiple conversations pause the recording after each one.
- If students find it very difficult, play the recording a final time and allow them to read the audioscript at the back of the book.

Background note

Picture a on page 87 is an installation: *Controller of the Universe* (2007) by Mexican artist Damián Ortega. Picture b is *Self-Portrait* (1787) by German painter Angelica Kauffmann.

1

Picture 1: The man likes it, the woman doesn't know.
Picture 2: The man likes it, the first woman doesn't like it, the second woman doesn't know.

2

Answers are in **bold** in the audioscript.

2.09–2.10

Picture 1

A: So, what do you think of this one?

B: Mmm, I can't decide. **I like the shape**. And **it's clever**, using those tools … But I find it … well, **a bit industrial**, if you know what I mean. Hmm, I'm not sure, really.

A: Well, personally, I think **it's amazing**. It's so **dynamic**, you can almost see the movement, like those tools are going to fly out and hit you any second … fantastic!

B: Mmm …

Picture 2

A: I really love this one. Look at those **beautiful pale colours**. And **the expression on her face** – so **calm** … lovely.

B: To be quite honest, I'm not that keen on it. **I'm not very fond of portraits**. And in my opinion this type of painting is **rather bland**. It just shows a pretty woman sitting down … **you don't get any impression of her personality** … How do you feel about it, Maria?

C: I can't make up my mind. I agree with you in a way … **it's a real chocolate box picture** but it's **well painted** … and interestingly it's a female painter, there weren't many of those in the 18th century, you know …

Language focus (SB page 74)

Aim: to draw students' attention to the items of functional language.

Tips:

- Make sure students have time to understand the form and meaning of the phrases, but you needn't translate them word for word.
- Students should be able to pronounce these phrases intelligibly, so drill them.

Asking for an opinion: 1, 7, 9, 11
Giving an opinion: 2, 4, 5, 6
Expressing uncertainty: 3, 8, 10

Speaking (SB page 74)

Aim: to allow students an opportunity to use this language in a meaningful, real-world context.

Tips:

- There is sometimes a choice of tasks. Any task involving reading a script will be easier than a task involving students making their own scripts. This gives you flexibility for mixed-ability classes.
- Give students time to prepare this activity, and circulate and monitor carefully.
- Correct sensitively, paying attention to the target language especially.
- If time allows, ask students to repeat the task, but with a new partner.

Global voices

These lessons in *Global* are designed to provide students with exposure to authentic speakers of English from both native and non-native English backgrounds. They all follow a similar format.

Warm up (SB page 75)

Aim: to introduce the topic and highlight potentially difficult vocabulary the students will encounter.

Tips:

- Be generous in helping students with the vocabulary here, but let them try to work it out first.
- Circulate and monitor any speaking task, but be careful not to over-correct.
- Follow up any short discussion pairwork with an open class discussion, asking students to report back what they said.

Listening (SB page 75)

Aim: to expose students to English spoken with a variety of accents.

Tips:

- Students will need to hear the recording at least twice, if not more times, to understand it. There are almost always two tasks.
- The first time they listen, tell them you don't expect them to understand every word; some of it will be hard. This is because the text has not been scripted or graded in any way. It's what they would hear in 'the real world'.
- The first task is easier and focuses on gist, the second task is more detailed.
- Pause after each speaker on the second listening, and don't be afraid to replay the whole thing if students appear to need it.
- Students can read the audioscript at the back of the book if you / they wish.
- It may be tempting to hunt for specific pronunciation or language errors, but we recommend against this. In real-world communication not everyone speaks perfect English all the time, not even native speakers.

1		2	
1	children	1	Patricia
2	money	2	Maura
3	weather	3	Yordanka
4	children	4	Patricia
		5	Alison
		6	Yordanka

2.11–2.14

Yordanka, Bulgaria

Well the last piece of good news I heard was only yesterday, and, um, it was some news about our baby, who is due in three or four weeks' time. And we heard that the baby is doing fine, he's growing well, and he's moving about happily. And we also found out that he's got a full head of hair, which is really funny.

Maura, Ireland

Um, the last piece of good news that I heard was when somebody at my work told me that I was paying too much tax, and suggested that I contact the tax office. So, I did, um … and I discovered that I'd been paying too much tax for about five years. So I was really happy and it was very, very good news indeed.

Patricia, Brazil

Um, the last piece of good news I heard was that this weekend is going to be great weather, so I'm very excited about it because I come from Brazil and where I come from in the north-east it's really hot, and we always have lovely sunny weather, and it's not like that here in England at all. So I'm very excited to know that this weekend I'll be able to go out and to enjoy a sunny, lovely day, and, um, I'll probably go for a picnic with my friends and um, I'm going to wear my lovely, summery dress, so … I think it's great.

Alison, England

Well I think I would have to say when I heard about the birth of my new niece, um … who, it was decided, would be called Sylvie. Um … It was especially exciting because we didn't know if it was going to be a boy or a girl um … and I knew that her … her older sister Martha would be really excited to get a new baby sister. Um, and of course everybody was delighted to have a new member of the family.

Language focus: *indeed* and *at all* (SB page 75)

Aim: to raise students' awareness of a particular piece of language present in the listening.

Tips:

- This language is not included in unit tests or reviews, it is included here to help students understand international English.
- The objective is awareness-raising, not production. Don't expect students to produce this language in an exercise or in conversation immediately.

1

positive statement: It was very, very good news **indeed.**

negative statement: It's not like that here in England **at all.**

2

very, very, indeed

not, at all

3

1 I wasn't expecting to hear that **at all**.

2 I was very excited **indeed**.

3 I thought it was a very nice surprise **indeed**.

4 I couldn't understand him **at all**.

5 I wasn't disappointed **at all**.

6 I felt very happy **indeed**.

2.15

It was very, very good news indeed.

It's not like that here in England at all.

Speaking (SB page 75)

Aim: for students to discuss the same or similar questions as the speakers in the listening.

Tips:

- The speaking tasks here are slightly more open to allow for students to explore the subject. Give them time to do this.
- If students are working in pairs, circulate and monitor. Make notes of incorrect language use to correct afterwards (or in a future class).
- As you go through the book and the *Global voices* lessons, ask students for feedback on these listening activities and their potential use of English with other people. Are they very difficult? Have students used their English as a 'lingua franca' with other non-native English speakers? How did they find it? What tips do they have on understanding or making themselves understood in an international context?

Writing: a description of a place

These lessons in *Global* are designed to provide students with extended writing practice. They all follow a similar format.

Reading (SB page 76)

Aim: to provide a sample text for students to analyse.

Tips:

- Many of these texts deliberately contain errors which the students will be asked to focus on and correct later in the lesson.
- At this stage of the lesson merely ask them to read the text and extract the information.
- There are often two questions for these texts: one which focuses on gist and the other on specific details.
- If a student does ask a question about an error in form, praise them for noticing it, and explain that they will be correcting them shortly.

1 All of these

2

Importance: one of the most important tourist attractions in China, listed as a UNESCO world heritage site.

Experience of visiting: wonderful experience to walk along the wall and feel the history and atmosphere – fantastic views.

Location: stretches from the east to the west of China.

History: built over two thousand years ago by the Ming Emperors.

Function or purpose: to protect the central part of China from being attacked.

Physical description: over 8,500 km long – some of the sections are in ruins, but other sections have been repaired.

Advice for tourists: take strong shoes and walk carefully visit in spring or Autumn.

Writing skills: avoiding repetition (SB page 76)

Aim: to give students a chance to develop their writing through various different micro skills.

Tips:

- Sometimes this section focuses on common student errors in writing.
- Clearly explain the focus and do an example of one of the questions first with the students before asking them to continue on their own.
- Let students check their answers in pairs or small groups, then correct in open class.

visit: go to	built: constructed
China: the country	the beacon towers: them
wonderful: amazing	sections: parts
the wall: the place	tourists: visitors

Language focus: expressing purpose (SB page 76)

Aim: to highlight and focus on a particular aspect of language that students can use to improve their writing.

Tips:

- Sometimes this section serves as revision or reinforcement of language that students have encountered passively before in the unit (for example, in the reading texts) – make this link clear where possible.
- Let students check their answers in pairs or small groups, then correct in open class.

1

… **in order to protect** the central part of China …

… **so that people on other towers could see them** and …

There is a cable car **to transport tourists**.

… **so that you can enjoy** mild weather …

2 Students' own answers.

Preparing to write (SB page 76)

Aim: to give students time to brainstorm ideas for the writing task.

Tips:

- Allow students to brainstorm ideas in pairs or small groups.
- At low levels, this may involve some use of L1 (the students' mother tongue); be tolerant of this, but be on hand to help with translations or English where needed.
- Ask students to make notes here, but not begin writing.

Writing (SB page 76)

Aim: to give students practice in more extended writing tasks.

Tips:

- This section can be done as homework.
- Remind students to refer back to the model text, but to be careful of the typical errors.
- Ask students to check their work carefully before they hand it in.

Global review

These lessons in *Global* are designed to provide students with an opportunity to review and consolidate the language they have studied in the unit.

Grammar and Vocabulary (SB page 77)

Aim: to give students revision of all the main grammar and vocabulary points that arose in the unit.

Tips:

- Demonstrate the activities by doing the first one as a whole class.
- Allow students time to do this, and encourage them to look back through the unit for help.
- When you come to correct this, do not simply go around the class asking for the right answer – encourage students to say *why* they think something is correct, and seek confirmation from others before moving on.

Grammar

1

One of **the** cheapest ways to have **a** conversation with **a** person in **a** foreign country is to use **the** internet. You can attach **a** microphone to your computer, and speak to **the** other person through **the** computer. If you attach **a** camera called **a** webcam to **the** computer, **the** person can even see you while you are speaking.

2

Daisy told Sophie that she was having a party the next day and (that she) had invited 20 people. She said she would be really busy and asked Sophie to arrive early to help. She told Sophie to phone her when she had received the message.

3

1 The picture was taken by Jon.
2 A taxi has been ordered.
3 We are being followed.
4 Conversations are recorded.

Vocabulary

1

1 demand
2 argue
3 discuss
4 whisper
5 overhear
6 mumble

2

1 cylinder
2 rectangle
3 oval
4 diamond

Speaking (SB page 77)

Aim: to provide extra speaking practice that will review and consolidate language presented in the unit.

Tips:

- Give the students time to read and understand the instructions.
- Circulate and monitor the students, encouraging them to use only English here.
- Make notes of any incorrect use of language, but refrain from correcting if students are in the middle of the task.

Study skills

These lessons in *Global* are designed to provide students with skills and strategies in learner training and learner autonomy. For more on learner autonomy and learner training, see the essay on page xxiii.

Developing fluency in speaking (SB page 77)

1 Ask students to do the quiz and decide and on their answers. Then they should check their answers in the key on page 130 (reproduced below).

Mostly As: You are doing the right things. These will help you become fluent and confident.

Mostly Bs: You are doing some of the right things but you could benefit from trying some of the ideas on page 77.

Mostly Cs: In order to improve your speaking you need to change your habits. Try some of the ideas on page 77.

2 Ask students to read the tips in the box or read through them with students. Students decide which suggestions they think would be best for them personally.

3 Students work in pairs and compare their choices from exercise 2. They should discuss ways they can follow the suggestions. In whole-class feedback ask students if they have other suggestions and tips for the class.

They should also think about why their choices are useful, eg an exchange with an English speaker is useful because you can learn about his / her culture as well as the language.

Ask students to consider other ways of improving fluency, eg listening to podcasts on subjects that interest them, or watching films and TV programmes in English. Many countries show these in the original language with subtitles – this can be a good way of listening to English while following the story. Sometimes the translations are not exact (colloquial expressions and jokes often do not translate literally) and students can look for the differences between the original version and the translation. This is a challenging exercise, but it is something students are likely to do naturally as their level of English improves.

Supply & Demand

Coursebook

Unit 7	Language	Texts	Communicative skills
Part 1 SB page 78	Grammar Defining relative clauses Vocabulary Inexact numbers	Reading *A good swap / Trash or treasure?*	Writing Describing objects for an auction Speaking Bartering
Part 2 SB page 80	Extend your vocabulary *-mania* Grammar Non-defining relative clauses Vocabulary and Pronunciation Word building: trade Word stress	Listening Tulipmania	Speaking The best way to make money
Part 3 SB page 82	Vocabulary Abstract nouns Grammar Countable and uncountable nouns	Reading *Meeting our demands*	Speaking Something you were motivated to do
Part 4 SB page 84	Extend your vocabulary Other ways of saying *funny* Grammar *wish* Pronunciation The letter *i*	Listening Three men on a desert island	Speaking Jokes
Function globally SB page 86	Making formal phone calls Getting through and leaving messages Roleplaying telephone conversations		
Global English SB page 87	A global language for business Rules for communicating more simply Simplified languages		
Writing SB page 88	Giving your opinion Considering both sides of an argument Agreeing and disagreeing with strong statements		
Global review SB page 89	Grammar and vocabulary review Extra speaking practice		
Study skills SB page 89	Learning word families		

Additional resources

eWorkbook	Interactive and printable grammar, vocabulary, listening and pronunciation practice Extra reading and writing practice Additional downloadable listening and audio material
Teacher's Resource Disc	Communication activity worksheets to print and photocopy
Go global: ideas for further research	**Supply** Ask students to find three interesting second-hand items for sale at online auctions and describe them to a partner. **Demand** Ask students to look for joke websites and find a joke they would like to tell the class.

Part 1

TEACH GLOBAL THINK LOCAL

Lead-in

Ask students where they usually buy things like furniture and household items, clothes, children's toys, etc. Ask if they ever buy and sell things second hand and how they do this.

Establish if students know what an *auction* is (a place or a website where people sell unwanted objects to whoever offers the highest price). Ask students if they have ever bought or sold anything at an auction or on an online site such as eBay™.

Writing (SB page 78)

1 Explain that students are going to sell an (imaginary) object at an auction. They should think of a household object and write a short description of it. Direct students to the *Useful phrases* for help.

2 Put students' descriptions up on the board or the wall, spread them on desks or make a space on the floor for them. Write a number on each description. Then ask students to walk round and read the descriptions. They should make a note of the number of the object they would like to buy and how much they would give for it.

3 Ask students to read out their description and then ask for 'bids' or prices. Students should call out their bids until the highest price has been given. That person then explains why he or she would like the object.

TEACH GLOBAL THINK LOCAL

Extra activity

If your students like practical activities, organise a real class auction. Ask students to bring in small inexpensive items they no longer want (old books or magazines, children's toys, knick-knacks, costume jewellery, etc).

Introduce some phrases used by the auctioneer:

The next item is …

What am I bid?

Do I have (20 cents)? Twenty-five?

Going, going, gone!

Students hold up their items in turn and describe them. Other students take it in turns to be the auctioneer. Students bid for the objects. Make sure the prices are low and fair and that everybody is happy with the outcome.

Reading (SB page 78)

1 Ask students to look at the pictures and the titles of the texts on page 79. Check that students understand the words *swap* (exchange), *trash* (rubbish, usually in American English) and *treasure* (valuable things).

Students predict what the texts are about.

2 Students work in pairs. Student A reads *A good swap* and Student B reads *Trash or treasure*? Students complete the table about their text.

A good swap

Organisation / Group	trade exchanges
Who it is for	businesses wordwide
How it works	members swap goods and services for trade credits, members use credits to buy goods and services from other members
Advantages	businesses can get things they need without cash and don't have to pay interest on bank credit, can help businesses find new customers
Cost	trade exchanges charge a fee for each swap

Trash or treasure?

Organisation / Group	online groups offering second-hand items for free
Who it is for	anybody who has internet access and becomes a member of a group
How it works	people join an online group and post messages offering things for free or asking for particular things
Advantages	you can get things for free; you can find unusual items that are difficult to find in a shop; decreases the amount of rubbish; helps other people
Cost	completely free

Language note

The text uses *credit* to mean both something that can be used as the equivalent of money (*These trade credits can then be used …*) and money that you borrow from a bank (*… pay interest on credit from a bank*). The second use is common in American English; the British English equivalent would be *loan*.

3 Students tell their partner about their text, using the table from exercise 2 to help them. Point out that students should ask their partner questions if they don't understand or want more information.

4 Discuss with the class what students think of the two systems. Encourage them to say if they have had experience of either of these. Ask what disadvantages there might be in using these systems.

Possible answers

Disadvantages could be:

trade exchange: the services and goods you need might not be available, especially if they are highly specialised; you might collect more credits than you can use if you have a popular service or goods

second-hand items: people might take advantage of the service by collecting free goods and then selling them; some people might always take and never offer items

TEACH GLOBAL THINK LOCAL

Reading extra

Focus on the vocabulary in the text.

Ask students to read the text they didn't read in exercise 2 and find words or phrases that mean:

A good swap

to swap things without money (*barter*)

to ask for money (*charge a fee*)

things that cost money (*goods*)

money that you arrange to borrow from a bank (*credit*)

Trash or treasure?

already used (*second-hand*)

using things again (*recycling*)

let somebody have something without payment (*give away for free*)

very different from each other (*diverse*)

Grammar (SB page 78)

Underline the relative clauses and elicit that they are used to describe something. Ask why *which* is used here (it refers to *restaurant*) and what other relative pronouns students know. Elicit examples for the others.

Point out that *each swap (that) they organise* is the object of the third example sentence, and the pronoun *that* can be left out: *each swap they organise*. This also applies to *which*. Also note that *that* can be used in place of *who* or *which*, more commonly in American English.

Ask students to read the example sentences and the rules and check that everything is clear.

1 Ask students if they know what *local currency* is. Tell students to read the first text, put in the correct relative pronouns and find out. Clarify what a local currency is (see answers for exercise 2). Then ask students to complete the other two texts with the correct relative pronouns.

1 which / that	5 which / that
2 who / that	6 which / that
3 where	7 whose
4 which / that	

2 Asks students to decide which sentences in the texts in exercise 1 contain object pronouns that can be left out. Students rewrite the sentence without the pronouns.

Local currency is money people can pay within a certain area.

It also has a local currency people use in the local villages.

The currency is part of a project villagers started.

TEACH GLOBAL THINK LOCAL

Extra activity

1 Write these nouns and sentence prompts on the board:

auction, bank, credit, currency, customer, fee, interest, member, owner

It's something / a thing which …

It's someone / a person who …

It's a place where …

Ask students to work in pairs. Student A describes a word to their partner, using relative clauses. Student B guesses their partner's word. Then they swap roles and repeat.

2 Students think of their own words and describe them. Their partner has to guess them as quickly as possible, eg:

It's something that you wear on your foot. It's made of wool or cotton. (sock)

G Grammar focus

Refer students to the language summary on defining relative clauses on page 144.

You can use exercise 1 on page 145 for:

a) extra practice now

b) homework

c) review a couple of lessons from now.

The answers are on page 143 of the Teacher's Book.

Vocabulary (SB page 79)

Language note

Vague language is very common in English when talking about numbers. It can be used to be deliberately vague if somebody doesn't want to give exact information, to round numbers up or down to make comprehension easier or when the speaker simply doesn't know the exact figure.

Note that *a couple of* does not literally mean 'a couple / two' but 'a few'.

The suffix *-ish* is added to round numbers to mean 'about'. It is often used for ages (*He's tall, fiftyish.*) and times (*She is coming at two-ish*). To talk about numbers of people or things we usually use *or so* (*I have five hundred books or so*).

Loads of is informal for *a lot of*.

1 Explain that when we refer to numbers or times we don't always give an exact figure. Explain how we use *-ish* and *loads of*.

Students then do the exercise.

1 a couple of things	4 loads of books
2 around two o'clock	5 about a hundred euros
3 ten minutes or so	6 thirtyish

2 Ask students to read through the sentences and check that they understand them. Then ask students to work in pairs and choose three questions. They take it in turns to ask and answer the sentences using expressions from exercise 1. Ask them to tell the class one thing about their partner.

Speaking (SB page 79)

1 Ask students to find two objects in their bag or pockets that they can use to play a barter game, eg car keys, a packet of tissues, a bar of chocolate, a nail file. Emphasise that this is only a game and students will get their items back!

2 Direct students to the *Useful phrases*. Tell them they are going to try to swap their items for something else. They should describe their objects so they sound really useful and attractive to other students. Students work in small groups and try to swap their objects.

3 Students tell the class if they were able to swap their items and what they swapped them for, or why they didn't swap anything.

Part 2

TEACH GLOBAL THINK LOCAL

Lead-in

With books closed, write the word *economy* on the board and ask students to brainstorm words and phrases they associate with the economy, eg money, banks, bankers, stocks, stock market, jobs, products, manufacturing, services, agriculture.

In multilingual classes, ask students what state their country's economy is in (good, bad, improving, getting worse, etc).

In monolingual classes, talk about the current state of your country's economy in simple terms. Ask how it affects students personally (difficult to get a job, higher taxes, etc).

Write *Supply & Demand* on the board. Elicit what 'supply and demand' is in the economy and what the relationship is between the two (*supply*: what products and services are available; *demand*: how much people want of these products and services; the relationship affects availability and prices).

Speaking (SB page 80)

1 Check that students understand the meaning of *invest* and *stocks*. Ask them to rank the ideas 1–7, with the best idea being number 1.

2 In pairs, students compare their lists, explaining their reasons. Establish if most students agreed on the best ideas and why / why not. As money can be a sensitive subject, keep the discussion objective.

Listening (SB page 80)

1 Draw a bubble on the board (or ask a student to do this) if students have difficulty in understanding. In monolingual classes, check comprehension by asking students to translate *bubble* in its different meanings.

Elicit what *dotcom* companies are and then what the dotcom bubble was. Do the same with the second question.

> In the 1990s the internet developed very quickly. Many people invested money in internet-based ('dotcom') companies and the price of stocks in these companies rose very quickly. The bubble burst because there were too many companies and their stocks were overvalued.
>
> In the first decade of the 21st century, many people became property owners because interest rates were low. The increased demand for housing meant prices increased and demand for property was high. Increased interest rates and unemployment meant that many people had to sell their houses, so supply was higher than demand. This happened in countries all over the world.

2 Ask students if they have heard of Tulipmania. Explain that one of the first economic bubbles focused on the buying and selling of tulips in the Netherlands. Clarify the meaning of each word in the box in words or pictures (see next page).

bulb: the part of plant that a flower like a tulip grows from
guilder: the former currency in the Netherlands
outstrip: become bigger than something
trader: somebody who buys and sells something
profit: the money that you make when you sell something

3 **2.16** Play the recording. Students listen and answer the question.

Tulips were a way to show wealth and many people wanted to buy them. But it takes five to ten years to grow a tulip bulb, so demand outstripped supply.

2.16

In the early 17th century, Holland was in its Golden Age. Many Dutch traders had become wealthy through trade with the East Indies. Tulips, which had been introduced to the Netherlands in the 1590s, were a popular way for people to show their wealth. Rare bulbs could be sold for hundreds or even thousands of guilders – at a time when the average income was 150 guilders a year.

In the early 1630s tulips started to sell for higher and higher prices as demand for the flowers outstripped supply. A tulip bulb, which only flowers for a few years, takes five to ten years to grow from seed. This meant that the supply of bulbs was limited. In 1636 a special traders' market was created to sell tulips: traders signed contracts in the winter to buy tulips in the summer when the bulbs had flowered. They hoped that the bulbs would be more valuable in the summer, so that they could make a profit. More and more traders bought tulips at higher and higher prices.

By February 1637 tulips cost *20* times more than in November 1636. One rare tulip was sold for 6,700 guilders, which was enough to buy a big house in Amsterdam. But suddenly buyers refused to pay the prices which the traders asked – and the market crashed. Prices for tulips fell as dramatically as they had risen. The tulip bubble had burst.

Today there is disagreement among economists about how strongly Tulipmania actually affected the Dutch economy. But for many, the story of Tulipmania remains a popular warning about the dangers of trying to make a quick profit.

4 Ask students to read through the questions and check they have understood them before answering. Students listen again and check their answers.

1 b 2 c 3 b 4 a 5 a 6 c

5 In pairs, students decide which statement they agree with. Refer them to economic developments in your country if appropriate. Circulate and prompt students who need help.

Extend your vocabulary (SB page 80)

Ask students to read the information about the suffix *-mania*. Then as a class or in groups, brainstorm new *-mania* words and collect them on the board. You could also ask students to look up *mania* on the internet using a search engine and report on the *–mania* words they find there.

Grammar (SB page 81)

Direct students' attention to the example sentences and the relative clauses in bold. Ask students if the sentence still makes sense if the clause in bold is taken out. Compare with a defining relative clause such as *The tulips I bought yesterday are beautiful* where the clause is necessary to understand the sentences.

Explain that these clauses are 'non-defining': they just add extra information. Point out the use of commas which are marked by pauses when reading out the sentences. Ask students to read the rules and check that they understand them.

1 Ask students to read the text about the South Sea Company. Students then complete the text by putting the relative clauses in the correct place.

Answers are numbered in the order they appear in the text.
1 c 2 d 3 a 4 b

2 Ask students to read the notes about the bubble economy in Japan. Clarify any difficulties. Ask students to write a paragraph using the notes. They should put the non-essential information in non-defining relative clauses. Ask students to check their paragraph with a partner. They should take it in turns to read out a sentence each, paying attention to pauses before and after the clauses.

The bubble economy years, which were years of great wealth, started around 1985. In Japan, where the interest rate had gone down, many people suddenly had a lot of money. The banks, which had mostly lent money to companies, gave loans to anybody. The Japanese economy, whose share prices had risen dramatically, crashed in 1990.

G Grammar focus

Refer students to the language summary non-defining relative clauses on page 144.

You can use exercise 2 on page 145 for:

a) extra practice now
b) homework
c) review a couple of lessons from now.

The answers are on page 143 of the Teacher's Book.

TEACH GLOBAL THINK LOCAL Extra activity

Students play the 'expanding sentences' game. Start off by giving students a simple sentence, eg:

Our town has a famous castle.

Students have to expand the sentence using as many non-defining clauses as they can, by adding one in turn, eg:

Our town, which dates back to the 15th century, has a famous castle.

Our town, which dates back to the 15th century and which is very beautiful, has a famous castle.

Our town, which dates back to the 15th century and which is very beautiful, has a famous castle, which is very popular with tourists.

Vocabulary and Pronunciation (SB page 81)

1 2.17 Do the first line of each table with students as an example. In pairs, they complete the two tables as far as possible, leaving a space if necessary. Then play the recording of the words for students to listen and check.

Noun	Adjective
economy	economic
finance	financial
profit	profitable
value	valuable
wealth	wealthy
poverty	poor

Verb	Noun (thing)	Noun (person)
supply	supply	supplier
invest	investment	investor
employ	employment	employer / employee
import	import	importer
produce	product	producer
trade	trade	trader

2 Play the recording for the first table. Students listen to the word stress and repeat. Ask in which words the stress 'jumps' to the next syllable. The stress is noted in the table above. Then play the recording for the second table, pausing after each line. Students say in which lines the stress changes.

Drill the pronunciation of the words in the tables by asking students to say them in different ways: loudly, quietly, sadly, happily, etc.

3 Ask students to choose the correct words to complete the sentences. Students compare with a partner, paying attention to pronunciation.

1 employees; economic	3 Wealthy; poverty
2 trade; import; suppliers	4 financial; investors

4 Students work in pairs and discuss whether they agree with the statements in exercise 3 or not, and why.

Part 3

TEACH GLOBAL THINK LOCAL Lead-in

Write this sentence on the board and ask students to complete it on a piece of paper with the first words that they think of.

_______ is / are the most important thing(s) in the world.

Make a list of students' ideas and note which were the most popular. Ask students to explain some ideas.

If the lists contain abstract nouns, use these to lead into the first vocabulary activity.

Vocabulary (SB page 82)

Language note

In English, abstract nouns are usually uncountable and used with zero article. They are not used with the definite article as in many other languages.

However, when we define these nouns with a defining relative clause or a noun phrase, then the definite article is used:

The power (that) he had over his audience was frightening.

The power in his hands was amazing.

1 2.18 Play the recording and ask students to complete the abstract nouns. Alternatively, ask students to complete the nouns with vowels as quickly as they can (you can give them a time limit) and then play the recording so that students can check their answers.

In monolingual classes, ask students to translate the words into their own language. In multilingual classes, ask students to check any meanings they are unsure of in a dictionary.

Elicit from students what all these nouns have in common (they are states, feelings and qualities). Explain that these are *abstract* nouns: nouns that have no physical existence, that you cannot touch, taste or smell.

Direct students to the *Language note*. Point out that in English we use abstract nouns without an article unless we are defining the word. In multilingual classes ask if students would use a definite article with these words in their language.

love	wealth
friendship	justice
creativity	power
peace	fear
respect	morality
health	beauty

2 Ask students to choose three of the sentences and complete them with words from exercise 1 to make sentences that are true for them. Students should think about their reasons for this.

3 Ask students to work in pairs and take it in turns to read out their sentences to each other. They should explain why they think this and their partner should say whether they agree or disagree.

Reading (SB page 82)

Background note

Abraham Maslow (1908–1970) was an American psychologist, born to Russian Jewish parents, whose hierarchy of needs was published in his 1943 paper *A Theory of Human Motivation.* While studying psychology at the University of Wisconsin, Maslow witnessed behavioural experiments with baby monkeys. He noticed that the monkeys attended to specific needs in a specific order and used these observations as a basis for his work on the hierarchy.

Today Maslow's theory is used in teacher training, in motivation training in business management, and in marketing as a way of understanding customer needs. Critics of the theory, however, claim it lacks empirical support and say there is no evidence that self-actualisation (realisation of one's full potential) can only take place once basic needs have been met: many famous artists produced outstanding work despite living in poverty, for example. Other critics have pointed out that the hierarchy is not relevant to all cultures as some place a higher value on, for example, social needs.

1 **2.19** Explain that students are going to read about a well-known theory of motivation. Ask them to read the first task about the intention of the person writing the text. Clarify the words *criticise*, *convince* and *influential*. Then ask students to read the text *Meeting our demands* on page 83 and answer the question. In full-class feedback ask students why they chose this answer (the text only gives us information, it doesn't contain language that says the theory is good or bad.)

The author's intention is (2) to give information about Maslow's theory of motivation.

2 Direct students' attention to the pyramid. Ask students to read the text again and complete the pyramid with the missing words, using words from the box. Encourage students to use a dictionary to help them.

physiological: food
safety: job security
love and belonging: family
self-actualisation: problem-solving, acceptance

3 Discuss the questions with the class. Prompt the class with further questions. Focus on the idea that the demands of each level need to be met before people can move up. Do we really need to feel love and belonging before we can realise our full potential? (Many highly intelligent or creative people are loners, for example.) Are higher needs more important for some people than basic needs?

Grammar (SB page 83)

1 Elicit from students examples of a countable and an uncountable noun, eg *book* and *water*. Elicit what the differences are between the two and how we use them.

Then ask students, alone or in pairs, to look at the highlighted words in the Reading text and decide if they are countable or uncountable. Encourage students to use a dictionary to help them. You might like to ask students to look up the first word in the text, *motivation*, and ask them whether it is given as C (countable) or U (uncountable).

In feedback after the task, point out that *crime* can be both countable and uncountable depending on the meaning. In the text it is uncountable because it refers to crime in general; *a crime* is a particular activity.

Ask students to look at the *Language note* and then give them other examples, eg:

a coffee = a cup of coffee, *coffee* is an unspecified amount
a cake = one cake, *cake* is an unspecified amount or a piece of cake

U: motivation, food, water, sleep, safety, love, belonging, friendship, esteem, respect
C: pyramid, job, family, group, people
U / C: crime

2 Ask students to read the example sentences and complete the rules with *countable*, *uncountable* or both. In feedback, ask students to give examples of the rules. In connection with the rule on the definite article, point out again that uncountable abstract nouns are generally used with zero article.

Second rule: countable
Third rule: uncountable
Fourth rule: countable and uncountable
Fifth rule: countable and uncountable

3 Ask students to complete the sentences with the correct word. Check the answers and refer students back to the rules if necessary. Point out that *weather* is uncountable but in the phrase *in all weathers* it can be used in the plural.

1 furniture
2 The violence
3 knowledge
4 weather is
5 advice
6 jokes

TEACH GLOBAL THINK LOCAL

Extra activity

Look at the completed sentences in exercise 3 and ask students to decide which of Maslow's hierarchy of needs each sentence is about.

furniture: possibly safety, as it is part of having familiar things around us

violence: safety

knowledge: self-actualisation

weather: safety

advice: esteem, or love and belonging

jokes: esteem, or love and belonging

G Grammar focus

Refer students to the language summary on countable and uncountable nouns on page 144.

You can use exercises 3 and 4 on page 145 for:

a) extra practice now
b) homework
c) review a couple of lessons from now.

The answers are on page 143 of the Teacher's Book.

Speaking (SB page 83)

1 Ask students what generally motivates them to do things. Then ask them to think of a particular time when they were motivated to do something and direct them to the list of questions. Students read the questions and think about (or make notes about) their answers. Give them sufficient thinking time to do this.

2 Students work in pairs. They tell their partner their story using the questions in exercise 1 to guide them. When they have heard each other's stories, students discuss if their experiences had anything in common. Invite one or two volunteers to tell the class briefly about their experiences and what (if anything) they had in common.

Part 4

TEACH GLOBAL THINK LOCAL

Lead-in

Tell students to imagine they can have three personal demands or wishes fulfilled. Ask students to note down what these three things would be.

Students work in pairs. They tell their partner what they wrote and why.

Listening (SB page 84)

Background note

The 'three wishes' joke exists in many variations but the basic sequence is usually the same. A magic being such as a genie or a fairy godmother appears and offers somebody three wishes. The last wish the person expresses undoes the first wish or causes a problem and therefore provides the punch line (the funny ending to the joke).

The joke in the listening is one variation of the joke.

1 Direct students to the pictures on the page. Model the pronunciation of these words. Tell students the pictures represent a well-known joke. Ask them to work in pairs and put the pictures in order to make the story.

Correct order: a, d, f, b, e (c is not needed)

2 **2.20** Ask students to listen and check the correct order of the pictures. Then ask them to draw speech bubbles for each man and write what each man wishes (answers in bold in the audioscript). Play the recording again if necessary.

2.20

OK, there's a desert island and there are three men. They've been there, alone, for a long time. One day, they're walking along the beach and they see a glass bottle. When they open the bottle, there is a loud crash and a genie appears. 'You have three wishes,' says the genie. The men look at each other, and decide to have one wish each.

The first man says to the genie: '**I wish I were back in London with my wife and three children**. I haven't seen them for ten years.'

The genie snaps his fingers and bang! the man is back in London in his family home.

It is the second man's turn. He looks at the genie and says, 'I've always wanted to see Hollywood. **I wish I could be in Los Angeles right now.**'

The genie snaps his fingers again and bang! the man is standing on Sunset Boulevard.

Now there is only one man left on the island with the genie. The genie looks at the man. The man looks at the genie.

'Well?' asks the genie.

The third man looks around, sighs and says, **'I wish my friends were here.'**

TEACH GLOBAL THINK LOCAL

Mixed ability

Pair stronger students up with weaker students. The stronger student retells the joke using the pictures and the speech bubbles. The other student listens and decides if the joke sounds right and adds any missing details.

3 Ask students if they thought the joke was funny or if they have heard it before. Ask students who know similar jokes to tell the class.

TEACH GLOBAL THINK LOCAL

Alternative procedure

If students don't know any similar jokes, tell the class another three wishes joke such as the one below.

A man is walking down the beach and comes across an old bottle. He picks it up, opens it and a genie appears. The genie says, 'Thank you. You have three wishes.' The man says 'First, I want a million dollars in a Swiss bank account.' There is a flash of light and a piece of paper with bank account numbers appears in his hand. He continues, 'Next, I want a new sports car.' There is a flash of light again and a bright red sports car appears. He continues, 'Finally, I want women to love me.' There is a flash of light and the man turns into a box of chocolates.

Extend your vocabulary (SB page 84)

Direct students to the vocabulary box. Model the pronunciation of the five words and ask students to repeat, paying attention to word stress.

amusing /əmˈjuːziŋ/

humorous /ˈhjuːmərəs/

comical /ˈkɒmɪkəl/

hilarious /hɪˈleəriəs/

witty /ˈwɪti/

Ask students to read the explanations and say which of the words they would describe the joke in the listening with. Then students work in pairs and think of examples of the things given. Ask students to feed back to the class.

Grammar (SB page 85)

1 Direct students to the example sentences. Read out the sentences and emphasise the word in bold. Ask students to read and complete the rules. Then go through the rules with students. Ask students what you would say if you wanted a bigger flat (*I wish / if only I had a bigger flat*) or if you wanted to be better at English (*I wish I were / was better at English*).

First rule: past simple

Second rule: were

2 Direct students to the illustrations. Ask them to write two captions for each picture using *I wish* and phrases from the box.

Top:
I wish it / the train wasn't so crowded.
I wish I had a car.

Bottom left:
I wish I didn't live on the 10th floor.
I wish the building had a lift / there was a lift.

Bottom right:
I wish it wasn't so expensive.
I wish I could afford it.

3 Ask students to complete the sentences of the poem with their own ideas. They can be true wishes or they can be humorous. Ask students to read their poem out to a small group. Then invite the group to read out the best or funniest poem to the class.

G Grammar focus

Refer students to the language summary on *wish* on page 144.

You can use exercise 5 on page 145 for:

a) extra practice now
b) homework
c) review a couple of lessons from now.

The answers are on page 143 of the Teacher's Book.

Pronunciation (SB page 85)

1 Ask students how the letter *i* in *wish* is pronounced: /ɪ/. Then ask students how the letter *i* is pronounced in *child*: /aɪ/. Write the word and the phonetic symbols for both on the board and repeat the sounds.

Ask students to say the words in the box silently to themselves and put them in the correct group according to sound.

Check the answers with the class. Ask if students can think of other words with these sounds. Make two lists on the board.

/ɪ/
dishes
finger
if
lift
swim
think
wish
(others: witty, silly, picture, swim, chicken)

/aɪ/
I
island
might
ride
sigh
tonight
wife
(others: right, smile, light)

2 Direct students to the rhyme and proverb. Model the two. Then drill pronunciation by going quickly round the class: students should read out the rhyme one after the other, with correct pronunciation of the *i* sound. Keep things moving quickly. Then go back the other way round the class with students reading out the proverb. In large classes you can do this in groups instead.

Then discuss with students what the proverb is trying to say and if they agree.

Speaking (SB page 85)

1 Ask students to read the beginnings and endings and match them to make four jokes.

1 a   2 c   3 d   4 b

2 Students work in pairs. They choose three of the questions and discuss them.

TEACH GLOBAL THINK LOCAL **Homework extra**

Students think of a joke they know or ask family or friends, and write it down in English. Or they look for a funny English joke on the internet. Remind students it should be suitable for the English class! Next lesson ask students to tell their joke to the class or a group.

Function globally: making formal phone calls

These lessons in *Global* are designed to provide students with immediately useful functional language. They all follow a similar format.

Warm up (SB page 86)

Aim: to introduce the topic via a quick speaking task or picture work.

Tips:

- Do not over-correct here, especially in speaking activities.
- Encourage students to use what language they can at this stage.

Listening (SB page 86)

Aim: to present the functional language in context via a conversation or series of conversations.

Tips:

- Ask students to read the exercises first before listening.
- Play the recording all the way through for each task (there are always two tasks).
- For multiple conversations pause the recording after each one.
- If students find it very difficult, play the recording a final time and allow them to read the audioscript at the back of the book.

1 Phone call 2 (The person the caller wishes to speak to isn't there.)

2

1 F (He wants to make an appointment.)
2 T
3 F (Miguel Hernández wants to speak to Mike Jones.)
4 F (A receptionist answers the phone.)
5 T
6 F (An automated message answers first.)
7 F (He is polite.)
8 T

2.21–2.23

Phone call 1

A: Hello, I'd like to make an appointment with Dr Singh.

B: Just a moment, please … erm, he's free this Wednesday at 8.30.

A: 8.30 … um, yes, that's fine.

B: Right … and your name?

A: David STYLES – that's S-T-Y-L-E-S.

B: That's 8.30 on Wednesday, then.

A: Thank you.

B: Goodbye.

Phone call 2

A: Good morning, Tyson's Engineering. May I help you?

B: Hello, this is Miguel Hernández. Could I speak to Mike Jones please?

A: I'm afraid he's in a meeting for the next hour or so. Can I take a message?

B: Could you ask him to call me back, please? He has my number.

A: Of course, what was your name again?

B: Miguel Hernández.

A: Miguel Hernández … Certainly, I'll do that. Thank you for calling.

B: Goodbye.

Phone call 3

A: Hello, this is GLB Bank. If you would like information about a new account, please press 1. If you have a query about an existing account, please press 2. Thank you. We are now processing your call. Please hold the line … Please hold the line …

B: Oh, come on …

C: Hello, Customer Services, David speaking. Sorry to keep you waiting. How can I help you?

B: Hello, I've lost my credit card and I'd like to cancel it.

C: Sorry, I'm afraid I'll have to put you through to another department for that … Please hold the line …

Language focus (SB page 86)

Aim: to draw students' attention to the items of functional language.

Tips:

- Make sure students have time to understand the form and meaning of the phrases, but you needn't translate them word for word.
- Students should be able to pronounce these phrases intelligibly, so drill them.

1 A	5 C
2 C	6 A
3 C	7 A
4 A	8 A

Speaking (SB page 86)

Aim: to allow students an opportunity to use this language in a meaningful, real-world context.

Tips:

- There is sometimes a choice of tasks. Any task involving reading a script will be easier than a task involving students making their own scripts. This gives you flexibility for mixed-ability classes.
- Give students time to prepare this activity, and circulate and monitor carefully.
- Correct sensitively, paying attention to the target language especially.
- If time allows, ask students to repeat the task, but with a new partner.

Global English

These lessons in *Global* have two main goals. The first is to give you and your students interesting information about English and language in general. The second goal is to provide students with practice in different kinds of reading comprehension tasks that they are likely to encounter in future study (for example, exams).

Warm up (SB page 87)

Aim: to engage students with the topic, and highlight potentially difficult vocabulary in the text.

Tips:

- be generous in helping students here with any unknown words in the first task.
- ask students to relate this task, wherever possible, to similar events or texts in their own lives. This will help them with the reading.

Reading (SB page 87)

Aim: to provide students with interesting information about English, and reading exam practice skills; where possible to focus on interesting or useful aspects of language in the text

Tips:

- Get students to read through the whole text once first before doing the tasks.
- Many of these texts have been graded slightly, or not at all. There is a glossary of difficult words. Get students to read that first as it will help them understand the rest.
- There are two tasks. The first is an easier task, often focusing on the gist of the passage. The second is a more difficult task, similar to reading exam questions.
- If there is a third question the purpose is to raise students' awareness about a language feature; do not expect them to produce it immediately.
- This language is not tested or reviewed in future units, which means you have more flexibility with this material as to when and where you use it.

1

1 T

2 F (They have so far had only limited appeal.)

3 T

2 In favour: efficient communication, simpler lingua franca than English, limited vocabulary and grammar

Against: vocabulary is too limited, doesn't solve communication problems which are not related to vocabulary

3

1 a

2 b

Speaking (SB page 87)

Aim: for students to relate the material in the reading to their own language, culture and experiences.

Tips:

- This is a short speaking activity and can be done in whole-class mode or in small groups.
- Wherever possible, ask students to think of and provide examples in their own language but explain them in English too.

As you go through these *Global English* lessons in the book, don't be afraid to ask students for opinions and reactions to the information in the text – not only answering the comprehension questions. Which do they find interesting? Do they know of similar experiences or facts in their own language or other languages? Some of your learners might be in your class because they are very interested in language, and these texts provide a great opportunity for you to capitalise on that motivation.

Writing: giving your opinion

These lessons in *Global* are designed to provide students with extended writing practice. They all follow a similar format.

Reading (SB page 88)

Aim: to provide a sample text for students to analyse.

Tips:

- Many of these texts deliberately contain errors which the students will be asked to focus on and correct later in the lesson.
- At this stage of the lesson merely ask them to read the text and extract the information.
- There are often two questions for these texts: one which focuses on gist and the other on specific details.
- If a student does ask a question about an error in form, praise them for noticing it, and explain that they will be correcting them shortly.

1 She agrees in general, although she thinks that it is a complex issue.

2 She makes these points: 2 (Most people are happy with small pleasures, like a walk in a park, a beautiful sunset or an evening with a friend.); 4 (I do not believe that money is the number one priority in life.); 5 (We need to learn to be satisfied with our lives, whether we are rich or poor.)

3 Students' own answers.

Writing skills: considering both sides of an argument (SB page 88)

Aim: to give students a chance to develop their writing through various different micro skills.

Tips:

- Sometimes this section focuses on common student errors in writing.
- Clearly explain the focus and do an example of one of the questions first with the students before asking them to continue on their own.
- Let students check their answers in pairs or small groups, then correct in open class.

1 I do not think: I disagree

I think: in my opinion / in my view

2

1 c

2 b

3 a

3

1 b

2 a

3 b

Preparing to write (SB page 88)

Aim: to give students time to brainstorm ideas for the writing task.

Tips:

- Allow students to brainstorm ideas in pairs or small groups.
- At low levels, this may involve some use of L1 (the students' mother tongue); be tolerant of this, but be on hand to help with translations or English where needed.
- Ask students to make notes here, but not begin writing.

Writing (SB page 88)

Aim: to give students practice in more extended writing tasks.

Tips:

- This section can be done as homework.
- Remind students to refer back to the model text, but to be careful of the typical errors.
- Ask students to check their work carefully before they hand it in.

Global review

These lessons in *Global* are designed to provide students with an opportunity to review and consolidate the language they have studied in the unit.

Grammar and Vocabulary (SB page 89)

Aim: to give students revision of all the main grammar and vocabulary points that arose in the unit.

Tips:

- Demonstrate the activities by doing the first one in whole class.
- Allow students time to do this, and encourage them to look back through the unit for help.
- When you come to correct this, do not simply go around the class asking for the right answer – encourage students to say *why* they think something is correct, and seek confirmation from others before moving on.

Grammar

1	1 was / were	4 who	6 had
	2 which / that / –	5 where	7 whose
	3 which / that		
2	1 **some** advice		
	4 new **furniture**		
	6 People **need**		
	2, 3 and 5 are correct		

Vocabulary

1	1 about / around	3 or so	
	2 pair of / couple of	4 about / around 30 / thirtyish	
2	1 financial	3 profitable	5 economic
	2 traders	4 interest	6 value
3	1 beauty	4 peace	7 justice
	2 respect	5 wealth	8 creativity
	3 morality	6 power	

Speaking (SB page 89)

Aim: to provide extra speaking practice that will review and consolidate language presented in the unit.

Tips:

- Give the students time to read and understand the instructions.
- Circulate and monitor the students, encouraging them to use only English here.
- Make notes of any incorrect use of language, but refrain from correcting if students are in the middle of the task.

Study skills

These lessons in *Global* are designed to provide students with skills and strategies in learner training and learner autonomy. For more on learner autonomy and learner training, see the essay on page xxiii.

Learning word families (SB page 89)

1 In pairs, students write down any words they can remember which are in the same family as the words in the box. Write students' words on the board, checking the meanings. Then ask them to read the tip. You could ask students to look up another word in their dictionaries and see how many related words are listed.

create: creative, creativity, creation
invest: investment, investor
produce: product, production, producer
safe: safety, safely, unsafe
weath: wealthy

2 Look at the dictionary extract with students. Direct students to the abbreviations used after each word and ask students what word class they stand for.

adj = adjective	n = noun
adv = adverb	v = verb

3 Ask students to look up the words in their dictionary and find the phonetic script for each word. Point out that /ˈ/ indicates which part of the word is stressed. Give students time to work out the pronunciation and practise saying the words with a partner. Then check pronunciation in whole-class feedback. Revise key phonetic symbols.

relate: /rɪˈleɪt/	relative: /ˈrelətɪv/
related: /rɪˈleɪtɪd/	relatively: /ˈrelətɪvlɪ/
relationship: /ˈrɪˈleɪʃənʃɪp/	unrelated: /ʌnrɪˈleɪtɪd/

4 Students complete the text using words from the word family in exercise 2. Check the answers with the class.

1 relationship	3 relatively
2 relatives / relations	4 unrelated

5 Direct students to the spidergram. They decide which word class each word belongs to and write the correct abbreviation next to it, using dictionaries if necessary. Check answers.

friend: n	friendship: n	friendliness: n
friendly: adj	unfriendly: adj	befriend: v

UNIT 8 # Lost & Found

Coursebook

Unit 8	Language	Texts	Communicative skills
Part 1 SB page 90	Grammar *would* Vocabulary Expressions with *lose* and *lost*	Reading *Life of Pi*	Speaking Describing a picture
Part 2 SB page 92	Grammar Second conditional	Reading *Lost in space* Listening Sending objects into space	Speaking A guessing game
Part 3 SB page 94	Vocabulary Expressions with *make* and *do* Extend your vocabulary With or without a plan Grammar Third conditional Pronunciation Expressing blame Intonation	Reading *Top five inventions and discoveries made by accident*	Writing How would your life have been different?
Part 4 SB page 96	Grammar Past modals of deduction Vocabulary Treasure	Reading and Speaking *Finding treasure* Listening Bulgaria's Thracian treasures	Speaking Speculating about treasures
Function globally SB page 98	Expressing sympathy Different kinds of difficult situations Roleplaying a conversation with a friend or colleague		
Global voices SB page 99	Listening to people talking about things they have lost or found Language for anecdotes		
Writing SB page 100	An essay Using discourse markers Expressing choices		
Global review SB page 101	Grammar and vocabulary review Extra speaking and writing practice		
Study skills SB page 101	Using your dictionary: learning fixed expressions		

Additional resources

eWorkbook	Interactive and printable grammar, vocabulary, listening and pronunciation practice Extra reading and writing practice Additional downloadable listening and audio material
Teacher's Resource Disc	Communication activity worksheets to print and photocopy
Go global: ideas for further research	**Lost** Ask students to find descriptions of the six books on the shortlist for the Man Booker prize this year and decide which one(s) you would or wouldn't like to read. **Found** Ask students to find a news article or watch a news video about treasure that has recently been found, and present it to the class.

Part 1

TEACH GLOBAL THINK LOCAL Lead-in

Books closed. Tell students they are going to be sent to a desert island for an unknown length of time. There is food and water on the island. Students can take a bag with five essential items of their choice. Ask students to make a list of the five items in their bag. Then put students in pairs and ask them to tell their partner about their items.

As a quicker alternative, you could ask students to decide on one item and share this in a group of five or six.

Speaking (SB page 90)

Background note

Pi Patel's family have a zoo in India. Pi grows up with the zoo animals and learns how to take care of them, control them and keep them content. The family decides to move to Canada and they set off on a boat with some of the zoo animals. But the boat sinks and Pi's family and most of the animals are drowned. Pi manages to get into a lifeboat with a tiger, a zebra, an orang-utan and a hyena. The animals fight and eat each other until only Pi and the tiger are left.

Pi catches fish and turtles to feed the tiger and uses his knowledge of animals to control it. Together they spend 227 days at sea until the boat reaches the coast of Mexico.

Tell students to look at the picture with the tiger. Model the pronunciation of *tiger*. Students work in pairs and follow the instructions for the task. In full class feedback, discuss students' ideas but don't give them any information about the book at this stage.

Reading (SB page 90)

1 Direct students to the information about the book and the author. Check students understand the words *shipwrecked* and *lifeboat*. Ask students how they think it is possible to spend 227 days in a boat with a hungry tiger.

Ask students to read the extract, using the glossary to help them, and find out what Pi, the boy in the boat, learns about himself.

Pi finds out that he has a strong will to live and that he will not give up.

2 Read out the lists of words. Students match them to make collocations from the text. Ask students to check their answers by scanning the text for the collocations and reading them in context. Check that students have understood the words.

1 c 2 d 3 a 4 b

3 Ask students to read the questions. Students read the text and answer the questions. Discuss the answers in full class feedback. Then give students the background to the situation in the boat (see *Background note*) and tell them how Pi managed to survive.

1 He felt anxious.
2 He thought of jumping overboard and swimming away.
3 He couldn't swim the long distance to land; he didn't know what he would eat and drink; he couldn't keep the sharks away; he couldn't keep warm; he didn't know which way to go.
4 He thought he was going to die.
5 He decided to survive and to work hard so that he would not die.

TEACH GLOBAL THINK LOCAL Reading extra

Tell students they are Pi. Ask them to write a paragraph in the first person explaining what happened when the boat reached the coast. Explain how they felt and what they did. Students compare paragraphs with a partner.

Grammar (SB page 91)

1 Direct students to the example sentences from the text and the rules about *would*. Students read the rules and choose the correct words to complete them. Check that students understand the word *hypothetical* (not real but possible in certain circumstances) – being in a boat with a tiger is a hypothetical situation for most of us. Ask students what they would do in this situation and elicit answers with *would*.

First rule: future (from the viewpoint of the speaker)
Second rule: unreal (hypothetical)

Discuss the other uses of *would* referred to in the rules. Elicit or give students examples:

advice: *I would do it if I were you.*

offers: *Would you like a drink?*

regular past actions: *When I was a child, I would often go to the zoo.*

polite requests: *I'd like two tickets, please.*

Language note

This use of *would* refers to a situation in the past that had not yet happened at the time of speaking, and so was in the future at that time. This is sometimes called the 'future in the past'.

2 Explain that *'d* is the 'contraction', the short form, of *would* and *had*. Ask students to decide if *'d* in sentences 1–7 is short for *would* or *had*. They rewrite the sentences without contractions.

1 I **had** never sat so close to a tiger before.
2 I **had** forgotten how big it was.
3 I wish my father were here; he **would** know what to do.
4 I **would** love to be back at home.
5 The tiger was quiet. He **had** eaten already that morning.
6 We **had** been at sea for some weeks.
7 I didn't want to sleep again; I was sure he **would** attack me.

3 Explain that the word *would* is missing from each conversation. Ask students to complete the conversations by adding *would* in the correct place. Point out that they should use contractions where possible. Ask them to compare and check their answers with a partner.

1 A: **Would** you like tea or coffee?
2 B: **Would** you like to sit down?
3 B: It **wouldn't** surprise me.
4 B: I'**d** get the bigger one.
5 B: Yes, we **would** walk there often when I was a child.

4 Ask students to look at the uses of *would* (a–d) and match them to conversations 1–5 in exercise 3.

a 4 b 1 c 5 d 3 e 2

Language note

The difference between an offer and a request can be unclear. In some situations, when we appear to be making an offer, we are actually asking someone to do something which is really a request or a polite instruction. In exercise 3 sentence 2, Speaker B is in a position of authority and the other person does not really have the option of saying no.

TEACH GLOBAL THINK LOCAL Extra activity

Outline the following situation to the class.

Your boss has requested a meeting with you. He tells you he is going to fire you from your job because you are always late for work. You know that your boss has been involved in some business dealings with a company that uses illegal workers because you received a copy of an email by mistake. You have the email as evidence. With this information you could blackmail your boss to get your job back.

What would you do in this situation? What would your decision depend on?

G Grammar focus

Refer students to the language summary on *would* on page 146.

You can use exercise 1 on page 147 for:

a) extra practice now
b) homework
c) review a couple of lessons from now.

The answers are on page 144 of the Teacher's Book.

Vocabulary (SB page 91)

1 Ask students to choose the best way to complete the explanations of expressions with *lose / lost*. Students should use dictionaries to help them. When students have completed the task, check that students have understood using concept questions, eg *When do people sometimes lose their mind for a short time? How do they feel? What might have caused this?; In what sort of situation might you have nothing to lose?*

In monolingual classes, discuss how these expressions are translated into your language. In multilingual classes, ask if these expressions can be translated in the students' language using one verb as in English *lose*.

1 a 2 b 3 b 4 a 5 b 6 a

2 Students work in pairs and choose one of the tasks. Ask students to feed back to the class.

Part 2

TEACH GLOBAL THINK LOCAL Lead-in

Write the following statements on the board.

I think spending money on exploring space is money well spent.

I think there is life on other planets.

If I had the opportunity, I would go into space.

Ask students to decide if they agree or disagree with the statements, or don't know. Then ask students to tell the class their answers and explain their reasons.

Reading (SB page 92)

1 Direct students to the picture of the round object on page 92. Students work in pairs and discuss what they think the object is, using the prompts given. Tell students that they have three guesses.

Students tell the class their ideas. Ask students to explain their ideas if appropriate but do not confirm or reject any of the guesses at this stage.

2 Ask students to read the text and the message in the information bubble and find out if their guesses were correct. Draw students' attention to the glossary to help them with the text. In class feedback, establish what the disc contained, where it was sent and who it was for.

The object is a phonographic disc that was included on the Voyager spacecraft in 1977. It contains sounds and images of life on Earth for life forms on other planets.

3 Students read the text again and explain the significance of the words and phrases in the list.

The disc is 12 inches in size.

President Carter was the American president who sent a message on the disc.

Carl Sagan organised the committee which collected the sounds, images and music.

It could take 40,000 years before Voyager is close to another planetary system.

The greetings on the disc are in 55 languages.

4 Ask students if they think the Voyager Golden Record is a good idea and to explain their reasons. They can do this first in pairs or groups and then in class feedback.

Listening (SB page 93)

1 **2.24** Direct students to the two questions. Play the recording. Students listen and choose the correct question.

They are answering question 2.

2.24

1 Me? I'd include a picture of a table. A big table covered in food.

2 If I could send something into space, I'd send a video of traffic. Lots of cars and how we are polluting our planet.

3 I'd include a photo of a group of people together … a group of people from different races. I'd include that if they asked me.

4 I would include the sound of a computer starting up – it's probably one of the most popular sounds on the planet now.

5 If I could put one song into space, it would be *Imagine* by John Lennon.

6 Some good photos of the planet Earth from space.

7 I'd include some images of accidents, like nuclear accidents, so that they don't think it's all good.

8 If I could send something into space, I'd send Einstein's famous formula.

9 I'd send my old red sock into space, so it can find the other one, which has been missing for years!

10 Art by Michelangelo and by Leonardo da Vinci. That's what I'd put.

11 If they asked me, I'd send a big note that says, 'Sorry, we made a mess of this world, can we come to yours?'

2 Play the recording again, pausing after each sentence to give students time to take notes. Students listen and note down the objects they hear. Then they work in pairs and compare their lists with their partner. In class feedback, ask students why the speakers said they would include these things or why you think they wanted to include them.

a big table covered in food

a video of traffic and lots of cars

a photo of a group of people of different races

the sound of a computer starting up

the song *Imagine* by John Lennon

photos of Earth from space

photos of nuclear accidents

Einstein's famous formula

one old red sock

art by Michelangelo and Leonardo da Vinci

a note which says we made a mess of our world

3 Ask students to tell their partner what they would send into space and why.

TEACH GLOBAL THINK LOCAL Alternative procedure

Instead of the pairwork in exercise 3, you could record your own class 'vox pops' of students explaining their ideas and opinions with a camcorder (or with a microphone and recording equipment). Ask students to prepare their answer, making notes if necessary, and then film each student in turn. Afterwards play the vox pops to the class.

Grammar (SB page 93)

1 Direct students to the examples sentences and the rules. Ask them to choose the correct words for the rules. Consolidate the rules by looking at the example sentences more carefully with students: look at the tenses in each clause and point out the use of the comma after the *if* clause.

First rule: unreal (hypothetical), future
Second rule: past
Third rule: main

2 Students make hypothetical sentences beginning with *If*. Remind them to use past simple in the *if* clause and *would* in the main clause. Do the first sentence together with students as an example.

1 If I could include a song, it would be *Imagine* by John Lennon.
2 If they asked me, I would send a big note that says *Sorry*.
3 If I could put something on the Voyager Golden Record, I would put a video of traffic.
4 If I had to include an image, it would be an image of a table covered in food.
5 If I could do anything, I would go on a space journey.

TEACH GLOBAL THINK LOCAL Mixed ability

For weaker students, prepare a version of the exercise with either the first clause or the second clause completed, so that students only focus on one pattern.

3 Before students do this exercise, point out that hypothetical sentences don't always start with the *if* clause: the main clause can sometimes come first, followed by the *if* clause. In this case there is no comma – as in questions 1, 5 and 6. Elicit again from students what tense is used in which clause.

Students complete the questions using the correct tense of the words in brackets.

1 How **would you feel** if **the teacher gave** you an exam tomorrow?
2 If **you could change** one thing about yourself, what **would you change?**
3 If **you didn't have** English class today, what **would you do?**
4 If **you won** a lot of money, what **would you buy** first?
5 What job **would you choose** if **you had** the chance to do any job in the world?
6 Where **would you go** if **you could visit** any country in the world?

4 Ask students to match answers a–f to the questions in exercise 3.

1 d 2 e 3 c 4 a 5 f 6 b

G Grammar focus

Refer students to the language summary on the second conditional on page 146.

You can use exercises 2 and 3 on page 147 for:

a) extra practice now
b) homework
c) review a couple of lessons from now.

The answers are on page 144 of the Teacher's Book.

Speaking (SB page 93)

1 Students work in small groups of four or five students. Ask students to turn to page 130 and follow the instructions.

One student in each group leaves the room. Then the rest of the group chooses one of the questions from the list on page 130. Each student thinks of an answer similar to those in exercise 4 on page 93: the answer should contain more than one word but not give the question away.

The student comes back into the group, listens to everybody's answers and has to guess the full question without looking at the list.

Groups repeat the activity with different students leaving the group.

Part 3

TEACH GLOBAL THINK LOCAL Lead-in

Brainstorm a list of important inventions and discoveries with the class. Then ask students to work in small groups and agree on their top five inventions, ranked from 1–5.

Groups feed back to the class, explaining their rankings.

Vocabulary (SB page 94)

Language note

Make usually means 'to create or produce' with emphasis on the result, not the action, eg *make a cake*.

Do usually means to carry out a specific action or activity, eg *do the dishes / the washing up*.

1 Explain that all the nouns are used with either the verb *make* or the verb *do*. Give the students general guidelines for using *make* or *do* (see *Language note* above). Ask students to decide if the words in the box go with *do* or *make*. Read out the words first to model pronunciation. Tell students to use dictionaries to help them. In feedback check that the meaning of all the phrases is clear.

make: decisions, a difference, a discovery, a mistake, progress, sense

do: an experiment, (somebody) a favour, a job, a test, nothing

2 Students complete the sentences with words from exercise 1. Point out that *make* or *do* is already given in each sentence to help them.

1 decisions
2 a favour
3 nothing
4 a job, a difference
5 sense

3 Students choose three sentences from exercise 2. Then students work in pairs and tell a partner if the sentences they have chosen are true for them. They should explain why they are true or why not.

TEACH GLOBAL THINK LOCAL Extra activity

Ask students to think of other words that go with *make* or *do*. Make a class list on the board and check that the meaning of all words is clear.

Ask students to work in pairs, pick three phrases from the lists and write a short story which includes all three words.

Alternatively, ask students to pick five phrases and make an exercise like exercise 1 for another pair. Two pairs then swap exercises.

Reading (SB page 94)

Background note

Many scientific discoveries and inventions have been made unexpectedly or through good luck. In many cases, accidental discoveries have happened while a scientist was looking for or experimenting with something else.

1 Refer students to the text on page 95. Clarify the title: explain or elicit that *by accident* doesn't mean literally that there was an accident but that it happened unexpectedly, without somebody planning to do this. Ask students to read the text quickly to find the main points. They should decide if they agree with the order of importance of the five discoveries and which discovery is most important in their life. Students then feed back to the class.

2 Ask students to read the text again in more detail and answer the questions.

1 sticky notes, cellophane
2 penicillin
3 penicillin, safety glass
4 sticky notes, cellophane
5 microwave oven
6 safety glass

TEACH GLOBAL THINK LOCAL Extra activity

Write this quote on the board from the French scientist Louis Pasteur:

'In the fields of observation, chance favours only the prepared mind.'

Discuss what this quote means. (The person who has discovered something accidentally must know the value of that information and how he or she can use it.)

Prompt students if necessary with these questions:

Can anybody make a scientific discovery totally by chance?

What sort of knowledge must the person who makes the discovery have?

What are the pre-conditions and requirements for a discovery such as the ones in the text?

Extend your vocabulary (SB page 94)

Direct students to the *Extend your vocabulary* box and ask them to read the explanations. Ask students the question and give them a moment's thinking time before they tell the class about their experiences.

Grammar (SB page 94)

Direct students to the first example sentence. Ask *Did Spencer invent the microwave?* (yes). Establish therefore that it is an unreal situation (modern eating habits are not different). Ask *Are we talking about past, present or future?* (past). Elicit the tense of the verb in the *if* clause (past perfect) and the form of the verb in the main clause (*might have* + past participle).

Ask students to read the rules to consolidate.

1 Students complete the sentences. Point out that different answers are possible but students should remember to use the correct form of the verb. In feedback, ask for different possible answers to each question.

1 he wouldn't have / might not have discovered penicillin.
2 hadn't been singing in church / hadn't lost his bookmarks in church.
3 wouldn't have discovered safety glass.
4 invented the microwave oven if a chocolate bar hadn't melted in his pocket / when he was testing a magnetron.
5 hadn't tried to make a tablecloth that didn't stain, he wouldn't have invented cellophane.

TEACH GLOBAL THINK LOCAL

Mixed ability

Exercise 1 is quite challenging. You could put weaker students in groups and give them the answers to exercise 1 on a worksheet as a list of jumbled clauses. They use these to complete the sentences. To make the exercise slightly more challenging, you could add one or two extra clauses.

2 Ask students to imagine how history would have been different without the inventions in the box. Direct them to the examples and ask them to write similar sentences about each of the inventions. Give them a sentence framework to work with:

If … hadn't been invented, … wouldn't have …

Then ask students to work in pairs and compare their ideas.

G Grammar focus

Refer students to the language summary on the third conditional on page 146.

You can use exercise 4 on page 147 for:

a) extra practice now
b) homework
c) review a couple of lessons from now.

The answers are on page 144 of the Teacher's Book.

Pronunciation (SB page 95)

1 2.25 Read out the situation in the box. Ask students who this person could be speaking to (to their husband, wife or partner; to a flatmate). Then direct students to the excuses in sentences 1 and 2. Ask them to listen to the sentences and note the pronunciation of *would have*: /ˈwʊdəv/ and *wouldn't have*: /ˈwʊdntəv/. Then ask students to listen and repeat.

2 Direct students to the list of situations. Ask students to work in pairs and choose three situations. They should write one or two sentences making excuses for each situation, similar to the excuses in exercise 1.

3 Students read their excuses to the class, paying attention to the pronunciation of *would have* and *wouldn't have*. The class decides who has the best excuse for each situation.

Pronunciation note

Ellison is a common feature of spoken English and weak vowels such as /ə/ may seem to disappear from contracted forms such as *would've* (/ˈwʊdəv/) and *wouldn't've* (/ˈwʊdntəv/). Students should be able to recognise this even if they do not use it themselves.

Writing (SB page 95)

1 Ask individual students to name a couple of important events in their life. Make a list on the board of useful phrases connected to the events they mention, eg:

My family moved house when I was 12.
I got married.
My son was born.
I was promoted.

Ask students to make a list of the important events in their lives. Circulate and help students with vocabulary.

2 Ask students to think what their lives would have been like if these things hadn't happened. Direct them to the example. Students write a paragraph describing how their life would have been different. When they have finished, ask them to swap their paragraph with a partner. Their partner should comment on what they read. Write some useful phrases on the board for students to do this, for example:

I didn't know you …
It's a good job you didn't …
It would have been a shame / pity if you had / hadn't …

To finish, you could ask students to edit their partner's work, focusing on the correct use of tenses.

Part 4

TEACH GLOBAL THINK LOCAL Lead-in

Write these newspaper headlines on the board. Ask students to work in pairs, choose one and write a short news story for a news report.

Rare treasure found in attic

Stolen paintings found in car

Gold jewellery found in field

Students should include:

- What was found? Where?
- Who found it? How?
- How did the items get there?

Ask students to read their stories to the class.

Reading and Speaking (SB page 96)

1 Direct students to the text. Students read it and answer the question. Make sure that students understand the word *buried*.

Ask students if they know what the law is regarding treasure in their country. If your students are from the same country, you could research this beforehand.

It depends on the law of the country. In some countries treasure belongs to the state. In some countries the finder can keep the treasure, and in some places treasure belongs to the landowner.

2 Direct students to the saying in the box and read it out, paying attention to the rhythm and rhyme. Elicit or explain that *weep* means 'cry'. Then ask students to work in pairs and answer the questions. In feedback, clarify the meaning of the saying, whether students agree with it and whether they have a similar saying in their language. If students express different attitudes about finding valuable items, then discuss these with the class.

The saying means that the person who finds something that belongs to somebody else should be allowed to keep it; it is just hard luck for the person who lost the item.

Listening (SB page 96)

Background note

The Thracians lived in present-day Bulgaria and parts of modern Greece, Romania, Macedonia and Turkey. They were warriors and horsemen who fought as allies of the Trojans against the Greeks in the Trojan War. They were also master goldsmiths.

There are thousands of burial mounds in Bulgaria and many have yet to be excavated by archaeologists. Unfortunately many have been excavated illegally and the treasures looted.

1 **2.26** Direct students to the three pictures of treasure and the information bubble. Ask students to read the information as background to the listening. Check that they understand the words *dug* and *archaeologist* (/ɑː(r)kɪˈɒlədʒɪst/).

Play the recording. Students listen and match the three treasure collections to the three pictures on page 96. They can note their answers after the numbers in the first row of the table in exercise 2.

1 b 2 c 3 a

2 Ask students to listen again for more details: when the treasure was found, how it was found and any other details about the treasure. Play the recording. Students listen again and complete the table. Pause after the information about each collection to give students time to complete their notes.

Play the recording a third time if necessary.

In feedback, establish what the three items in the photos are.

Collection 1

Year found: 1924

How found: two brothers were working in their field

Other details: 13 gold objects, cups, dishes, maybe used for religious purposes

Collection 2

Year found: 1949

How found: workers were digging for clay

Other details: gold tableware, four drinking cups shaped like animal heads; made third century BC, may have belonged to a Thracian king

Collection 3

Year found: 2004

How found: archaeologists noticed a woman in a shop wearing an old gold necklace; found by her husband in his field

Other details: 20,000 pieces of gold jewellery from 3000 BC, buried as offerings to the gods

2.26

Treasure collection 1

In 1924 two brothers found this treasure when they were working in their field. They found 13 gold objects: cups and dishes with lids and an object with three almond-shaped dishes. At first the farmers didn't know what they had found and tried to use them as farm tools. Present-day experts think that the objects could have been used for religious purposes.

Treasure collection 2

This treasure was found in 1949 when workers were digging to find clay. They discovered a set of gold tableware including four drinking cups shaped like the heads of animals. Archaeologists think that the set was made about the beginning of the third century BC and may have belonged to the Thracian king Seuthes III.

Treasure collection 3

This treasure was discovered in 2004. One day two archaeologists went into a shop and noticed a woman wearing an old gold necklace. Her husband, a farmer, had found it in his field. Over the next three years archaeologists found more than 20,000 pieces of gold jewellery including thousands of small gold rings. The jewellery dates back to the third millennium BC. It is thought that the Thracians must have buried the jewellery as offerings to the gods.

These are only some of the many collections of treasure which have been found in Bulgaria. Unfortunately today many of Bulgaria's valuable treasures are being taken illegally from archaeological sites. They are then taken out of the country or sold quietly to private collectors.

3 Ask students to read the questions and check that they understand them. Students work in pairs and discuss the questions. Students feed back to the class. Ask what important treasures have been found in their country and from what era.

Grammar (SB page 97)

Language note

Past modals of deduction (for example, *He might have gone home*) refer to 'unreal' situations – we don't know whether they happened or not. These shouldn't be confused with past modals which describe real situations, eg *I had to go home, I couldn't go home*.

Look at the first example sentence with the class. Ask *Were the objects used for religious purposes?* (archaeologists don't know but think it's possible). Then look at the second example. Remind students that the jewellery was buried in a field. Ask *Was it buried as an offering to the gods?* (archaeologists believe it was). Explain that these forms are called 'past modals of deduction' and are used to make guesses about the past. Establish how these past modals are formed.

Ask students to read the rules.

1 Direct students to the text about the Winchester hoard and read out the first sentence. Clarify the meaning of *metal detector*. Ask students to read the rest of the text and complete it using the correct modal verbs. Point out that they should use the context (the information in other parts of the text) to help them choose the correct verb.

Answers are numbered in the order they appear in the text.

1 must have buried
2 might have been
3 must have worn
4 may have belonged

2 Ask students to rewrite the conversations using past modals so that the meaning stays the same. Do the first sentence as an example with students if necessary.

1 They must have belonged to the man who used to live here.
He might / may / could have wanted to hide them.
2 It can't have been cheap.
It must have been for special occasions.
3 My mum must have bought this vase in China.
She might / may not have bought it there.

G Grammar focus

Refer students to the language summary on past modals of deduction on page 146.

You can use exercise 5 on page 147 for:

a) extra practice now
b) homework
c) review a couple of lessons from now.

The answers are on page 144 of the Teacher's Book.

Vocabulary (SB page 97)

1 Read out the words in the box and drill the pronunciation. Check that they understand the headings for the categories. Ask students, in pairs, or on their own, to put the words in the correct category. Point out they can use a dictionary if necessary. Check the answers.

Jewellery: bracelet, brooch, chain, necklace
Containers: bowl, chest, jug, vase
Precious metals and jewels: diamond, gold, platinum, silver

2 Ask students to name the objects for the definitions. You can do this orally, explaining any difficult words (*rectangular, wrist, liquid, pin*) with gestures or examples. Ask questions about jewellery people in the class are wearing: *Is anybody wearing a necklace / bracelet? Is it gold / silver?, etc.*

rectangular container: chest
colourless stone: diamond
jewellery worn on wrist: bracelet
container for liquids: jug
grey metal: platinum
jewellery with pin: brooch

TEACH GLOBAL THINK LOCAL

Extra activity

Students think of definitions for the other things in the table. Then they work in pairs and tell their partner their definition. Their partner says the right word.

Speaking (SB page 97)

Background note

All the objects shown on the right of the page can be found in the British Museum. They were all found as treasure.

1 Refer students to the six pictures at the right of the page. Tell students they are going to speculate about the function of these objects. Draw their attention to the *Useful phrases*. Students work in pairs and discuss the objects.

2 Ask students to feed back their ideas to the class. Then ask them to turn to page 131 and check their ideas.

For answers see SB page 131.

Function globally: expressing sympaty

These lessons in *Global* are designed to provide students with immediately useful functional language. They all follow a similar format.

Warm up (SB page 98)

Aim: to introduce the topic via a quick speaking task or picture work.

Tips:

- Do not over-correct here, especially in speaking activities.
- Encourage students to use what language they can at this stage.

Listening (SB page 98)

Aim: to present the functional language in context via a conversation or series of conversations.

Tips:

- Ask students to read the exercises first before listening.
- Play the recording all the way through for each task (there are always two tasks).
- For multiple conversations pause the recording after each one.
- If students find it very difficult, play the recording a final time and allow them to read the audioscript at the back of the book.

1	1 picture b	2 picture a
2	Conversation 1: 3	Conversation 2: 3
3	Conversation 1: the other person tries to cheer him up	
	Conversation 2: the other person expresses sympathy	

2.27–2.28

Conversation 1

A: What's the matter? Are you all right?

B: Yes, fine. My computer's just crashed again.

A: Oh, that's a pain. That's always happening to me.

B: It's just so annoying … I've lost an hour's work.

A: Well, come on, cheer up, it's Friday. Why don't we go for a drink after work?

B: Um … why not? Thanks. I'll ring computer support now. Perhaps they can find my document.

Conversation 2

A: What's wrong?

B: I've just had a phone call from my sister-in-law. My brother has just been taken to hospital.

A: Oh, no. I'm really sorry to hear that. What happened?

B: He was in a car accident on the motorway. Luckily they think he'll be all right.

A: Oh, that's good. It must have been a terrible shock. Look, can I make you a cup of coffee? Or perhaps you should go home?

B: No, I'm fine now. A coffee would be good – thanks.

A: OK, I won't be a minute.

Language focus (SB page 98)

Aim: to draw students' attention to the items of functional language.

Tips:

- Make sure students have time to understand the form and meaning of the phrases, but you needn't translate them word for word.
- Students should be able to pronounce these phrases intelligibly, so drill them.

1 a, e, g
2 c, d
3 b, h
4 f

Speaking (SB page 98)

Aim: to allow students an opportunity to use this language in a meaningful, real-world context.

Tips:

- There is sometimes a choice of tasks. Any task involving reading a script will be easier than a task involving students making their own scripts. This gives you flexibility for mixed-ability classes.
- Give students time to prepare this activity, and circulate and monitor carefully.
- Correct sensitively, paying attention to the target language especially.
- If time allows, ask students to repeat the task, but with a new partner.

Global voices

These lessons in *Global* are designed to provide students with exposure to authentic speakers of English from both native and non-native English backgrounds. They all follow a similar format.

Warm up (SB page 99)

Aim: to introduce the topic and highlight potentially difficult vocabulary the students will encounter.

Tips:

- Be generous in helping students with the vocabulary here, but let them try to work it out first.
- Circulate and monitor any speaking task, but be careful not to over-correct.
- Follow up any short discussion pairwork with an open class discussion, asking students to report back what they said.

Listening (SB page 99)

Aim: to expose students to English spoken with a variety of accents.

Tips:

- Students will need to hear the recording at least twice, if not more times, to understand it. There are almost always two tasks.
- The first time they listen, tell them you don't expect them to understand every word; some of it will be hard. This is because the text has not been scripted or graded in any way. It's what they would hear in 'the real world'.
- The first task is easier and focuses on gist, the second task is more detailed.
- Pause after each speaker on the second listening, and don't be afraid to replay the whole thing if students appear to need it.
- Students can read the audioscript at the back of the book if you / they wish.
- It may be tempting to hunt for specific pronunciation or language errors, but we recommend against this. In real-world communication not everyone speaks perfect English all the time, not even native speakers.

1

Speaker	Item	Lost or found?
1 Christina	ring	found
2 Muneer	wallet (with money)	found
3 Dotrothy	diamond	lost
4 Richard	money	lost
5 Leslie	bracelet	lost

2

1 Muneer 2 Dorothy 3 Richard
4 Leslie 5 Christina

2.29–2.33

Christina, Germany

So one evening I went out with my friends and suddenly I saw something blinking on the ground and I was looking after it, but I first thought it's like the head of a beer bottle, um, but it was a ring, a finger ring with many stones on it.

Muneer, Saudi Arabia

Actually I – I still remember when I was a child I found, in my country of course, I found an amount of money, a big amount of money inside a wallet and it was in the street and I got it and took it to my mom and told her about it. She said that we shouldn't take something which doesn't belong to us, and yeah, we told … er we got it to the police and they found the owner of this money.

Dorothy, Scotland

It was my very last day at work before I left to have a family. When I got home that evening I discovered that a ring which was very precious to me had lost its stone. I went back to the office to look for it but to this day I was never able to find the stone. I still have the setting for it. One day perhaps someone will buy me a diamond.

Richard, England

I regularly lose money out my back pocket which is usually sort of £10, £20 in one hit … and I usually only find about 2p or 5p on the floor. That's all I ever find I'm afraid.

Leslie, Switzerland

Hmm, I think the most valuable thing I have ever lost was, uh, a bracelet and yeah, it was out of silver and I lost it when I was in Disneyland with my friends in Paris and it was absolutely impossible to find it again.

Language focus: language for anecdotes (SB page 99)

Aim: to raise students' awareness of a particular piece of language present in the listening.

Tips:

- This language is not included in unit tests or reviews; it is included here to help students understand international English.
- The objective is awareness-raising, not production. Don't expect students to produce this language in an exercise or in conversation immediately.

2.34

1

1 one evening
2 suddenly
3 first
4 It was my very last day
5 before
6 When I got home
7 to this day

2

1 one evening; it was …
2 suddenly
3 to this day
4 when I got home

Speaking (SB page 99)

Aim: for students to discuss the same or similar questions as the speakers in the listening.

Tips:

- The speaking tasks here are slightly more open to allow for students to explore the subject. Give them time to do this.
- If students are working in pairs, circulate and monitor. Make notes of incorrect language use to correct afterwards (or in a future class).
- As you go through the book and the *Global voices* lessons, ask students for feedback on these listening activities and their potential use of English with other people. Are they very difficult? Have students used their English as a 'lingua franca' with other non-native English speakers? How did they find it? What tips do they have on understanding or making themselves understood in an international context?

Writing: an essay

These lessons in *Global* are designed to provide students with extended writing practice. They all follow a similar format.

Reading (SB page 100)

Aim: to provide a sample text for students to analyse.

Tips:

- Many of these texts deliberately contain errors which the students will be asked to focus on and correct later in the lesson.
- At this stage of the lesson merely ask them to read the text and extract the information.
- There are often two questions for these texts: one which focuses on gist and the other on specific details.
- If a student does ask a question about an error in form, praise them for noticing it, and explain that they will be correcting them shortly.

1 Some small, personal items, a diary of her personal life and a first-generation computer.

2 find out about how people lived in the past; remember their grandmother; gain wisdom; understand what sort of person she was; take care of their possessions

3 Students' own answers.

Writing skills: using discourse markers (SB page 100)

Aim: to give students a chance to develop their writing through various different micro skills.

Tips:

- Sometimes this section focuses on common student errors in writing.
- Clearly explain the focus and do an example of one of the questions first with the students before asking them to continue on their own.
- Let students check their answers in pairs or small groups, then correct in open class.

1

1 However
2 First of all
3 For this reason
4 For example
5 in this way
6 Secondly
7 such as
8 Moreover

2

Example: for example, such as
Result/Consequences: for this reason, in this way
First point: firstly
Additional point: secondly, moreover
Contrast: however

3

Possible answers

1 they would learn more about their family history.
2 I'd put them in a photo album.
3 it might also be valuable one day.
4 I might put in an old newspaper.
5 they might learn how to use it.

Preparing to write (SB page 100)

Aim: to give students time to brainstorm ideas for the writing task.

Tips:

- Allow students to brainstorm ideas in pairs or small groups.
- At low levels, this may involve some use of L1 (the students' mother tongue); be tolerant of this, but be on hand to help with translations or English where needed.
- Ask students to make notes here, but not begin writing.

Writing (SB page 100)

Aim: to give students practice in more extended writing tasks.

Tips:

- This section can be done as homework.
- Remind students to refer back to the model text, but to be careful of the typical errors.
- Ask students to check their work carefully before they hand it in.

Global review

These lessons in *Global* are designed to provide students with an opportunity to review and consolidate the language they have studied in the unit.

Grammar and Vocabulary (SB page 101)

Aim: to give students revision of all the main grammar and vocabulary points that arose in the unit.

Tips:

- Demonstrate the activities by doing the first one in whole class.
- Allow students time to do this, and encourage them to look back through the unit for help.
- When you come to correct this, do not simply go around the class asking for the right answer – encourage students to say *why* they think something is correct, and seek confirmation from others before moving on.

Grammar

1 would you do, had
2 could go, would travel
3 had known, would have handed
4 wouldn't have lost, hadn't crashed
5 must have done
6 might / must

Vocabulary

1 chest: the others are jewellery
2 desperately: the others have the same meaning
3 jug: the others are metals
4 successfully: the others have the same meaning
5 a decision: the others are used with *do*
6 nothing: the others are used with *make*
7 fault: the others make collocations with *lose*

Speaking and Writing (SB page 101)

Aim: to provide extra speaking practice that will review and consolidate language presented in the unit.

Tips:

- Give the students time to read and understand the instructions.
- Circulate and monitor the students, encourageing them to use only English here.
- Make notes of any incorrect use of language, but refrain from correcting if students are in the middle of the task.

Study skills

These lessons in *Global* are designed to provide students with skills and strategies in learner training and learner autonomy. For more on learner autonomy and learner training, see the essay on page xxiii.

Using your dictionary: learning fixed expressions (SB page 101)

Direct students to the explanation about fixed expressions. Ask them if they know the meaning of the expressions mentioned.

1 Ask students to read the sentence and choose the best meaning for the expression in bold. Remind them to use the context for help. Ask students why they chose their answer but don't correct at this stage.

a had the right idea

2 Students read the dictionary entry and check their answer.

3 Ask students to work in pairs and decide what the sentences in bold mean. Ask students for their ideas. Then establish what the keyword in each sentence is (*jump*) and ask students to check their ideas in their dictionary. Review the answers in whole-class feedback.

1 make a decision about something too quickly without knowing all the facts
2 to take an opportunity that is offered to you in a very enthusiastic way
3 to move in front of people who have been waiting for longer than you have

4 Ask students to look at the sentences carefully and choose the correct word to compete the sentences. Tell them to consider which words would be more logical and why. Ask them for their answers and their ideas about what the expression means. Then ask them to check their ideas in their dictionaries. In feedback, check the correct meanings. Then refer students to the study tips at the end of the page.

1 in the same **boat**: in the same difficult or unpleasant situation
2 feel like a **fish** out of water: be in a situation that you know nothing about or are not used to

UNIT 9 # Love & Hate

Coursebook

Unit 9	Language	Texts	Communicative skills
Part 1 SB page 102	Vocabulary and Pronunciation Stereotypes Grammar Verbs followed by *-ing* and infinitive with *to*	Listening The relationship between the English and the French	Speaking English and French satirical images
Part 2 SB page 104	Grammar Comparatives and superlatives Extend your vocabulary *I mean* Vocabulary Love	Reading and Speaking *A Short History of Tractors in Ukrainian*	
Part 3 SB page 106	Pronunciation Word stress and meaning Grammar Verbs followed by prepositions	Reading *Room 101*	Speaking Categories
Part 4 SB page 108		Listening and Speaking Sports Reading *Classic sporting rivalries*	Writing Expanding sentences
Function globally SB page 110	Giving and accepting compliments Listening to conversations in social situations Roleplaying a conversaton at a party		
Global English SB page 111	Strong language Identifying and correcting 'bad' English Discussing language change		
Writing SB page 112	An informal email Using dashes Expressing affection and enthusiasm		
Global review SB page 113	Grammar and vocabulary review Extra speaking and writing practice		
Study skills SB page 113	Improving your listening skills		

Additional resources

eWorkbook	Interactive and printable grammar, vocabulary, listening and pronunciation practice Extra reading and writing practice Additional downloadable listening and audio material
Teacher's Resource Disc	Communication activity worksheets to print and photocopy
Go global: ideas for further research	**Love** Ask students to look for the website of the Fitzwilliam Museum in Cambridge and find out more about the paintings to discuss in class. **Hate** Ask students to find out about three unusal phobias and report on them to the class.

Part 1

TEACH GLOBAL THINK LOCAL **Lead-in**

Divide the board into two columns. On one side write English, and on the other side write French. Ask students to think of things that they see as 'typically English' or 'typically French', as seen from their culture. Elicit examples and fill the board. Then begin with *Speaking* exercise 1.

Speaking (SB page 102)

1 Pairwork. Ask students to compare and contrast the two paintings. Remind them of useful language on how to do this (from Unit 4 *Friends & Strangers* Part 1), eg *In this picture … whereas in this one …*

Circulate and monitor. Remember that this task is similar to those in many international English exams, so if your students are thinking of taking one of these then give feedback at the end on common problems or particularly good examples of English that you heard.

2 Ask students to read the bubble containing information about where these two paintings were shown. Clarify the meaning of *satirical* (using humour to criticise people or things and make them seem silly) and *prints* (in this text, a picture that is a copy of a painting). Students then answer the two questions.

Background note

Vive la Différence was an art exhibition at the Fitzwilliam Museum in Cambridge in 2007. It displayed prints from the years 1720–1815, a time when there was a lot of travel and cross-cultural influence between the two countries but also a time when they were enemies. The Fitzwilliam Museum website provides additional background information to the exhibition.

Possible answers

In the first picture, stereotypes could be:

French women have silly hairstyles (in fact French women of the time did wear their hair tall).

French women are too concerned with their appearance.

In the second picture, stereotypes could be:

The English are fat.

The English do not dress very well.

The English are stiff and uncomfortable.

You could say of these pictures that the French and the English appear to be friendly, but are actually very critical of each other.

Vocabulary and Pronunciation (SB page 102)

1 Reproduce the first three rows of the table on the board and write the title *Stereotypes* above it. Do the first example with the class, clarifying what *assume* and *assumption* mean (if you *assume* something, you believe it is true, even though you have no proof; an *assumption* is something you believe is true even though you have no proof). Elicit the next line of the table. Students then continue completing the table themselves, using a dictionary if necessary.

Noun	Verb	Adjective
assumption	assume	–
generalisation	generalise	general
judgement	judge	judgemental
misconception	misconceive	–
satire	satirise	satirical
stereotype	stereotype	stereotypical
tolerance	tolerate	tolerant

2 2.35 Now play the recording to let students check their answers. Go over the spelling of the words by inviting students to come up and complete the table on the board. Play the recording a second time, asking students to listen and determine which is the stressed syllable (underlined in table above). Students then listen a third time and repeat the words.

3 Students now complete the sentences with the words in the box. Stress that they do not have to change the form of the words; they are all in the correct form. Feed back on the answers by asking different students to read them out loud. Correct any errors of pronunciation with the target words.

1 satirical
2 assume
3 stereotypical
4 misconception
5 generalise
6 judge
7 tolerate

4 Ask students to read the sentences again. Which ones do they agree with? Ask them to tick the sentences they agree with, put a cross next to the sentences they don't agree with and put a question mark next to sentences they are not sure about. They then compare answers with a partner.

Listening (SB page 103)

This is part of a lecture about the relationship between the English and the French.

1 2.36 Ask students to read the introduction to the lecture first. Explain that 'The Sweet Enemy' was a term sometimes used by the English in the past to refer to the French (and vice versa). Concept-check the phrase *the relationship … has been hot and cold* by asking *Does this mean it has been good, bad or a bit of both?* Students then listen and put the topics in order.

Correct order

b 1066 Norman conquest of England

e Allies and enemies in wars

a English borrows words from French

f French borrows words from English

d Both make fun of each other's cooking

c More love than hate

2 After checking the answers to exercise 1, tell students to look at the sentences in exercise 2. Explain that each one contains a factual error. Ask students to try to correct the errors from memory first. Then play the recording again for them to check their answers.

1 After the Norman conquest, **England** was ruled by **France**.

2 France and England were **allies / friends** in the 20th century.

3 The English use French words from cooking, **music** and the arts.

4 The French use English words from food, **technology** and pop culture.

5 The French make jokes that English cooking is **boring** and **bland**.

6 The English make jokes that French cooking is **inedible**.

2.36

The date 1066 is a very well-known year for English people. It is the year that the Normans, under William the Conqueror, invaded and managed to conquer England. For several decades, England was ruled by the French.

Since then the English and French have fought in many wars. They were enemies in the 14th, 18th and 19th centuries. But they were also allies in the Crimean War in the 19th century, in both World Wars of the 20th century and in recent conflicts. The French and English military continue serving together in the United Nations.

In terms of language, each country has borrowed many words from the other. The English use French words such as *chef*, *café* or *fiancé*, as well as others from cooking, music or the arts. And contemporary French uses words like *weekend*, *hotdog*, *hamburger* and *parking*, as well as other modern English expressions from technology and pop culture.

Both countries enjoy making fun of the other's food. For the French, English cooking is boring and bland. The English have a higher opinion of French cooking but many English people still like to make jokes that French food is inedible (for example, snails or frogs' legs).

Despite this, the relationship between the two countries today is a good one. French is still among the most popular foreign languages for English students to learn, and English is the most common foreign language studied in France. 200 years. It is thought that there are more than 300,000 French people living in Britain, and more than 600,000 British people living in France. While the French still call the English 'rosbif' and the English call the French 'frogs' the realities of today's Europe mean that there will probably be more love than hate between the two countries in years to come.

Background note

Although English people tend to see the Norman conquest as the first battle between the English and the French, in reality the two groups of peoples were quite ethnically diverse. Both the Norman and the English leaders had Viking heritage, and the localpopulations also included peoples from Saxon, Frankish, Gallic and Briton tribes.

3 Students work in small groups. Ask them to choose two of the questions to discuss in the group. Assign each group a group leader, who will report back on the answers. Circulate and monitor. Feed back on the answers.

TEACH GLOBAL THINK LOCAL Mixed ability

If you are working with a mixed-ability class, give each group a particular goal for the speaking activity, eg that every student must contribute two ideas. This means that stronger students do not automatically dominate the whole discussion, and weaker students have an achievable goal. Provide support as well, perhaps by writing the following sentence stems on the board:

Personally, I think that …

I honestly believe that …

As for me, I believe / think / agree that …

Grammar (SB page 103)

Write the sample sentences on the board. Ask students to work in pairs. One student copies down the sample sentences while the other consults the rules in the book. Then the student with the book open quizzes the other student, using the rules given. This could be as simple as reading out part of the rule and prompting the other student to finish it.

1 Students rewrite the sentences using the word given. Do the first one as an example.

1	I've decided to go to France.
2	I expect to have a better life there.
3	I enjoy eating French food.
4	I began learning French last year.
5	I managed to pass my first exam.
6	Do you fancy coming with me?
7	I can't afford to go.

2 Ask students to read the text through first before completing the gaps. Ask *Why do French people go to live in England and English people go to live in France?* Then students complete with the correct form of the verb.

Answers are numbered in the order they appear in the text.

1	to live
2	to go
3	to live
4	moving

G Grammar focus

Refer students to the language summary on verbs followed by *-ing* and infinitive with *to* on page 148.

You can use exercises 1 and 2 on page 149 for:

a) extra practice now

b) homework

c) review a couple of lessons from now.

The answers are on page 144 of the Teacher's Book.

TEACH GLOBAL THINK LOCAL Homework extra

Depending on the country you live in, you could ask the students to write a short composition about relations between their home and a neighbouring country. If you are teaching in a country where relations with neighbours are very strained then perhaps you may not want to do this!

Part 2

TEACH GLOBAL THINK LOCAL Lead-in

Before the class, find some proverbs about love that exist in your students' language (this works better in monolingual classes but can also be done in a multilingual class). Write these on the board, leaving out the last word or words. For example, the proverbs from Speaking exercise 1 would look like this:

Love is …   *Love knows no …*   *All's fair in love and …*

Ask students to finish the proverbs off in their own language, then explain / translate them in English.

Reading and Speaking (SB page 104)

The text is an extract from the novel *A Short History of Tractors in Ukrainian* by Mariana Lewycka. It is the opening page of the novel, which focuses on the relationship between a woman, her father and his new bride-to-be who is a much younger woman.

1 **2.37** Students read the English sayings and decide if there are any similar ones in their language. Ask them if they agree with the sayings.

2 Pre-teach the following words which are key to understanding the text: *bonkers* (crazy), *indulgent* (allowing someone what they want), *outraged* (very angry), *bourgeois* (typical of middle-class people and their attitudes, a disapproving word for this). Students then read and listen to the text. Ask them to choose two adjectives which they think best describe the narrator's feelings. Explain *astonished* and *delighted* if necessary.

1	Nadezhda's father is getting married again only two years after his wife's death, to a much younger woman.
2	The 'correct' answers are *astonished* and *angry*. However, if students can give you good reasons for one or the other adjectives then accept these!

3 Now ask the students to read the text more carefully to answer the questions. Tell them they should underline or otherwise mark the part of the text that gave them the answer.

1	a	*Please let it be a joke!*
2	c	*The traitor! And our mother barely two years dead.*
3	c	*'After marriage you can meet.'*
4	a	*It seems very sudden.*
5	b	*'Why you want to meet? You not marrying her.' / (He pronounces* [what] *'vat'.)*

4 Ask students to discuss the questions in pairs. To help give this a more specific focus, ask them to make notes of their answers. Circulate, monitor and do whole-class feedback.

Background note

Monica Lewycka is a Ukrainian born in Germany and brought up in England. *A Short History of Tractors in Ukrainian* was her first book. The book centres on the old man's obsession with the younger woman and how this affects the rest of the family. Critics have said that Lewycka has the unique ability to observe life in Britain both from the position of an insider and an outsider.

TEACH GLOBAL THINK LOCAL

Reading extra

Ask students to close their books. Tell them you are going to read aloud the text, but you will pause at certain places. They have to chant the missing word. Then continue reading.

Pause at places where few answers are possible linguistically, or only one, eg:

My father's voice, quavery with excitement, crackles down the ... (pause, class chants LINE).

I remember the rush of blood to my ... (pause, class chants HEAD).

This is good practice for collocations or word chunks.

Grammar (SB page 104)

1 Ask students to answer the questions in small groups. Allow them some time to read the sample sentences and think of the rules. They should try to brainstorm together answers to as many of the questions as possible. Ask students from each group to come up to the board and explain different rules for the use of comparatives. Tell them to check their answers with the full grammar rules in the *Grammar focus* section on page 148.

2 Write the five adjectives on the board and check that students understand what they mean. Elicit a sentence using one of those adjectives to compare Valentina and the father, eg *She is younger than him.*

Try to push students to say this in other ways, using the same adjective, eg *He isn't as young as her. She's much younger than him.* Then ask students to make as many different sentences as they can using the other adjectives. Give them a time limit, then ask students to write their answers on the board.

G Grammar focus

Refer students to the language summary on comparatives and superlatives on page 148.

You can use exercises 3 and 4 on page 149 for:

a) extra practice now

b) homework

c) review a couple of lessons from now.

The answers are on page 144 of the Teacher's Book.

Extend your vocabulary (SB page 105)

Go through the explanation and the example sentence. Check if students have a similar expression (it may be a different word or words) in their language. The words *I mean* are also very useful for learners to buy time and reformulate something when they are speaking! Students then complete the sentences with their own ideas.

Vocabulary (SB page 105)

1 Tell students that the words below are all phrases or parts of phrases to talk about liking or loving someone. Ask them to complete the sentences, using a dictionary to help them.

1 fancies
2 keen
3 fond
4 adores
5 spot
6 crazy

2 2.38 Play the recording for students to listen and check their answers. Clarify the difference between to *like* someone, to *fancy* someone (to feel attracted physically to him / her) and to *adore* someone (to love him / her very much).

3 This activity is best done if you do an example first with the students. Write four sentences on the board using the target language, three of which are true and one of which is false. Ask students to guess which one is the false sentence. They should do this by asking you questions first about all four sentences.

Students then write their own sentences.

4 Pairwork. Students read each other their sentences and ask questions to guess the false ones. Circulate and monitor. Feed back by asking one or two students to read their sentences to the whole class for the other students to guess.

Part 3

TEACH GLOBAL THINK LOCAL Lead-in

Before the lesson, think of a personal anecdote about you (or a close friend) and an encounter with an animal or insect you are or were particularly afraid of. This could be a scary dog, a horse, a snake, a spider or a rat. The story should be quite short. Tell your story, and then ask students to retell it to each other in pairs. Ask them if they have any similar stories.

Pronunciation (SB page 106)

1 **2.39** Write the target sentence on the board and ask the class to read it chorally, then drill individuals. Explain that you are going to play a recording of the sentence said five times by five different people. Each person will stress a different word, giving a different meaning to the sentence. Students must first listen and write the word they hear most stressed each time.

1 I **hated** rats when I was a child.
2 I hated **rats** when I was a child.
3 I hated rats when **I** was a child.
4 I hated rats when I was a **child**.
5 **I** hated rats when I was a child.

2 Play the recording again, pausing after the first one. Repeat the sentence again yourself. Ask students to read through the possible meanings and choose the one they think matches the intonation.

a 5 b 1 c 4 d 3 e 2

Language note

This is not easy, especially if students have a very different intonation to English! They may need to hear the sentences several times, both on the listening and through teacher models. However, the main stress in a sentence - the 'tonal unit' – is quite important to conveying meaning as English word order is relatively fixed (ie you can't stress something simply by putting it first).

3 Now students practise in pairs. One says the sentence in different ways and the other guesses the meaning. Circulate and monitor, helping where needed. This might even be harder for students to produce accurately from the first attempt, so don't expect miracles!

Reading (SB page 106)

The text is an extract from George Orwell's *1984* and an explanation of the history and cultural significance of Room 101.

1 **2.40** Ask students to close their books. Play the recording so they can listen to the extract from *1984* (the first part of the text). Pause after … *happens to be rats*. Ask students to work in pairs and say what they think this text is about. Then let students open their books, play the recording again and let them read and listen all the way through.

The room is a place where everyone has to confront the thing they hate or are afraid of most in the world.

2 Ask students to read the second part of the text again more carefully and answer the questions. Check that students understand *BBC* (British Broadcasting Corporation, the public service broadcaster in the UK).

1 rats
2 in the Ministry of Love, the headquarters of the secret police
3 an office in the BBC
4 Erich Mielke, the head of the Stasi
5 contestants say what things annoy them the most and that they would put in Room 101

3 Ask students if they have heard of this room before. Ask them to think of what they would put in the room and write it down on a piece of paper. Students then share what they wrote in small groups. Elicit some of the most interesting answers in open class.

Background note

George Orwell's *Nineteen Eighty-Four*, often written *1984*, is one of the most famous political novels of the 20th century. It is the story of Winston Smith, a government worker who defies the law by falling in love and trying to join the resistance. He is finally captured and brought to Room 101 where he is tortured until he gives in. The cultural impact of *Nineteen Eighty-Four* is significant and includes such terms as *Room 101*, *Big Brother*, *doublethink* and *Thought Police* which are commonly used in describing contemporary totalitarian regimes.

Grammar (SB page 106)

1 Learning verbs and their dependent prepositions is as much about getting a sense for the language as memorising them. When they try to do this exercise, tell students to refer to the text for help, or to think of sentences with the verbs in them.

on: depend, rely, spy
of: dream, know (less common), remind somebody, taste
in: believe, succeed
for: apologise, apply, wait
about: dream, know (more common), talk
at: shout, stare

Language note

Some of these verbs and prepositions are more fixed than others. The verb *talk*, for example, can be used with *about* (*we talked about the weather*), with *for* (*we talked for hours*) and with *at* (*he didn't listen, he just talked at us*). The majority of the verbs presented are fixed with that particular preposition. Where there are other possibilities for this level, we have included the most common uses.

To remind somebody of something/someone has two similar meanings. It can mean 'to make someone remember something in the past' (*he reminded me of my promise*) or it can mean 'to make someone think of someone else because they are very similar' (*she reminds me of that actress on television*).

2 Ask students to read the comments about what other people would put in Room 101. Tell them to tick the ones they think are funny or interesting. Feed back on this. Then tell them to put the missing prepositions into each sentence.

1 rely on
2 apologises for
3 talk about
4 shout at
5 dream about
6 believe in
7 stare at
8 spies on
9 applied for
10 taste of

G Grammar focus

Refer students to the language summary on verbs followed by prepositions on page 148.

You can use exercises 5 and 6 on page 149 for:

a) extra practice now

b) homework

c) review a couple of lessons from now.

The answers are on page 144 of the Teacher's Book.

Speaking (SB page 107)

1 Ask students to read the categories in the list and choose five of them. They should write a brief answer for each one they choose, without writing what the category is. Give them time for this. While they are working, do the same yourself for two or three categories.

2 It's best to demonstrate the activity by doing it. Write your own answers up on the board. Ask a student to guess what category they come from. Help them with the question (see the example). When students guess the category encourage them to ask *Why?* and give an answer.

In pairs, students then do the same with the answers they wrote down. Feed back by asking one or two students to perform their dialogues aloud.

TEACH GLOBAL THINK LOCAL
Homework extra

Ask students to find out more about George Orwell and his work. Have his books been translated into their language? They could look for the meaning and modern usages of the following terms which were all used in *Nineteen Eighty-Four*: *Big Brother*, *Thought Police*, *doublethink* and *Newspeak*.

Part 4

TEACH GLOBAL THINK LOCAL Lead-in

Put students into groups. Write *Sports* on the board. Tell them they have to brainstorm 12 sports in two minutes. Let them do this, and call out *Stop!* after the time has elapsed. Ask them to call out their lists and correct any language mistakes you hear. Now ask them to take their list and divide it into different categories. Tell them they can use typical categories (eg sports with a ball, sports without a ball) but encourage them to be more creative (eg sports that are popular in their country, sports that can be played with a wheelchair). Feed back.

Listening and Speaking (SB page 108)

1 **2.41** Ask students to put away their books and listen carefully (if you like, ask them to close their eyes, or cross their arms and put their heads down). Tell them they are going to hear different sports. They don't have to write or do anything, just listen.

Play the recording. Ask students to work in pairs and discuss what they heard. Then play the recording a second time, pausing after each sport and asking students to describe more in detail, using the *Useful phrases*.

1 football
2 swimming
3 running
4 horse racing

2.41

1 *sounds of football match: whistle blowing, ball being kicked, cheering*
2 *sounds of swimming race: whistle blowing, splash of competitors jumping into water*
3 *sounds of running race: voice saying 'on your marks, set', starter gun, cheers*
4 *sounds of horse race: jockey shouting, horses' hooves galloping*

2 Ask students to stay with the same partner. They now open their books and do exercise 2. Alternatively, let them leave their books closed and write the questions on the board and give the instructions for the task verbally. Circulate, monitor and feed back.

Reading (SB page 108)

This is a text about five classic rivalries in the world of sports.

1 Books closed. Write the following on the board: *It's not whether you ______ or ______ , it's how you ______ the ______.* Ask students to complete the gaps. If this is too difficult, dictate the words *game*, *play*, *lose*, *win* and ask them to complete the sentence. They then check their answer in the book and ask and answer the questions with a partner.

2 Ask students to read *Classic sporting rivalries* and answer the questions.

international politics: India vs Pakistan, Bobby Fischer vs Boris Spassky
sport, religion and politics: Celtic vs Rangers
violence: Monica Seles vs Steffi Graf
two close cities: New York Yankees vs Boston Red Sox

3 Ask students to read the texts again and insert the missing sentences.

1 not needed
2 New York Yankees vs Boston Red Sox
3 Monica Seles vs Steffi Graf
4 India vs Pakistan
5 Celtic vs Rangers
6 not needed
7 Bobby Fischer vs Boris Spassky

Once you've checked the answers you could ask the students the following questions: *Have you ever heard of these sporting rivalries? Are there any other sporting rivalries you know of?*

Background note

The 'Cold War' refers to the unfriendly relations and tension that existed between the former Soviet Union and the West from the end of the Second World War to the 1980s.

TEACH GLOBAL THINK LOCAL Reading extra

If you want to do more focused work on the vocabulary in this section, ask students to find expressions that are connected to rivals, enemies or competition (*rivalry*, *enmity*, *beat*, *political dispute*, *war*, *shooting*, *outbreak of violence*, *dominant*, *come under threat*, *challenge*, *etc*).

Writing (SB page 109)

1 Demonstrate the activity first by doing the example sentences on the board. Then put students into small groups and ask them to take turns making the sentence longer. Circulate and monitor, correcting if needed. Students should do this task in writing, meaning they should write their sentences down each time and then read them to the group.

2 Ask different groups to report on the best or most interesting sentences they produced.

TEACH GLOBAL THINK LOCAL

Alternative procedure

If you don't have a big class, you could do this a whole-class activity. Write the sentence on the board. Each team consults on how to make it longer and then sends a person to the board to rewrite the sentence. Don't help them with this. Teams take turns until they make a grammatical or spelling mistake or the sentence becomes too long (you have to be the judge of this!).

Function globally: giving and accepting compliments

These lessons in *Global* are designed to provide students with immediately useful functional language. They all follow a similar format.

Warm up (SB page 110)

Aim: to introduce the topic via a quick speaking task or picture work.

Tips:

- Do not over-correct here, especially in speaking activities.
- Encourage students to use what language they can at this stage.

Listening (SB page 110)

Aim: to present the functional language in context via a conversation or series of conversations.

Tips:

- Ask students to read the exercises first before listening.
- Play the recording all the way through for each task (there are always two tasks).
- For multiple conversations pause the recording after each one.
- If students find it very difficult, play the recording a final time and allow them to read the audioscript at the back of the book.

1

Conversation 1: d
Conversation 2: a
Conversation 3: b
Conversation 4: c

2

garden; food; appearance/clothes; dancing

2.42–2.45

Conversation 1

A: Would you like something to eat?

B: Yes, please … This is a great party … You have a lovely garden.

A: Thank you, we love it.

Conversation 2

A: This is great food.

B: Thanks, I'm glad you like it.

Conversation 3

A: Nice to see you again.

B: Nice to see you too … thank you for the invitation.

A: What a lovely dress. You look wonderful.

B: Do you think so? Thank you.

Conversation 4

A: Are you enjoying the party?

B: Yes, thanks. Good music.

A: Um, yes … You're a good dancer.

B: Thanks. You're not so bad yourself!

Language focus (SB page 110)

Aim: to draw students' attention to the items of functional language.

Tips:

- Make sure students have time to understand the form and meaning of the phrases, but you needn't translate them word for word.
- Students should be able to pronounce these phrases intelligibly, so drill them.

1 b, c	3 b, c, d
2 b, c	4 a, c

Speaking (SB page 110)

Aim: to allow students an opportunity to use this language in a meaningful, real-world context.

Tips:

- There is sometimes a choice of tasks. Any task involving reading a script will be easier than a task involving students making their own scripts. This gives you flexibility for mixed-ability classes.
- Give students time to prepare this activity, and circulate and monitor carefully.
- Correct sensitively, paying attention to the target language especially.
- If time allows, ask students to repeat the task, but with a new partner.

Global English

These lessons in *Global* have two main goals. The first is to give you and your students interesting information about English and language in general. The second goal is to provide students with practice in different kinds of reading comprehension tasks that they are likely to encounter in future study (for example, exams).

Warm up (SB page 111)

Aim: to engage students with the topic, and highlight potentially difficult vocabulary in the text.

Tips:

- be generous in helping students here with any unknown words in the first task.
- ask students to relate this task, wherever possible, to similar events or texts in their own lives. This will help them with the reading.

1 spelling: *separated*
2 double negative: *didn't know anything*
3 misused apostrophe: *coffees*
4 incorrect superlative: *happiest / most happy*
5 incorrect comparative with countable noun: *fewer holidays*

Reading (SB page 111)

Aim: to provide students with interesting information about English, and reading exam practice skills; where possible to focus on interesting or useful aspects of language in the text.

Tips:

- Get students to read through the whole text once first before doing the tasks.
- Many of these texts have been graded slightly, or not at all. There is a glossary of difficult words. Get students to read that first as it will help them understand the rest.
- There are two tasks. The first is an easier task, often focusing on the gist of the passage. The second is a more difficult task, similar to reading exam questions.
- If there is a third question the purpose is to raise students' awareness about a language feature; do not expect them to produce it immediately.
- This language is not tested or reviewed in future units, which means you have more flexibility with this material as to when and where you use it.

1 sentence 2

2 word stress (*controversy*); grammatical constructions (split infinitives: *to really know*); muddled meanings of words (*uninterested* and *disinterested*)

3

1 b

2 a

3 b

Speaking (SB page 111)

Aim: for students to relate the material in the reading to their own language, culture and experiences.

Tips:

- This is a short speaking activity and can be done in whole-class mode or in small groups.
- Wherever possible, ask students to think of and provide examples in their own language but explain them in English too.

As you go through these *Global English* lessons in the book, don't be afraid to ask students for opinions and reactions to the information in the text – not only answering the comprehension questions. Which do they find interesting? Do they know of similar experiences or facts in their own language or other languages? Some of your learners might be in your class because they are very interested in language, and these texts provide a great opportunity for you to capitalise on that motivation.

Writing: an informal email

These lessons in *Global* are designed to provide students with extended writing practice. They all follow a similar format.

Reading (SB page 112)

Aim: to provide a sample text for students to analyse.

Tips:

- Many of these texts deliberately contain errors which the students will be asked to focus on and correct later in the lesson.
- At this stage of the lesson merely ask them to read the text and extract the information.
- There are often two questions for these texts: one which focuses on gist and the other on specific details.
- If a student does ask a question about an error in form, praise them for noticing it, and explain that they will be correcting them shortly.

1 She is enjoying life. She likes her house, she has several good friends, she goes out a lot and she's going on holiday soon.

2

1 F (I'll tell you all about it when I'm back in Korea.)

2 F (At first, there was a bit of friction over cleaning the house … we've sorted that out now and we get along fine.)

3 F (I really hate doing housework!)

4 T (I like to cook them Korean food.)

5 T (Some of my friends have already gone back to their countries.)

6 T (I can't wait to see you, I miss you so much.)

Writing skills: using dashes (SB page 112)

Aim: to give students a chance to develop their writing through various different micro skills.

Tips:

- Sometimes this section focuses on common student errors in writing.
- Clearly explain the focus and do an example of one of the questions first with the students before asking them to continue on their own.
- Let students check their answers in pairs or small groups, then correct in open class.

1

I'm fine – I hope you're OK as well.

She's a really nice person – whenever I have a problem she's always willing to help me.

It was my fault – I really hate doing housework!

It was so spicy for them that they almost cried – it was really funny!

We sometimes go out to a museum or an art gallery – we have a great time together.

I can't wait to see you – I miss you so much.

2

1 c

2 d

3 b

4 a

Language focus: expressing affection and enthusiasm (SB page 112)

Aim: to highlight and focus on a particular aspect of language that students can use to improve their writing.

Tips:

- Sometimes this section serves as revision or reinforcement of language that students have encountered passively before in the unit (for example, in the reading texts) – make this link clear where possible.
- Let students check their answers in pairs or small groups, then correct in open class.

1

1 so

2 wait

3 dying

4 miss

5 to

6 special

2 Students' own answers.

Preparing to write (SB page 112)

Aim: to give students time to brainstorm ideas for the writing task.

Tips:

- Allow students to brainstorm ideas in pairs or small groups.
- At low levels, this may involve some use of L1 (the students' mother tongue); be tolerant of this, but be on hand to help with translations or English where needed.
- Ask students to make notes here, but not begin writing.

Writing (SB page 112)

Aim: to give students practice in more extended writing tasks.

Tips:

- This section can be done as homework.
- Remind students to refer back to the model text, but to be careful of the typical errors.
- Ask students to check their work carefully before they hand it in.

Global review

These lessons in *Global* are designed to provide students with an opportunity to review and consolidate the language they have studied in the unit.

Grammar and Vocabulary (SB page 113)

Aim: to give students revision of all the main grammar and vocabulary points that arose in the unit.

Tips:

- Demonstrate the activities by doing the first one as a whole class.
- Allow students time to do this, and encourage them to look back through the unit for help.
- When you come to correct this, do not simply go around the class asking for the right answer – encourage students to say *why* they think something is correct, and seek confirmation from others before moving on.

Grammar

1	**2**
1 i	1 as interesting **as**
2 e	2 more difficult **than**
3 h	3 **much friendlier** / much more **friendly**
4 j	4 correct
5 b	5 this is the **prettiest**
6 a	6 correct
7 c	
8 d	
9 g	
10 f	

Vocabulary

1	**2**
1 generalisations	1 crazy
2 satirise	2 soft spot
3 tolerant	3 keen
4 stereotypical	4 fond
5 misconception	
6 judgemental	

Speaking and Writing (SB page 113)

Aim: to provide extra speaking practice that will review and consolidate language presented in the unit.

Tips:

- Give the students time to read and understand the instructions.
- Circulate and monitor the students, encouraging them to use only English here.
- Make notes of any incorrect use of language, but refrain from correcting if students are in the middle of the task.

Study skills

These lessons in *Global* are designed to provide students with skills and strategies in learner training and learner autonomy. For more on learner autonomy and learner training, see the essay on page xxiii.

Improving your listening skills (SB page 113)

1 Ask students to think of a reason to improve their listening skills. Elicit various ones and write them up on the board. Then tell students to write down the three best ones and compare with a partner.

Feed back, incorporating the points in the first box about how to practise listening.

Possible answers
to understand films in English
to talk to people from English-speaking countries
to understand lectures in English
to pass exams in English
to understand people from all over the world
to understand English songs

Ask the class how they have found the listening exercises in the course so far. They can do this in pairs, or as a whole-class activity. The kinds of listening activities that feature in *Global* are: listening for gist (the general idea), listening for specific details, listening as part of pronunciation practice and read-and-listen activities.

You could also ask students to talk about what listening they have done outside of class, for example with the eWorkbook. It's worth recommending here that students do extra listening exercises in the eWorkbook, as well as download audio of words, phrases, conversations and literary extracts to practise listening on the move.

2 Now ask students to go over the different ways of improving their listening skills. They tick the ones they have already tried. Ask if they have any other suggestions, and write these up on the board. Then ask students to choose one of the suggestions from the book or the board that they haven't tried (but could conceivably do!) and try it before the next class.

3 In pairs, students compare ideas and say why they like the ideas they have chosen. Ask for suggestions for other ways to improve their listening skills, and write these on the board.

UNIT 10 Beginnings & Endings

Coursebook

Unit 10	Language	Texts	Communicative skills
Part 1 SB page 114	Extend your vocabulary Beginnings and endings Pronunciation Silent letters Vocabulary Books and reading	Listening and Reading *Great opening lines*	Speaking Reading questionnaire
Part 2 SB page 116	Vocabulary Celebrations Grammar and Speaking Verb form review	Reading and Speaking *Birthday customs*	Writing A thank-you note
Part 3 SB page 118	Vocabulary and Listening Death Grammar Reflexive pronouns	Reading *Unhappy endings: the wives of Henry VIII*	Speaking A presentation
Part 4 SB page 120	Extend your vocabulary *farewell* Vocabulary Leaving	Reading *Famous farewells*	Writing A farewell email or speech
Function globally SB page 122	Saying goodbye Formal and informal farewells Roleplaying the end of a conference or a student leaving a host family		
Global voices SB page 123	Listening to people talking about their favourite films Tenses to talk about films		
Writing SB page 124	A speech Writing a speech Wishes and hopes		
Global review SB page 125	Grammar and vocabulary review Extra speaking and writing practice		
Study skills SB page 125	Using your dictionary: exploring synonyms		

Additional resources

eWorkbook	Interactive and printable grammar, vocabulary, listening and pronunciation practice Extra reading and writing practice Additional downloadable listening and audio material
Teacher's Resource Disc	Communication activity worksheets to print and photocopy
Go global: ideas for further research	**Beginnings** Ask students to find the origins of a common tradition or custom in their country and prepare a short presentation for the class. **Endings** Ask students to find examples of humorous or moving epitaphs and present them to the class.

Part 1

TEACH GLOBAL THINK LOCAL Lead-in

Books closed. Write the title of the unit *Beginnings & Endings* on the board. Ask students what happens at the beginning of each lesson, and the sort of topics they think might be included in this unit. Elicit ideas.

Ask students to flick through the unit and see what topics there are: beginnings of novels, beginning of life (birthdays), end of life (death) and saying goodbye. Ask if students had any of these topics on their lists.

Listening and Reading (SB page 114)

Background note

Pride and Prejudice, published in 1813, was written by the English novelist Jane Austen (1775–1817).

Moby Dick, published in 1851, was written by American author Herman Melville (1819–1891).

The Great Gatsby, published in 1925, was written by the American author F Scott Fitzgerald (1896–1940).

Rebecca, published in 1938, was written by English author Daphne du Maurier (1907–1989).

Tracks, published in 1988, was written by American author Louise Erdrich (born 1954).

Captain Corelli's Mandolin, published in 1994, was written by English author Louis de Bernières (born 1954).

1 Direct students to the book covers. Ask students if they have read any of them or seen a film version. If students have read any of the books, ask them if it was in English or in translation.

2 **2.46** Check that students understand the words in the box. Then ask them to listen and match each novel to a topic in the box. Play the recording, pausing after the description of each novel.

The Great Gatsby: money
Rebecca: family secrets
Captain Corelli's Mandolin: war
Tracks: Native American culture
Pride and Prejudice: marriage
Moby Dick: adventure

2.46

The Great Gatsby by F Scott Fitzgerald is set in the 20s in New York. It is narrated by Nick Carraway, who rents a house next door to the extremely wealthy Jay Gatsby, a man who uses his money to get what he wants. Gatsby is in love with Nick's cousin Daisy, who is unhappily married. He persuades Nick to help him to arrange a meeting with Daisy, leading to a series of tragic events.

Rebecca by Daphne du Maurier is a romantic mystery. After knowing Maxim de Winter for only a week, the narrator (whose name we don't know) marries him and moves with him to his house in Cornwall. Her husband's servants and friends make it clear she can never take the place of Maxim's first wife, Rebecca. In the end the narrator learns the surprising truth about Rebecca's death.

Captain Corelli's Mandolin by Louis de Bernières begins in 1940. The novel follows the daily life of Pelagia, who lives on the Greek island of Cephalonia. The Italian army has just invaded Greece and Pelagia's fiancé has left to fight against the Italians. While he is away Pelagia begins a secret relationship with Antonio Corelli, an Italian captain who is sent to live with Pelagia and her father, and whose greatest passion is music.

Tracks by Louise Erdrich is the story of Fleur Pillager, a member of a Native American tribe who is said to be a witch. Through Fleur's story we hear about the problems facing Native American tribes in the early 20th century: their fight to save their lands, the long winters and lack of food and disease brought by the white man.

Pride and Prejudice by Jane Austen was published in 1813 when women were expected to behave in a certain way and their parents decided who they should marry. Elizabeth is the second of five sisters and her mother wants to find good husbands for all of them. The novel follows Elizabeth's up-and-down relationship with Mr Darcy.

Moby Dick by Herman Melville is a dramatic tale of adventure at sea. Moby Dick is a huge white whale who is being hunted by Captain Ahab. Ahab lost one of his legs to Moby Dick and is determined to kill the whale. A sailor called Ishmael joins the crew on Captain Ahab's boat. In Ishmael's voice, the book tells the story of the whale hunt which ends in tragedy.

3 Explain that students are going to listen to the descriptions again and then tell their partner what the novel is about. Encourage them to make notes but not write down every word. Play the recording, again pausing slightly after each novel. Students work in pairs and take turns to tell their partner about one of the novels. Their partner can help them with details if necessary.

4 **2.47** Direct students to the opening lines of the six novels on page 115. Students read and listen to the text and match the opening lines with the correct novels. In feedback, ask students which words helped them to match the lines to the novels.

'Dr Iannis had enjoyed …': *Captain Corelli's Mandolin*
'We started dying …': *Tracks*
'It is a truth …': *Pride and Prejudice*
'In my younger …': *The Great Gatsby*
'Call me Ishmael …': *Moby Dick*
'Last night …': *Rebecca*

5 Ask students to work in pairs and discuss the questions. Then they feed back to the class.

6 Read out the rubric and invite suggestions from the class. Students should explain their reasons. Tell students the answer and ask whether they were surprised.

1 *Moby Dick*
2 *Pride and Prejudice*

7 Read out the questions. Students answer them orally as a class. You could also ask students if they ever read the ending of a book first.

TEACH GLOBAL THINK LOCAL

Homework extra

Students choose the novel in their language which they think has the best opening line. They should write a short description of the book and include its opening line translated into English. They should also find out when it was published.

In monolingual classes discuss what books students have chosen. In multilingual classes, ask students to swap their descriptions with another student and read about each other's books.

Extend your vocabulary (SB page 114)

Direct students to the *Extend your vocabulary* box. Ask them to read the explanations and example sentences. Students then complete the sentences with the correct phrase.

1 at the end of
2 In the beginning
3 at the beginning of
4 in the end

Pronunciation (SB page 114)

1 Ask students to close their books. Write the words *acknowledged*, *would*, *while* on the board and read them out.

Ask students what all these words have in common in terms of pronunciation. Read them out again. Elicit (or tell) students that they all contain 'silent' letters. Ask students what the silent letters are.

The underlined letters are not pronounced.
acknowledged
would
while

2 Ask students to look through the list of words quickly and look up the meanings of any words that are unknown to them in their dictionaries. Then students underline the silent letters in the words.

When they have done the task, ask students to read out a word in turn and say which is/are the silent letter(s). Check and correct individual pronunciation, then drill all the words as a class – perhaps as a chant in groups of three words.

answer	doubt	light
autumn	high	sandwich
ballet	hour	scissors
castle	island	though
climb	knife	Wednesday
column	know	comb

Language note

'Silent' letters are so called because they are not articulated, but their presence may change the sound of the word, typically the vowel sound. For example, in *wrong* the *w* is genuinely silent, ie the pronunciation would be the same with or without it, but in *night*, the 'silent' *gh* changes the sound of the vowel. This commonly occurs with words ending in *e*, eg in *acknowledge* the final *e* is silent but it changes the sound of the preceding *dg*. In some words the pronunciation of the silent letter is optional, eg *Wednesday* can be pronounced /ˈwenzdeɪ/ or /ˈwedənsdeɪ/.

3 Students work in pairs. Ask them to write two sentences which each contain at least three of the words in exercise 2. Point out that they can be logical sentences (*I climbed up to the castle on Wednesday*) or nonsense sentences (*I doubt you can cut sandwiches with scissors*).

Students read their sentences out to the class, paying attention to the pronunciation of the words with silent letters.

TEACH GLOBAL THINK LOCAL

Mixed ability

Ask early finishers to look at their sentences again. They should edit them to try to include more words from the list.

Vocabulary (SB page 115)

1 Read out the pairs of words to model pronunciation. Ask students to work in pairs and take turns to explain the difference between the pairs of words. Tell them they can use a dictionary for help if necessary. Do the first one or two pairs or words with the class as an example. Students feed back to the class.

A novel is a book about imaginary people. A biography is a book about the life of a real person.

A guidebook gives you tourist information about places. An atlas shows you where places are on a map.

A self-help book gives you help with problems in your life. An instruction manual tells you how to use a machine or piece of equipment.

A magazine contains articles on general subjects. A journal contains articles relating to a particular subject or profession.

A textbook contains information about a particular subject. A notebook contains blank pieces of paper which you can write on.

A hardback is a book with a hard cover. A paperback is a book with a soft cover.

An audio book is a book which is recorded so that you can listen to it. An e-book is a digital copy of a book which you can read on a screen.

A bookshop is a place where you buy books. A library is a place were you borrow books.

2 Direct students to the text about the British Library in London. Students complete it using words from exercise 1.

Answers are numbered in the order they appear in the text.

1 journal
2 biography
3 self-help book
4 textbook
5 e-books
6 audio books

3 Ask students to look at the verbs in the box and decide which ones can collocate with books and magazines. Students cross out the verbs which can't be used.

Verbs which can be used: borrow; buy; enjoy; lend; listen to (audio books); order; publish; play (audio books); subscribe to; write

Not used: join; watch

Speaking (SB page 115)

1 Ask students to read through the statements about reading habits and check that they understand them. Put students in pairs. Each student decides if the statements are true or false about their partner and notes this down.

2 Students ask their partner questions to check their answers. They note down their partner's answers and compare them with their own guesses.

Students can ask additional questions to find out more information, eg *Who's your favourite detective novel author? How often do you go to the library?*

3 Ask students how well they guessed about their partner's reading habits. Then ask students to tell the class one or two interesting things they found out about their partner.

Part 2

TEACH GLOBAL THINK LOCAL Lead-in

Ask students how they feel about their birthday. Do they look forward to it? Do they hate the idea of being another year older? Or do they ignore the day because they feel it has no particular meaning? Has their attitude changed as they have got older? Do they worry about telling people their age?

Vocabulary (SB page 116)

1 In pairs, students match the verbs and nouns to make phrases about birthdays. Check answers.

1 e 2 g 3 d 4 h 5 a 6 c 7 f 8 b

2 **2.48–2.52** Tell students they are going to listen to five situations. They should say what is happening in each one using phrases from exercise 1. Play the recording. Pause after each one and ask students to describe the situation.

1 People are drinking a toast to somebody called Ryan. (It's his 40th birthday.)
2 A man is giving somebody a birthday present.
3 A man is blowing out the candles on his birthday cake.
4 A woman is going to post a birthday card.
5 The speaker is giving a speech. (She says thank you to the guests and her parents.)

2.48–2.52

1

A: Now, er, I'd like to ask you to lift your glasses and join me in wishing Ryan a happy 40th birthday … to Ryan.

B: To Ryan!

2

A: Happy birthday. Here's a little something from us all – I hope you like it.

B: Oh, thank you. Can I open it now?

3

A: Right, go on then. Remember to make a wish.

B: Yeah, I did it!

4

A: I'm just going to put this in the post. I nearly forgot, it's my brother's birthday tomorrow.

B: Oh, can you take that other letter if you're going? You know, the one about the telephone bill. Thanks.

5

Can I have your attention, please? ... Thank you. Well, I'd like to start by saying a huge thanks to everyone who's here today. It's been a fantastic day so far and a lot of that is down to my parents, of course. Mum and Dad: thanks for everything today and … well, for always really … A big clap for them please …

Reading and Speaking (SB page 116)

Background note

In many countries people have a name day as well as a birthday. On name days people celebrate the day which is linked to their name – usually the feast day of the Catholic or Orthodox saint that they were named after.

1 Direct students to the text on page 116. Students read the text and find out when ordinary people started celebrating birthdays. Check the answer with the class. You may want to drill the pronunciation of 12th *(twelfth:* /twelfθ/) which many students find difficult.

If you teach in a country which has name days or have students who come from those countries, focus on this in class.

The 12th century

TEACH GLOBAL THINK LOCAL

Reading extra

Focus on some of the useful vocabulary in the text. Ask students to find words in the text for …

- large meals for lots of people (*feasts*)
- traditions (*customs*)
- being kept safe from harm (*protection*)
- relating to an old religion which had many gods (*pagan*)
- usual (*common*)

2 Students work in groups of three: A, B and C. Explain that each student is going to read a different text on an aspect of birthday celebrations. Ask students to read the rubric and follow the instructions. As read the text on page 127 and Bs on page 129. Cs read the text on page 117. Then they should answer the two questions.

A Birthday cards

1 People send birthday greetings using cards and postcards. They also give cards with presents. People also send e-cards as a quick, environmentally friendly alternative.

2 The custom probably started in England in the early 19th century when the first postage stamp was issued.

B Birthday song

1 People often congratulate others on their birthday by singing them a song – often *Happy Birthday to You*.

2 The music for the song was written by two sisters in America in 1893 with different lyrics. In 1935 the writers' sister won copyright of the song.

C Birthday cake and candles

1 Today people have candles on a birthday cake to show how old they are. People blow out the candles and sometimes make a wish.

2 The custom might have started in Greece about 3,000 years ago. It could also have started in Germany in the Middle Ages.

3 Students tell the other members of their group about the text they have read, using their answers to the questions in exercise 2. Students can also refer to other details.

4 Students work in AB pairs. They choose to talk about either birthday customs (option A) or another celebration (option B) in their country.

In monolingual groups, ask students to work together and talk about the questions. They can focus on what happens in their particular family as well as generally in their country.

In multilingual groups, ask students to prepare a presentation for their partner using the questions given. Students then tell their partner or another pair about their birthday customs or celebration.

In class feedback with monolingual groups, focus on personal differences and similarities. In multilingual groups, ask students to say something about their partner's customs.

Grammar and Speaking (page 117)

1 Tell students they are going to review the verb tenses and forms they have studied in the book. Direct them to the list of structures and ask them to find at least two examples of each structure in the reading texts on pages 117, 127 and 129.

There are many examples of tenses in the texts; the table shows the first occurrence of each tense category.

	Cake	Cards	Song
Present tenses	celebrate	send	is
Past tenses	started	sent	had originally written
Future forms	will come true	will e-cards replace	will probably congratulate
Passives	were put	is not known	are sung
Conditionals	would become	couldn't wish	would have ended
Reported speech	said that it symbolised		

2 Students work in pairs and compare their examples. They should try to explain to their partner when the tense or form in their example is used. If students have any difficulties or questions, they should review that structure in the *Grammar focus* section. In full-class feedback, discuss any particular difficulties students had.

3 Direct students to the text on national holidays. Ask them to skim the text quickly for the main ideas. Ask students which four people are mentioned in the text and if they are familiar with them (Julius Caesar, George Washington, Martin Luther King, Mahatma Gandhi).

Then ask students to read the text carefully again and choose the correct verb form to complete the text. Students can do this alone or in pairs. When you have taken feedback on the answers, ask students how they would answer the question in the text: whose birthday would they make into a national holiday in their country?

Answers are numbered in the order they appear in the text.

1 introduced	4 honours	7 would
2 was marked	5 was killed	8 has been
3 have	6 is celebrated	9 had

TEACH GLOBAL THINK LOCAL Alternative procedure

In monolingual groups you could make the last part of exercise 3 into a vote. Individual students nominate people and explain why they have chosen them. Other students support or reject the nominations and give their reasons. Finally the class takes a vote and decides on the person they would like to honour.

4 Explain that students are going to do an information gap activity using two pictures which are similar but have some differences. First, elicit vocabulary to describe where things are in pictures and write it on the board:

on the right / on the left / in the middle of the picture
in the foreground / background
in the bottom right / top left corner

In pairs, As should turn to page 127 and Bs to page 129. They describe their pictures and find five differences. Ask them to talk about what the people *are doing*, what they *are going to do* and what they *have done*.

1 Picture A: the man in the bottom right corner is going to eat a piece of cake.
Picture B: he has eaten the cake.

2 Picture A: the girl on the right has blown out her candles.
Picture B: she is going to blow the candles out.

3 Picture A: a couple in the foreground are about to hug.
Picture B: they are hugging.

4 Picture A: a woman in the background on the left is not wearing a party hat.
Picture B: the woman is wearing her party hat.

5 Picture A: a woman in the background is sitting at the table.
Picture B: the woman is getting up.

5 In pairs, students tell each other about a particular celebration in the past that they attended, and their plans for future celebrations.

G Grammar focus

Refer students to the verb form review on page 150.

You can use exercises 1 and 2 on page 151 for:
a) extra practice now
b) homework
c) review a couple of lessons from now.

The answers are on page 144 of the Teacher's Book.

Writing (SB page 117)

1 Ask students if they write thank-you letters and notes when they get a present. Ask them to read the rubric in exercise 1 and draw their attention to the *Useful phrases*. Students write a thank-you letter for the present given.

2 Students work in pairs. They read their partner's letter and decide if it is appropriate to the task.

Part 3

TEACH GLOBAL THINK LOCAL Lead-in

With books closed, ask students to work in pairs.

Student A looks at the picture on page 118 and describes it to Student B. Student B should say where they might expect to see such a statue.

Vocabulary and Listening (SB page 118)

1 Read out the words in the box to model pronunciation. Drill pronunciation of *funeral* (/ˈfjuːnərəl/) and *grief* (/griːf/). Ask students to read the definitions and match them to the words in the box. Ask students to check their answers in pairs: one reads out the definition and their partner says the answer. In feedback check that all the words are clear.

1 a grave
2 a funeral
3 a widow (woman)/a widower (man)
4 a will
5 a body
6 grief

2 Ask students to make collocations using the verbs and words from exercise 1. Check the answers in class feedback. Make sure students understand what is meant by *view a body*. In multilingual classes you could ask students if this is common in their country or according to their religion.

1 attend a funeral	4 view a body
2 become/be a widow/widower	5 visit a grave
3 show grief	6 write a will

TEACH GLOBAL THINK LOCAL Extra activity

Death is a sensitive topic and one that people often avoid discussing. If you think it is appropriate in your class, you could give students further practice of the collocations in exercise 2 by talking about these questions in pairs.

In your country, or according to your religion:

What funeral customs are common?

Are there any rules about how a widow or widower should behave after their partner's death (for example concerning clothes or remarriage)?

Do children typically participate in funerals or are they protected from death?

Is it usual to visit the grave of dead relatives?

Who has the right to a state funeral?

Do most people write a will?

3 2.53 This exercise practises the collocations in exercise 2 in context, and prepares for the Reading text. Discuss what could go in the first gap. Then ask students to read the text and think about what information could go in the gaps. Play the recording. Students listen and complete the text, then compare their texts with a partner. Play the recording again if necessary.

2.53

In 16th century England, life expectancy was low. People usually died at home and **viewing the body** was common. People believed that the more people who followed the funeral procession to **the grave**, the better the dead person's chances of **a life after death**, so people were often paid **to attend funerals**. After the death of a relative or close friend, people were expected to **show their grief**. This was called *mourning*. A widow was expected to wear black clothes to mourn her husband and not show herself in society. **Widowers** often wore a black hat and gloves and could continue with their work and daily lives as usual. In 1540 a law was passed so that **people could write wills** and choose who should receive their property. Married women, however, **were not allowed to write wills** at this time.

Reading (SB page 118)

Background note

Henry VIII (1491–1547) became the ruler of England in 1509. His wish to end his marriage to Catherine of Aragon due to the lack of a male heir led to the English Reformation: the break with the Catholic church in Rome and the foundation of the Church of England. Before this time the Pope was responsible for religious matters in England and church taxes were paid to Rome. Henry married Anne Boleyn in 1533 and was excommunicated from the Catholic church, which did not recognise his divorce and considered that he was still married to Catherine of Aragon. In 1534 an Act of Parliament made Henry the head of the Church of England.

1 Direct students to the text on page 119. Ask them to look at the title of the text, the rhyme (top left) and the pictures. Ask students what this tells us about King Henry VIII and his wives and what else they know. Go through the rhyme with students if necessary and elicit the meaning of *wedded* and *beheaded* in the rhyme.

2 Ask students to read the text, using the glossary to help them. Students note down when and how each marriage ended.

1 Catherine of Aragon: divorced in 1533
2 Anne Boleyn: beheaded in 1536
3 Jane Seymour: died in 1537
4 Anne of Cleves: divorced in 1540
5 Catherine Howard: beheaded in 1542
6 Catherine Parr: survived Henry who died in 1547

3 Look at the questions with students. Students read the text again and answer the questions.

1	Jane Seymour
2	Catherine Parr
3	Anne Boleyn
4	Catherine of Aragon
5	Anne of Cleves
6	Catherine Howard

TEACH GLOBAL THINK LOCAL

Reading extra

Students produce a timeline (a chronological and visual representation) of the events in the texts. Ask students to include the dates of the start and end of each marriage and any details they would like to add (details about the wives, children, etc).

Ask students to compare timelines with a partner.

4 Check that students understand the word *treat*. Ask students to choose two sentences and complete them. Students then work in pairs and compare their sentences with a partner. Students feed back to the class.

Grammar (SB page 118)

Direct students' attention to the example sentences. Ask students who Catherine and her lovers were unable to save (Catherine and her lovers). Point out that the subject and object are the same so we use *themselves*. Explain that this is called a 'reflexive' pronoun.

Ask students who Henry fell in love with (Jane) and who Jane fell in love with (Henry). Write the two names on the board and use arrows to show that the subject and object of the verb are different. In this case we use *each other*.

Check that student have understood the difference and give further examples if necessary.

Background note

Mary Stuart (1542–1587) was Queen of Scotland from 1542 to 1567. She was the daughter of King James V of Scotland.

Elizabeth I (1533–1603) was the Queen of England from 1558 to 1603. She was the daughter of Henry VIII and Anne Boleyn. She succeeded to the throne after the deaths of her half-brother Edward VI and half-sister Mary I.

Direct students to the text about Mary Stuart. Ask students to complete the text with *themselves* or *each other*. Do the first sentence as an example with the class.

Answers are numbered in the order they appear in the text.

1 each other	3 each other	5 each other
2 themselves	4 themselves	6 themselves

G Grammar focus

Refer students to the language summary on reflexive pronouns on page 150.

You can use exercises 3, 4 and 5 on page 151 for:

a) extra practice now
b) homework
c) review a couple of lessons from now.

The answers are on page 144 of the Teacher's Book.

TEACH GLOBAL THINK LOCAL

Mixed ability

Exercise 3 deals with a limited list of reflexive pronouns. For stronger students, refer to the complete list in the *Grammar focus* section on page 150 and ask students to make sentences using the verbs given there (*blame*, *embarrass*, etc). Other verbs that commonly take reflexive pronouns are *dress*, *prepare*, *shave*, *see*, *wash*.

Speaking (SB page 119)

2 Explain that students are going to do a presentation about a historical person who came to a tragic end. Explain what type of presentation this should be (entirely oral, with the help of pictures or a poster, using presentation software, etc). Ask students to read tasks A and B and choose one task. They should do some research to find out about the person they have chosen.

2 Students make notes about the person they have chosen, using the questions given to help them.

3 Before students give their presentations, review general guidelines for presentations (students should speak loudly and clearly, make eye contact, use their notes to help them but not read directly from them). Draw students' attention to the *Useful phrases*. Students give their presentations to the class (or to small groups in large classes). Ask listeners to listen carefully and think of any questions they would like to ask. Encourage students to comment on each other's presentations, making both positive comments and suggestions for improvement.

TEACH GLOBAL THINK LOCAL

Alternative procedure

To give listeners a more structured listening experience and keep them focused on the presentation, ask them to make notes to answer the questions in exercise 2.

Part 4

TEACH GLOBAL THINK LOCAL Lead-in

In multilingual classes, write *Saying goodbye* on the board and ask students to come to the board and write the words in their languages for 'goodbye'. Establish if there are different words in these languages for saying 'goodbye' for a short or long time. Write the word *farewell* on the board. Explain that this is an old-fashioned word for saying 'goodbye' but that it is still used to say goodbye when you think you might not see somebody for a long time – or at all.

In monolingual classes, ask them what English words they know for saying goodbye (*goodbye*, *bye*, *see you*). Write the word *farewell* on the board and explain as above.

Reading (SB page 120)

Background note

Lawrence Oates (1880–1912) was an English Antarctic explorer. He was a member of Robert Scott's Terra Nova Expedition team which set out in 1911 and tried to be the first to reach the South Pole. They reached the South Pole on 18 January 1912, only to discover that the Norwegian Roald Amundsen and his team had arrived there on 16 December.

On the way back Oates suffered from frostbite and was unable to walk as quickly as the others. The team had to walk a certain amount every day in order to reach the places where they could pick up food. On 16 March 1912 Oates walked out into a storm in the freezing cold so that the team could travel faster without him. His body was never found. Unfortunately, his companions did not survive the journey either.

1 Direct students to the picture and the quote by Lawrence Oates. Ask students where they think Oates is and what he meant by the quote. Point out the clothes they are wearing and the flags. Elicit ideas. If necessary, explain that Oates was part of Robert Scott's attempt to be the first men at the South Pole.

2 Direct students to the information on page 131 to find out about Captain Oates.

3 Students read *Famous farewells* on page 121. Ask them to skim the text and look at the names of the speakers. Do they know anything about the speakers? If any names are completely unknown, help students with information.

Background note

American aviator Amelia Earhart (1897–1937) was the first woman to fly solo across the Atlantic.

King Edward VIII (1894–1972) was the British king from January to December 1936. When he gave up the throne his brother George VI became king.

Samuel Pepys (/piːps/) (1633–1703) is known for his famous diaries which gave information about many important events in London from 1660–1669.

Kofi Annan (born 1938) is a diplomat from Ghana who was Secretary General of the United Nations from 1997–2006.

The 1942 film *Casablanca* stars Humphrey Bogart as the owner of a nightclub in Casablanca, Morocco, during World War II.

Romeo and Juliet is a tragic play about two young lovers, written by the playwright William Shakespeare (1564–1616).

Oscar Wilde (1854–1900) was an Irish writer famous for his wit.

Napoleon Bonaparte (1769–1821) became Emperor of France in 1804. He was defeated by a coalition of countries which included Russia and the UK. He was forced to abdicate and go into exile on the Mediterranean island of Elba, but he later escaped.

4 Ask students to read the text again and answer the questions. Explain that the answer can be one or several people.

real people: Earhart, Edward VIII, Pepys, Annan, Wilde, Bonaparte

characters: Rick in *Casablanca*, Juliet in *Romeo and Juliet*

last words: Earhart, Wilde

said to a group: Edward VIII, Pepys, Annan, Bonaparte

written down: Earhart, Pepys

5 Ask students to find words or phrases in the text to match the definitions. Tell them to use context to help them.

1 hazards
2 burden
3 quit
4 parting
5 sorrow

6 Look at the questions with the class. Clarify the meanings of *down-to-earth* (practical and sensible) and *patriotic* (feeling love towards your country). Ask students to work in pairs and try to agree on an answer. Feed back to the class.

7 Read out the first question. Ask students to answer the question and explain their reasons.

Extend your vocabulary (SB page 120)

Ask students to read the collocations in the box.

1 Students work in groups. Explain they are going to plan an *imaginary* farewell party for their last English class. Students should decide together on the list of points in the task.

2 Groups feed back to the class and present their ideas. Decide which group has the best ideas. If your situation allows it, put the ideas into practice and hold a real farewell party for the class.

Vocabulary (SB page 120)

1 Look at the sentences with the class. Explain that all the words in bold mean 'to leave' in one way or another. Ask students to work in pairs and take turns to explain the meaning of the words in bold. Point out that students can use a dictionary to help them if necessary. Students feed back to the class.

1 stopped working because he had reached the official age to stop
2 died
3 gone to a different place to live
4 have ended their relationship
5 left home to live somewhere else
6 told her employer she was leaving her job
7 finished university
8 was told to leave his job

2 Students match the two halves of the sentences. Check the answers.

1 g	5 f
2 h	6 c
3 e	7 a
4 b	8 d

3 Look at the two sets of questions with the students. Students work in pairs. Ask them to choose A or B and discuss the questions. Then ask them to work with a pair who have chosen the other task and exchange ideas.

Writing (SB page 121)

1 Direct students' attention to the writing tasks. Look at each task in turn with the class and elicit ideas about:

- the content, eg problems at work, good and bad memories, advantages and disadvantages of living alone
- the sort of language to be used: formal or informal, neutral, funny, emotional.

Students choose a task and do their piece of writing.

2 Students work in pairs and swap their writing. Ask them to evaluate their partner's writing using the criteria given.

Function globally: saying goodbye

These lessons in *Global* are designed to provide students with immediately useful functional language. They all follow a similar format.

Warm up (SB page 122)

Aim: to introduce the topic via a quick speaking task or picture work.

Tips:

- Do not over-correct here, especially in speaking activities.
- Encourage students to use what language they can at this stage.

Listening (SB page 122)

Aim: to present the functional language in context via a conversation or series of conversations.

Tips:

- Ask students to read the exercises first before listening.
- Play the recording all the way through for each task (there are always two tasks).
- For multiple conversations pause the recording after each one.
- If students find it very difficult, play the recording a final time and allow them to read the audioscript at the back of the book.

1 Conversations 1 and 4

2

compliment: 2
thank: 1, 2 and 3
talk about another meeting: 2 and 4
send a message: 3 and 4
talk about the trip back: 2 and 4

2.54–2.57

Conversation 1

A: Time to go. Take care of yourself.
B: You too. Thanks for everything.
A: Bye! Keep in touch.
B: Yes, will do. Bye bye.

Conversation 2

A: I'm afraid I have to go now.

B: Well, it was very nice to meet you.

A: Yes, you too. I've enjoyed working with you. Have a good trip.

B: Thanks. I look forward to seeing you again sometime.

Conversation 3

A: It's been nice seeing you again … Please give my regards to your wife.

B: Thank you. And thanks again for all your hospitality.

A: Goodbye.

Conversation 4

A: Bye then, all the best.

B: And to you. Give my love to the family.

C: Drive safely!

A: I will … See you soon.

Language focus (SB page 122)

Aim: to draw students' attention to the items of functional language.

Tips:

- Make sure students have time to understand the form and meaning of the phrases, but you needn't translate them word for word.
- Students should be able to pronounce these phrases intelligibly, so drill them.

1

1 b	4 g	7 j	10 c
2 l	5 a	8 d	11 e
3 h	6 i	9 k	12 f

Speaking (SB page 122)

Aim: to allow students an opportunity to use this language in a meaningful, real-world context.

Tips:

- There is sometimes a choice of tasks. Any task involving reading a script will be easier than a task involving students making their own scripts. This gives you flexibility for mixed-ability classes.
- Give students time to prepare this activity, and circulate and monitor carefully.
- Correct sensitively, paying attention to the target language especially.
- If time allows, ask students to repeat the task, but with a new partner.

Global voices

These lessons in *Global* are designed to provide students with exposure to authentic speakers of English from both native and non-native English backgrounds. They all follow a similar format.

Warm up (SB page 123)

Aim: to introduce the topic and highlight potentially difficult vocabulary the students will encounter.

Tips:

- Be generous in helping students with the vocabulary here, but let them try to work it out first.
- Circulate and monitor any speaking task, but be careful not to over-correct.
- Follow up any short discussion pairwork with an open class discussion, asking students to report back what they said.

Listening (SB page 123)

Aim: to expose students to English spoken with a variety of accents.

Tips:

- Students will need to hear the recording at least twice, if not more times, to understand it. There are almost always two tasks.
- The first time they listen, tell them you don't expect them to understand every word; some of it will be hard. This is because the text has not been scripted or graded in any way. It's what they would hear in 'the real world'.
- The first task is easier and focuses on gist, the second task is more detailed.
- Pause after each speaker on the second listening, and don't be afraid to replay the whole thing if students appear to need it.
- Students can read the audioscript at the back of the book if you / they wish.
- It may be tempting to hunt for specific pronunciation or language errors, but we recommend against this. In real-world communication not everyone speaks perfect English all the time, not even native speakers.

1, 2 Students' own answers.

3

Titanic: love; sea; ship

The Lord of the Rings: curse; hobbit; ring

Breakfast at Tiffany's: Fifth Avenue; night out; shop window

Mamma Mia: father; island; wedding

4 Students' own answers.

2.58–2.61

Maria Pilar, Spain

My favourite film is *Titanic* and the beginning is in a very big ship on the sea and is the principal idea, or the main character is a handsome man, Leonardo di Caprio … and I think that the history is about the love in a ship and the love is, uh, very bad because suddenly the ship broke in the middle of the sea and all the people in the ship died.

Marc, France

One of my favourite films is *The Lord of the Rings* which is a film that has been – which is … founded on the book of Tolkien – *The Lord of the Rings* and the beginning of the story is about a small hobbit, Bilbo … that wants to get rid of his ring, a ring he has found years before and he gives it to his nephew. And in fact the ring is a kind of cursed ring and, um, the idea – the quest that his nephew has to deal with is to get rid of the ring and to destroy it.

Mireille, US

One of my favourite films is *Breakfast at Tiffany's* and it starts off – you see the character Holly Golightly, she is standing in front of – standing on Fifth Avenue in front of Tiffany's, looking in the shop window, eating a croissant. It's very early in the morning, she had been out all night and she just sits in there eating her croissant and drinking her coffee. That's how the movie starts.

Nicole, Switzerland

So my favourite film is called *Mamma Mia* and the beginning of the film, so, the beginning – the film starts with a girl who is singing, or is singing, yeah, a song of Abba, and she's throwing in a letter in a box. And er … we know then that she ask her three possible fathers to come to her wedding and then you can see the … what the fathers are doing, or what the men are doing and how they get to the airpor… to the harbour and to come to the wedding. So they meet another – the other …, so the three meet together and come together to the island.

Language focus: tenses to talk about films (SB page 123)

Aim: to raise students' awareness of a particular piece of language present in the listening.

Tips:

- This language is not included in unit tests or reviews; it is included here to help students understand international English.
- The objective is awareness-raising, not production. Don't expect students to produce this language in an exercise or in conversation immediately.

to describe events: present simple

to describe a particular scene: present continuous

Speaking (SB page 123)

Aim: for students to discuss the same or similar questions as the speakers in the listening.

Tips:

- The speaking tasks here are slightly more open to allow for students to explore the subject. Give them time to do this.
- If students are working in pairs, circulate and monitor. Make notes of incorrect language use to correct afterwards (or in a future class).
- As you go through the book and the *Global voices* lessons, ask students for feedback on these listening activities and their potential use of English with other people. Are they very difficult? Have students used their English as a 'lingua franca' with other non-native English speakers? How did they find it? What tips do they have on understanding or making themselves understood in an international context?

Writing: a speech

These lessons in *Global* are designed to provide students with extended writing practice. They all follow a similar format.

Reading (SB page 124)

Aim: to provide a sample text for students to analyse.

Tips:

- Many of these texts deliberately contain errors which the students will be asked to focus on and correct later in the lesson.
- At this stage of the lesson merely ask them to read the text and extract the information.
- There are often two questions for these texts: one which focuses on gist and the other on specific details.
- If a student does ask a question about an error in form, praise them for noticing it, and explain that they will be correcting them shortly.

1

The reason is Alex's retirement.

The audience members are Alex and his work colleagues.

2

1 c 2 d 3 e 4 a 5 b

Writing skills: writing a speech (SB page 124)

Aim: to give students a chance to develop their writing through various different micro skills.

Tips:

- Sometimes this section focuses on common student errors in writing.
- Clearly explain the focus and do an example of one of the questions first with the students before asking them to continue on their own.
- Let students check their answers in pairs or small groups, then correct in open class.

1

Paragraph 1: **Ladies and gentlemen**, welcome to this special party …; **As you know**, Alex is leaving us …

Paragraph 2: **First of all**, I'd like to thank …; **Indeed**, the great success …

Paragraph 3: **Well**, your dream has come true.; **On top of that**, last year you won the prize …

Paragraph 5: **So, on behalf of everybody here**, I'd like to …

2 She follows all of these points except for discourse markers.

Introduction, conclusion, organisation: see Reading exercise 2

Address the audience: *You* / *Alex*, and *we* / *us*

Examples: *In my opinion the office will feel very empty without him … I remember meeting Alex on his first day in the office and he told me that his ambition was to become a top-class reporter.*

Humour: *we need your bad jokes and funny stories to remind us why we come into work every morning … I hope you will come and visit us often and give us advice on how to improve our reports.*

Language focus: wishes and hopes (SB page 124)

Aim: to highlight and focus on a particular aspect of language that students can use to improve their writing.

Tips:

- Sometimes this section serves as revision or reinforcement of language that students have encountered passively before in the unit (for example, in the reading texts) – make this link clear where possible.
- Let students check their answers in pairs or small groups, then correct in open class.

1 hope 2 wish 3 hope 4 wish 5 hope

Preparing to write (SB page 124)

Aim: to give students time to brainstorm ideas for the writing task.

Tips:

- Allow students to brainstorm ideas in pairs or small groups.
- At low levels, this may involve some use of L1 (the students' mother tongue); be tolerant of this, but be on hand to help with translations or English where needed.
- Ask students to make notes here, but not begin writing.

Writing (SB page 124)

Aim: to give students practice in more extended writing tasks.

Tips:

- This section can be done as homework.
- Remind students to refer back to the model text, but to be careful of the typical errors.
- Ask students to check their work carefully before they hand it in.

Global review

These lessons in *Global* are designed to provide students with an opportunity to review and consolidate the language they have studied in the unit.

Grammar and Vocabulary (SB page 125)

Aim: to give students revision of all the main grammar and vocabulary points that arose in the unit.

Tips:

- Demonstrate the activities by doing the first one as a whole class.
- Allow students time to do this, and encourage them to look back through the unit for help.
- When you come to correct this, do not simply go around the class asking for the right answer – encourage students to say *why* they think something is correct, and seek confirmation from others before moving on.

Grammar

1

Answers are numbered in the order they appear in the text.

1 is read	6 used
2 were produced	7 would save
3 have been written	8 said
4 have never seen	9 would not be published
5 still prefer	

2

1 each other 2 themselves 3 each other

Vocabulary

1 throw	5 blow
2 grave	6 away
3 subscribe	7 notice
4 fired	8 bookshop

Mystery word: hardback

Speaking and Writing (SB page 125)

Aim: to provide extra speaking practice that will review and consolidate language presented in the unit.

Tips:

- Give the students time to read and understand the instructions.
- Circulate and monitor the students, encouraging them to use only English here.
- Make notes of any incorrect use of language, but refrain from correcting if students are in the middle of the task.

Study skills

These lessons in *Global* are designed to provide students with skills and strategies in learner training and learner autonomy. For more on learner autonomy and learner training, see the essay on page xxiii.

Using your dictionary: exploring synonyms (SB page 125)

1 With books closed, ask students to think of words with the same meaning as *leave* and *arrive*. Write students' ideas on the board. Ask students which prepositions we use with *arrive* (*at* and *in*). You might like to ask them to think of example sentences too. Then ask students to open their books and read the tip box about synonyms.

2 Direct students to the dictionary entries and ask them to check their ideas from exercise 1.

3 Ask students to complete the sentences with the correct synonym for *arrive* or *leave*. In feedback, check the answers with the class and clarify any problems. Then refer students to the study tips at the end of the page.

1 depart
2 get
3 stormed out
4 set off
5 Go away!
6 reached

Grammar focus answer key

Unit 1

1 **1** do you mean **4** appear
2 I don't understand **5** sounds
3 are changing **6** never forget

2 **1** **a** drives **b** is driving
2 **a** speaks **b** is speaking
3 **a** am working **b** work
4 **a** translate **b** are translating

3 **1** understand
2 are studying
3 takes
4 are (you) going
5 don't remember
6 are living
7 is learning
8 don't want

4 **1** is **2** is **3** Does **4** Do **5** are

5 **1** How often do you go
2 When did you go
3 Why did you choose
4 What do you like

6 **1** live there
2 do most people live
3 do the people speak
4 make up the government

7 **1** Who wrote *Frankenstein*?
2 What time do Americans usually eat lunch?
3 How many famous authors come from Dublin?
4 What do Brazilians celebrate on 7 September?
5 Which 20th century world leader spent 27 years in prison?
6 How often does India have a national election?

Unit 2

1 **1** had **6** prepared
2 was living **7** were living / lived
3 was travelling **8** was working
4 heard **9** helped
5 joined

2 **1** He was living in Russia when he met his wife.
2 I was working when the fire alarm went off.
3 She was listening to the teacher when her phone rang.
4 I was having a meal in a restaurant when someone took my bag.
5 The boy was playing on the roof when he fell down and broke his leg.

3 **1** moved; had argued
2 had finished; went
3 stopped; had fallen out
4 visited; had returned
5 refused; had lied

4 When Josh was **very** young, around six years old, his father read him books at bedtime. They were usually **very** / **quite** simple stories about animals or spacemen. However, one day Josh's father brought home a book of **very** old fairytales. While Josh listened to these stories, he sometimes got **quite** / **very** frightened and hid under the blankets. However, he preferred the fairy tales to the other stories, which he found **very** / **quite** boring.

5 **1** This place isn't very pretty.
2 Her son isn't very friendly.
3 Those curtains aren't a very nice colour.
4 That restaurant isn't very clean.
5 He isn't very clever.

6 Correct forms (*When I was a child* applies to all sentences):
1 used to / would
2 used to / would
3 didn't use to
4 used to / would
5 used to

7 Many people **used to believe** that there **was** a city somewhere in England called Camelot. They **used to think** that forests and plains **surrounded** it and that the famous King Arthur **lived** there. In the castle of Camelot there **was** the famous Round Table. The king **would hold** meetings with his knights around this table. Outside the castle there **was** a large green field where the king and his knights **would participate** in fairs and jousts.
(This means that they believed it in the past but no longer believe it.)

OR

Many people believe that there **used to be** a city somewhere in England called Camelot. They think that forests and plains **used to surround** it and that the famous King Arthur **used to live** there. In the castle of Camelot there **used to be** the famous Round Table. The king **would hold / used to hold** meetings with his knights around this table. Outside the castle there **used to be** a large green field where the king and his knights **would participate / used to participate** in fairs and jousts.
(This means many people believe now that there was such a place and that it is no longer there.)

Unit 3

1 **1** are launching / are going to launch
2 are going to offer
3 are beginning / are going to begin
4 is going to start
5 aren't going to stop
6 are going to continue

2 **1** A is going to / will
B will
2 A are going to / will
B will
3 A is going to
B will
4 A will
B is going to

3 **1** This morning I was so tired that I fell asleep at my desk.
2 Yesterday it was such a hot day that we spent the day in the park.
3 It was so late that the shops were closed.
4 He worked so hard that his back hurt.
5 It was such a bad storm that the airport was closed.
6 The roads were so icy it was impossible to drive.

4 **1** certain
2 not certain
3 certain
4 certain
5 not certain
6 not certain
7 not certain
8 certain

5 A: I'll
B: it's
A: we'll
A: buy
B: Will

Unit 4

1 **1** have called
2 painted
3 killed
4 gave
5 have found
6 used

2 **1** did (you) meet
2 have (you) known
3 Did (you) go
4 Have (you ever) lost touch
5 Have (you ever) had

3 **1** yet **4** yet
2 yet **5** yet
3 already **6** already

4 **1** He has already walked up the wall.
2 He hasn't walked down the wall yet.
3 He has already looked to the right.
4 He has already looked to the left.
5 He hasn't eaten lunch yet.
6 He hasn't polished his helmet yet.

5 **1** might / may
2 must
3 can't
4 must
5 may / might
6 might / may
7 must

6 **1** anybody
2 Nobody
3 everybody
4 somebody
5 anybody
6 Everybody

Unit 5

1 **1** mustn't
2 don't have to
3 mustn't
4 don't have to
5 mustn't
6 don't have to
7 don't have to
8 mustn't
9 don't have to
10 mustn't

2 **1** had to
2 could
3 couldn't / weren't allowed to
4 had to
5 couldn't / weren't allowed to
6 didn't have to

3 **1** 've been teaching
2 've lived
3 've been running for
4 's been doing her homework
5 've eaten pasta since

4 **1** Can you pick some tomatoes up? / Can you pick some up?
2 If you put chocolate and chilli together … / If you put them together …
3 I've mixed the cake ingredients up. / I've mixed them up.
4 I'll wash the dishes up later. / I'll wash them up later.
5 Remember to turn the oven off. / Remember to turn it off.

Unit 6

1 **1** started
2 took
3 was recognised
4 became
5 were photographed by
6 was taken
7 did not get
8 have been made

2 **1** Job applications are not currently being accepted.
2 Refunds on purchases will not be given.
3 Bears have been seen in the park.
4 All our prices have been cut.
5 Security cameras are being used in this area.
6 Bad behaviour towards airport staff will not be tolerated.
7 Part-time staff are required for general duties.
8 Cash is not kept in the kiosk overnight.

3 **1** an
2 an
3 a
4 A
5 the
6 the
7 The
8 the
9 the
10 the
11 the
12 a

4 **1** an
2 a
3 the
4 a
5 the
6 The
7 a
8 the
9 a
10 the
11 the

This describes the blue and yellow picture on page 68.

5 **1** was / would be
2 would do / was doing / was going to do
3 was
4 didn't know
5 had met
6 would call

6 **1** They said they don't speak / didn't speak English.
2 He said he really wanted that coat.
3 The teacher told us that the capital of Peru is / was Lima.
4 She asked me where my boots were.
5 She said she had phoned him the day before / yesterday.
6 He asked me what I was doing there.
7 She told them to listen to her and (to) do as she said.
8 We asked them if / whether they worked there.

7 **1** She asked me to sit down.
2 She asked me to show her my exam number.
3 She told me to listen carefully.
4 She asked me to tell her about myself.
5 She told me to look at her and not to look at my feet.

Unit 7

1 Correct forms:
1 who / that
2 that / which
3 who / that
4 that / which
5 where
6 that / which

2 **1** Smith's bank, which is one of the oldest banks in the country, was the centre of an enormous scandal last year.
2 Many of the bank's accounts, which belonged to old age pensioners, were empty.
3 It seems the bank managers used the money to make investments in the property market, which crashed soon after.
4 When they lost all the money the managers, who knew they were in trouble, tried to hide the evidence.
5 The bank managers, who were trying to leave the country, have been arrested.

3 **1** accommodation
2 cash
3 clothes
4 information
5 respect (less commonly, *respect* can be countable: *In this respect he is right*; and *need* can be uncountable: *a friend in need*)
6 traffic
7 luggage
8 work

4 **1** a coffee; coffee
2 a cheese; cheese
3 a long hair; long hair
4 salad; a salad

5 **1** I didn't like it so much
2 I could be there
3 I had more energy
4 it was / were a bit warmer
5 I could see better
6 it was / were a bit bigger
7 I had something to eat

Unit 8

1 **1** e
2 d
3 a
4 c
5 b

2 **1** included
2 wouldn't be
3 were
4 would put
5 found
6 would smell
7 would give
8 did

3 **1** If you answered my calls, I would call you.
2 If I spoke Chinese, I would understand this.
3 If it was / were a nice day, we could go to the beach.
4 If it wasn't / weren't a secret, I would tell you about it.
5 If I didn't have a lot of work to do, I could go out tonight.

4 **1** If it hadn't been a hot day, the scientists wouldn't have decided to open the window.
2 If they hadn't decided to open the window, a bird wouldn't have flown into the laboratory.
3 If the bird hadn't flown into the laboratory, it wouldn't have flown around and (it wouldn't have) knocked over some containers.
4 If it hadn't knocked over the containers, the liquids wouldn't have come into contact.
5 If the liquids hadn't come into contact, they wouldn't have mixed together.
6 If they hadn't mixed together, the scientists wouldn't have found the cure they had been looking for.

5 **1** I'm sure you left them on the table.
2 I'm not sure if he was there.
3 I'm sure it wasn't Sue.
4 I don't believe she failed either.
5 It's possible that school finished early, but I'm not sure.

Unit 9

1 **1** to find
2 getting started
3 setting up
4 to be
5 to be
6 to start

2 **1** trying
2 sitting
3 noticing
4 doing

3 **1** smart (*smarter*; others take *more* + adjective)
2 cold (*colder*; others have double consonant)
3 cheap (*cheaper*; others end in *-ier*)
4 small (*smaller*; others take *more* + adjective)
5 sad (*sadder*; others are irregular)
6 lovely (*lovelier*; others end in *-er*)

4 **1** He is older than her / she is.
2 She is much younger than him / he is.
3 He isn't as lonely as he was before.
4 She was happier in the Ukraine than (she was) in England.
5 Things are better than they seem.

5 **1** about
2 of
3 for
4 of
5 on
6 for
7 on
8 of
9 in

6 **1** d
2 f
3 e
4 b
5 a
6 c

Unit 10

1 **1** is having / is going to have
2 is going to be / will
3 has/have been waiting
4 represents
5 died
6 reached
7 would probably survive
8 has been considered
9 has existed
10 is given
11 is
12 picks
13 will become

2 **1** to marry him
2 didn't think
3 hadn't known
4 wasn't going to rush
5 to think
6 would marry

3

I	me	myself
you	you	yourself
he	him	himself
she	her	herself
we	us	ourselves
they	them	themselves

4 **1** each other
2 themselves
3 themselves
4 each other

5 Correct forms:
1 got up
2 showered
3 correct
4 shaved
5 correct
6 correct
7 got dressed
8 remembered
9 correct
10 correct
11 correct
12 felt tired
13 correct
14 lay down

Global Teacher's Resource Disc

The *Global* Teacher's Resource Disc includes a comprehensive range of resources.

The Communication activities section contains a number of photocopiable worksheets for classroom use provided as printable PDFs. There are two worksheets directly linked with the content of each of the units in the Coursebook. In addition, there are generic worksheets appropriate for different points of the course (eg beginning of the year).

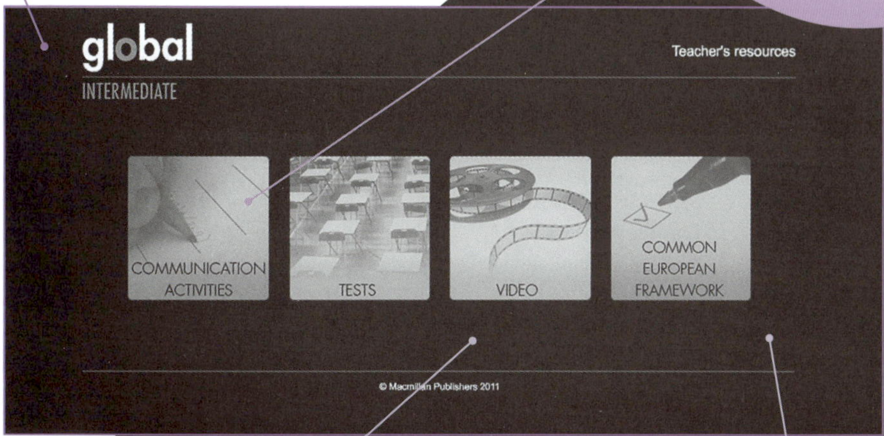

Also included are video clips for classroom use, with their corresponding worksheets and teacher's notes provided as printable PDFs.

Each level of *Global* is mapped against the corresponding level in the Common European Framework.

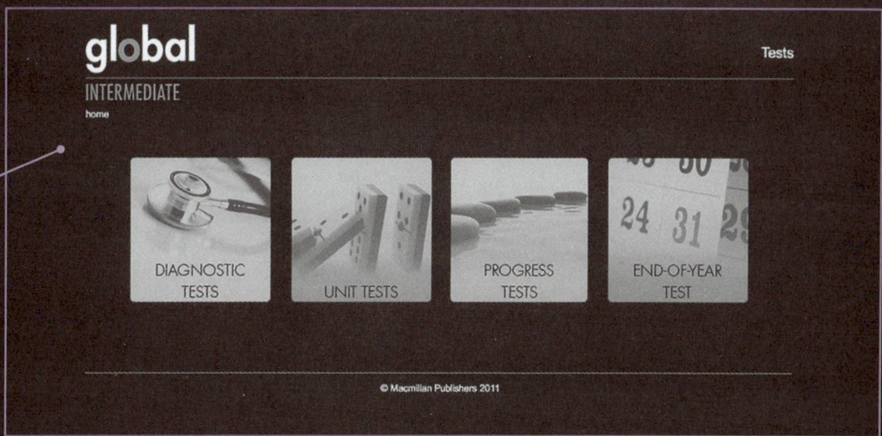

The Teacher's Resource Disc also contains numerous *Global*-related tests for use in class.